The class leader didn't accept my help and rested against the headboard of the bed. Because the metal bars of the headboard was cold and hard, I passed her the pillow. She didn't refuse and cushioned it behind her back.

The class leader closed her eyes and allowed me to roll up the legs of her trousers.

What a tight pair of pants. When I slightly rolled it up, I could see her even whiter skin under her white socks. It was a dazzling existence under the rays of the sun.

Even though I tried not to touch the class leader's skin to reduce her anxiety, she was still nervous. Her muscles were wound up and made it hard for me to do my job, and I also hurt her a couple of times.

The class leader opened her eyes angrily, "What future prospects do you have if you can't even do this properly?"

Huh? Are you saying I would be successful in the future if I'm good at removing a girl's pants? If you think I'm not skilled enough, we can practice some more later on.

Chen YingRan who was standing on the sides quietly couldn't hold back and said: "If you think the legs are too tight, you can take it off from the sides& are you wearing underwear?"

The class leader looked at the school doctor with a terrified expression.

Chen YingRan continued to speak: "I never wore underwear in gym class because it would chafe my legs, but later I was called into a small and dark room by the gym teacher uncle."

Damn, don't speak about 18+ topics. Did it actually happen or are you just messing with us? Did that molester gym teacher receive punishment? And when are you planning to stop being a molester doctor?

After some efforts, her two white legs were exposed in the open air.

But her injury was pitiful. The skin was cut open and blood was on her pants, but fortunately, it didn't fully congeal.

She bent her legs so her knees pointed up and prepared to receive medication.

Chen YingRan chased me away so she could sit at the end of the bed facing the class leader's injuries.

She opened the bottle of disinfectant and a strange smell immediately spread through the air.

Fuck, so strong, so fishy, so smelly. The class leader also furrowed her brows. Even though I knew good medicine is bitter, but what kind of disinfectant is this! I stretched my neck to take a look, why is it milky white, why it sticky and disgusting? Are you going to spread that on her legs?

Chen YingRan quickly closed the bottle and went towards the cabinets while laughing at herself:

"Shit, I took the wrong bottle. I almost put shota juice on&."

How many shotas did you molest to squeeze out that much juice! Don't tell me Shu Zhe's is also a part of that, please don't give that stuff to the sister, it would be a tragedy! Besides, if it was actually effective, I have tons on me.

Perhaps it was to lessen the awkward atmosphere, Chen YingRan pointed to a banana with some black spots that was sitting on the treatment table and said:

"Do you want a banana?"

"No thanks." I wasn't in the right mood to act so leisurely.

Chen YingRan covered her mouth and laughed: "Don't worry, I washed it properly."

Do you even need to wash a banana? You can eat it right away after peeling it. What exactly did you do with the banana?

After a while, Chen YingRan finally finished applying the normal medicine on the class leader's injuries. The class leader laid on the bed a while to rest, but no matter what, she refused to return with me.

Is she afraid I would carry her again? Do you think there would be a lecher outside waiting for you now that the area below your knees are bare?

"Can you tell Xiao Xiong&. no, tell Geng YuHong to come here." the class leader ordered, but she was not looking at me.

"Can you also tell her to bring my bag along. You can leave now."

What, are you leaving early because of your injury? I thought you said your injury wasn't a big deal. Or are you unable to show your face because I carried you across the schoolyard?

It turns out I was mistaken, the class leader was stronger than I believed. The reason why she wanted Loud Mouth to bring her bag was because she wanted to change out of her blood-stained gym uniform.

When I met her again, she was wearing her school uniform skirt she wore this morning. She also recovered the calmness and confidence that belongs to a class leader.

But the bandages on the class leader's fingers wasn't a big deal& I mentioned before that because the class leader's legs were too long, the school skirt that's supposed to be under the knees, ended up above the knees for her. With the addition of the bandages on her knees, it makes you have bad thoughts.

Eunuch Cao, who didn't learn his lesson, ran in front of the class leader after class and asked with a solemn expression:

"Class leader, I& I want to ask& when you enter the classroom, are you more used to using the back or the front door? Since your seat is so close to the back door, you should like using the back door more. Does that mean compared to the front, you like it more from the back?"

The class leader, who was already in a bad mood, put both her elbows on the desk and put her fingertips together. Then she commanded in a gloomy but clear voice:

"Xiong YaoYue, drag Cao JingShen out and give him a beating."

The class leader usually calls her "Xiao Xiong" at her request, but when she called her whole name, Xiong YaoYue knew the class leader was really angry.

But to any girl, giving Eunuch Cao a beating would be a form of entertainment (Eunuch Cao wouldn't hit back and his body of fat wouldn't hurt your hands). That's why Xiong YaoYue was delighted to hear her order and Loud Mouth followed her when she was dragging Eunuch Cao out of the classroom.

"Count me in." Loud Mouth rolled up her sleeves and revealed her thick and nutritious arms.

The class leader added in from behind:

"Find someplace with nobody around. Don't let the headteacher see."

After she sentenced Eunuch Cao, she turned around to look at me as if I was the culprit for all evil in the world.

I'm not that important. If you have the time to watch me, you might as well keep an eye on Shenzhou-11. I heard my dad was watching a live stream from his hotel room. He was extremely excited because he had old classmates who were involved.

"Boo hoo (gt;_lt;)&. the secondary female protagonist is too sly."

Xiao Qin was next to me fiddling with her pencil. I wasn't sure if she was talking about character designs or the class leader.

"She actually tripped on purpose so she could be carried by Ye Lin classmate. Next time, she'll probably purposely fall on top of Ye Lin classmate's bed. I have to take action, should I also participate in PE&"

Xiao Qin turned towards me and said with a smile:

"Ye Lin classmate, since it's Friday, let's have a romantic candlelight dinner after school, my treat."

I held up a finger up to my mouth to tell her to be quiet so Niu ShiLi wouldn't hear.

"Hey, you're my secret girlfriend, did you forget you have to keep it a secret that we're dating."

Xiao Qin pouted, "But it's been so long. It's tiring to always keep it a secret."

"&besides my mom already knows about our relationship, even the hemorrhoid warrior from the cast knows."

Is the hemorrhoid warrior Kyle, the one who's infatuated with warrior culture and has the word hemorrhoid tattooed on his arm? It seems you really like giving others nicknames.

"That's not the same." I said, "Auntie Ren is not an outsider. As for Kyle, he's a foreigner, he's too much of an 'outsider', it doesn't matter if he knows& anyways pay attention when we're at school."

Xiao Qin lowered her head and became silent.

I suddenly became aware that the one I didn't want to find out was the class leader.

If Niu ShiLi heard conclusive evidence, he would tell the class leader. What would happen if she stops our relationship because I was already taken?

Wait, didn't I want to start a harem? If I'm to become a man with a harem, why should I worry about my concubines' opinions? Wouldn't a ton of cute girls hurl themselves at me once I release my kingly aura?

"Ye Lin, choose me tonight."

"No, he should choose me, he's already been at your place for two nights in a row."

"Stop fighting, it's embarrassing& why don't we all do it together."

Ah, and so on and so on, but in the end, it's still just a delusion.

Since Xiao Qin mentioned dinner, I thought about how the class leader wouldn't be able to cook with her injured hand. Shu Zhe can't do anything but eat, so what would they eat tonight? I heard the class leader is vehemently opposed to takeout, would she actually try and cook with her injuries?

I ignored my acting girlfriend Xiao Qin to carry out some neglect play, then I purposely walked in front of the class leader's desk while sneaking glances at Xiao Qin. I wanted to know if my womanizer plan has any effect.

"Class leader, what are you eating tonight?" I stared at her injured hand.

"It's none of your business." The class leader responded coldly.

"You can order takeout." I suggested, "Even though it wouldn't taste as good as your cooking, it would still fill Shu Zhe's belly."

"Takeout is unhygienic. It's still better to make it yourself if you could."

It looks like the class leader is being stubborn again. If I never suggested to order takeout, then she might have actually ordered takeout with her brother for the first time. But now that I mentioned it, she might force herself to cook.

So I shrugged and said, "Why don't I go to your house and cook for you guys?"

"Cook for us?" The class leader seemed to be looking down on me, "Do you even know how to cook?"

Of course, for a single parent family like mines, I would have to bear with my dad's cooking if I didn't learn. My dad always reads a magazine while cooking and has mistaken sugar for salt multiple times.

Thus I proudly pointed at myself with my thumb and said:

"Who says I don't know how to cook. I might not know anything complicated, but I can still make simple dishes. How about I treat you guys to my noodle?"

Ah, I've already used this dirty joke three times, I should hurry and apologize before she turns really angry.

I coughed and changed my previous remark:

"If you don't want noodles, I can make tomatoes and egg, or even over easy eggs."

The class leader showed a bit of interest. She sat down at her seat, carefully rested her face on her bandaged hands and asked: "What else?"

I racked my brains and replied:

"Stir fried julienne potatoes, onions and meat, fried garlic shoots, those I can kind of make. I'm not great at cooking spinach soup or winter melon soup, but it's still passable& to be honest most of my expertise revolves around noodles&"

The class leader thought quietly for a few seconds before lightly patting the desk and said: "Fail."

Huh, are you trying to score me on how well I would act as a stay-at-home husband? Are you really going to focus on your career after marriage and let a man cook for you like Loud Mouth mentioned?

As the master chef of class 2-3, the class leader looked at me in contempt before she began to order dishes:

"I want to eat braised chicken with mushrooms, do you know how to make it?"

What?? Can't you order a simpler dish when it's my first time as your head chef?

"No, I can't." I replied honestly, "I'm only an entry-level chef, I can't make high-level dishes, but if you don't mind me buying half-finished goods&"

"Don't." The class leader interrupted, "I have a frozen chicken in my fridge at home. If you're willing to cook, then I can guide you."

Are& you trying to make a joke of me? Do you want to see a large man like me wear your small apron while being confounded by a frozen chicken? Shu Zhe might even come in to laugh at me, is this how you siblings repay your benefactors?

Class leader, aren't you usually pretty magnanimous? You still find time to give Xiong YaoYue study sessions even when she gives you a lot of trouble, but why do you hate me so much?

I suddenly remembered Xiao Qin made sea cucumber and braised bamboo chicken with Auntie Ren before. The methods should be pretty similar to braised chicken with mushrooms.

I told the class leader to wait for a second and went to ask Xiao Qin: "Do you know how to make braised chicken with mushrooms?"

"Of course, as long as it's something Ye Lin classmate loves to eat, I'll force myself to learn even if I don't know how to make it."

"No, no." I said, "Even though I do like to eat it, this time it's not for me, it's for the class leader. You probably already know the class leader injured her hand, so that means she can't cook tonight. Can you head to the class leader's home after school and cook braised chicken with mushrooms for everyone?"

Xiao Qin's expression made it seem as if she was sent from heaven to hell. I mean it's expected since she was planning to have a romantic candlelight dinner with her boyfriend, but she was treated as a tool, a tool to help me with the favour of another woman& you should kill scum like me, you might as well dump me right now.

I couldn't really hold back when I saw Xiao Qin's look of disappointment, so I supplemented: "I won't make you cook alone, I'll be your assistant."

Xiao Qin's eyes lit up again.

"If I can cook together with Ye Lin classmate& then the meaning is completely different. By the way, it seems I did eat a lot of the class leader's cooking at my house last time, so I should repay her. Then it's decided, let me show you cooking skills only a real girl would know."

No one said you weren't a real girl. But you better know how to actually cook braised chicken with mushrooms. When I went to your house with the class leader last time, most of the food you cooked were all fast food like fried chicken. If you turn the braised chicken with mushrooms into a mysterious black goop, then have fun watching everyone's reactions at the dinner table.

After Xiao Qin agreed, I ran to the class leader and told her not to worry. Xiao Qin would come over to cook, so their food worries would be solved.

"Hehe, Xiao Qin will come with me to cook. You can just wait outside for the food."

The class leader didn't seem that happy when she heard the news. She looked at Xiao Qin who was two tables away and said quietly:

"Is that so& it's fine if Xiao Qin comes and helps, but I hope it doesn't affect her studies&"

Huh, you seem disappointed you can't guide me in the kitchen. Do you want to laugh at me that badly? Do you not care even if I turn the dish into a nuclear disaster?

After school, the class leader used supervising the students in charge of cleaning the class as an excuse to wait until everyone left before coming to find us at the school gates.

Are you embarrassed walking home with me? Then you should have just left with Xiao Qin.

The class leader still wasn't riding her bike today, it seems her butt is still swollen. I guess helping her cook will be my atonement.

The three of us walked with Xiao Qin on the left, the class leader on the right, and I was in the middle. The two girls were completely silent and it was a bit awkward.

Two girls from QingZi Academy High school division was walking towards us. The class leader's height made them check her out, but they covered their mouths and laughed when they saw the bandages on her knees.

"She should pay more attention when wearing a vest in the summer&"

"She should wear knee pads if doing it on top of a bamboo sleeping mat. She looks smart, but I guess she doesn't have any common knowledge."

"The guy looks pretty built, but it's pretty obvious he's not the caring type&"

"Why are they all walking together? Is the one on the left his sister?"

Who did it with the class leader on a bamboo mat? Who said Xiao Qin was my sister? Get the hell out of here!

For some reason Xiao Qin came to a halt when she heard their words.

"Ah, I think sis Ying Ran taught me that posture before&" Xiao Qin stood still while muttering to herself, "She even said only those who have knee injuries have actually loved&"

"How sly, I'm the one who loves Ye Lin classmate the most."

Xiao Qin suddenly began to sprint before she finished her sentence, then she bent her knees and directly kneeled on the road without reducing her speed.

It was basically like footballers who would slide on the grass as celebration after they score a goal.

But grass is grass, this is a mother fucking asphalt road! Xiao Qin was wearing a dress today, so her legs was bare. Her legs were about to have intimate contact with the road.

Xiao Qin's knees were covered with fresh blood before I could even react. The blood stained the edge of her skirt, but she had a splendid smile.

"Hehe~~~ now I expressed my greater love for Ye Lin classmate. The people who are harboring bad thoughts will definitely fail."

My first reaction was extreme anger.

I clutched Xiao Qin's collar to raise her off the ground, then I yelled at her:

"Are you retarded? Why can't you walk on the ground properly? Do you think you have an iron body or something?"

At this point in time, the pain was slowly creeping up on Xiao Qin, and she said with a bitter smile:

"This& is how I show love for Ye Lin classmate. I feel at ease now that I'm also injured&"

I said in a quiet voice only Xiao Qin would hear:

"Don't think I would like you because you keep injuring yourself&"

I accidentally let the truth slip out in the heat of the moment. I practically admitted I was only leading her on and she would always be a secret girlfriend.

Xiao Qin didn't seem to be surprised. She shifted her slightly dark gaze and said in a similarly quiet voice:

"Because I've also hurt Ye Lin classmate many times, you probably won't feel at ease if I don't experience the same amount of pain. I don't care how you treat me in the future&"

"You& at least don't hurt yourself." I hissed, "If you keep hurting yourself, I'll& remove you as my girlfriend."

"Is it because you want to give that spot to the class leader?"

"You&."

I suddenly felt someone kicking my calf. I turned around to take a look, isn't this the class leader? Why are you kicking me angrily, does your knees not hurt anymore?

"Why are you being so mean to Xiao Qin." The class leader took Xiao Qin in her arms and angrily rebuked me, "Xiao Qin tripped by accident, you don't have to comfort her, but why are you yelling at her. So, do you still have a grudge against her?"

Huh, how did you know I have a grudge against her? I've never even told my dad I was bullied by Xiao Qin.

Xiao Qin was snatched over by the class leader, she had no idea how to react when suddenly embraced with motherly love.

The class leader gently patted Xiao Qin, then continued to scold me:

"It's because your little brother got lost when playing hide-and-seek with Xiao Qin when you were young& even if Xiao Qin was at fault, you can't hate her for life."

Oh, I thought you were going to say something else. You still haven't forgotten the lie Xiao Qin told you? Even I almost forgot about it.

"I don't have a little brother." I said, "Xiao Qin was lying, didn't I already explain it to you?"

The class leader ignored me. She bent down to check on Xiao Qin's injuries while ignoring her own.

"How pitiful, there's so much blood&"

I took a glance and my chest did throb a bit.

It was indeed more serious than the class leader's injury. After all, asphalt is not the same as synthetic track. Those two streaks of red were horrible to look at.

But she has many years of fundamentals in martial arts, so even if she wanted to injure herself, she would have subconsciously lessened the impact. So instead of badly mangles knees, she only had some serious scrapes.

The class leader carefully blew away the dirt on Xiao Qin's injury, then she took out some napkins to soak up some of the blood. When Xiao Qin made a pained expression, the class leader stopped and asked: "Did I hurt you?"

"It's okay& it's okay&" Xiao Qin could only respond with those words.

"I have a medical kit at home, it's 5 minutes away. Shall we go there to take care of the rest?" The class leader inquired.

Xiao Qin nodded.

The class leader turned to me and gave me an order.

"It's time for you to carry Xiao Qin."

"Hah?" I widened my eyes.

"What's wrong?" The class leader cast glances at me, "Aren't you strong? Now that Xiao Qin is hurt. You should at least be able to carry her to my house."

I stammered, "But there's a lot of people on the streets."

The class leader became even more upset, "Today at school& there was also a lot of people."

I could only carry Xiao Qin after being intimidated by the class leader. Xiao Qin was naturally overjoyed.

But& it's a bit heavy. I'm not comparing Xiao Qin's weight and the class leader's weight, but I'm currently hungry and Xiao Qin and I are both carrying backpacks.

I wanted to change a posture because Xiao Qin's bag was in an uncomfortable position. Then the class leader took off her backpack and hung it around my neck without even asking.

Damn, that hurts. I can't catch my breath, how heavy is your backpack? How many Chinese-English dictionaries are you carrying inside of here? I clearly offered to help hold your bag before we left school and you refused, but are you regretting it now?

What are girls even thinking about? Why are they sometimes gentle, but sometimes worse than a demon? I'm carrying a person and three bags, do you want to kill me?

This time, two men who looked like otakus were walking in our direction. One of them saw us then paused and pushed up his glasses.

"Damn, what's going on? Both of the girls have injured knees, did he do this by himself?"

"Shhhh." His companion lowered his voice, "Quiet down, also it's not easy getting two at once, look how tired he is."

Damn right I'm tired. But I never did anything, I only got mad at my childhood friend and somehow ended up in this predicament.

Many other people of all ages pointed at laughed at me when they saw me. Why are they not afraid of me? Do you not see my appearance? Is it because I don't qualify as a human anymore as a human tool?

I felt like I was a pack mule instead of a person.

TN: Hi guys, just wanted to let you know I posted the prologue of a new novel here. Give it a read and feel free to give feedback, I want to see if others enjoy it. I will also be making changes to the website and Patreon stuff over the next weeks while I have time because of quarantine. Stay safe guys. Enjoy.

My head was covered in sweat and each step was difficult to take as the class leader treated me like a pack mule. Soon, I was about to fall down and take my last breath.

As for a Spartan like me who constantly undergoes serious training, usually, something like this wouldn't take my life. But the class leader hanging her bag around my neck was the fatal strike, it's strangling me and I can't breathe properly. If I was actually strangled by your bag, I'll definitely come back to haunt you so no one else would marry you.

I'm not sure if it was because she heard my cursing inside my head, but the class leader adjusted her bag so I would be able to breathe. I was able to successfully carry Xiao Qin in front of the class leader's building, and the class leader was able to avoid her fate of being unable to get married.

People used to say, the last part of a journey was the hardest. It looks like it came true.

Not only did I have to carry Xiao Qin up to the fifth floor, but we also bumped into a group of people here to pick up the bride and groom and the stairs were packed to the brim.

I'm not sure which southern province the bride and groom were from, but I didn't expect there would actually be customs of getting married at night. If it was people from Dong Shan City, it would only be for second marriages.

There was a band playing downstairs with a black stretch limo parked on the side. Under the relatives' watch, the groom carried the bride down the stairs. The groom had a fairly small and skinny body, so each step seemed to be quite difficult to make.

By chance, they ran right into the class leader and I carry Xiao Qin, trying to go up the stairs.

Marriage is a major event in one's life, so the class leader turned to the side to let them through. I also tried to lean against the wall as much as possible so the marriage group could pass.

The groom who was carrying the bride, and me who carried Xiao Qin, glanced at each other as he passed by. I had no idea what he was thinking.

The person following from behind seemed to be the bridesmaid. She had a lively personality and she joked with me and Xiao Qin:

"Hey, are you guys getting married at such a young age? What are you planning to do upstairs?"

I didn't even have the time to respond before Xiao Qin said with a smile:

"(*^__^*) Of course, we're going to consummate the marriage."

What, you're going to consummate the marriage at the class leader's home? What kind of guest are you?

The bridesmaid didn't expect Xiao Qin to respond so audaciously and was stunned.

Xiao Qin continued to speak with excitement:

"I'll learn from the bride and hurry up and give birth to Ye Lin classmate's children."

What Xiao Qin said was terribly untactful, because when the bride passed by, we could all see the bulge on her stomach. It was clear this was a shotgun marriage. Even if the times are different now, it was still awkward pointing it out in front of all their relatives.

The bridesmaid walked down the stairs with embarrassment and the class leader sighed.

"Xiao Qin, watch what you say, besides, there's something wrong with your feelings for Ye Lin."

She was probably referring to the lie Xiao Qin told her. She told her she used to like my younger brother, but began to like me after he went missing, like the bridge scene from TOUCH. The class leader probably thinks Xiao Qin is using me as a substitute for my younger brother.

It's not true, but I do admit there are problems with Xiao Qin's feelings for me.

Xiao Qin then began to whisper in my ear: "Did you hear that? Woman number two is saying bad things about me, she's definitely an antagonist."

You're the antagonist! Think about the times when you broke the class leader's shoes, forced her to show her breasts to you, then wrote her name in the Death Note!

The class leader spoke again when the marriage party all left:

"The bride is too careless. If they were planning on getting married, why couldn't they just hold it in a bit? I hate when people get the order wrong."

I think you're the one who's getting the order wrong! They're only getting married because she's pregnant. Besides, aren't you usually a feminist? Why do you act conservatively in these cases? I heard some feminists in other countries advocate other women to act like men. A female offender who killed her husband received the praise of many feminists because she proved that women can also kill people.

Wait, it might not be her views on love, if she doesn't want to get the order wrong, this is clearly her OCD! The class leader seemed to have the order "Dating ' Marriage ' Kids" in her mind, similar to how when you're cooking you add oil, then open the fire, then add the ingredients& then does that mean she's planning to keep herself pure before she gets married not because of her conservative views, but because of her OCD?

After we entered the class, we could see Shu Zhe sitting behind the dining table with an impatient expression.

"Sis, why did you take so long to get home?" Shu Zhe complained, "We did shot put in gym class today, so I'm starving."

Do you not see the injuries on your sister's hand and knees? Why didn't the sexy white rose panties slip out from your shorts when you were doing shot put and make you the laughing stock of the class?

Shu Zhe stared blankly when Xiao Qin and I entered, but he stood up from the chair.

"Ah, bro Ye Lin, why are you here? Also& did sis Xiao Qin get injured?"

Sis Xiao Qin, hmph, even though you talked behind her back, you're still calling her with sweet names.

The class leader briefly explained the situation to Shu Zhe and told me to carry Xiao Qin to her room so she could disinfect the wound.

Since the injury was on her knees and she may have to lift up her skirt, I was chased out of the room and only the two girls remained.

Even though the class leader's hand still hurt, she forced herself to not show any pained expression when treating Xiao Qin's injuries. But Xiao Qin was the who shuddered every time she was touched with a cotton swab.

I stood in the living room and started chatting with Shu Zhe.

"Bro Ye Lin, you came at a bad time. My sister's hand seems to be broken, so she can't cook for you."

Who was looking forward to her cooking? I came to help your sister cook, shut up and feel some gratitude.

"Hey, there's nothing wrong with the goods, right?" I asked like a drug dealer.

Shue Zhe looked at the class leader's room's door a bit awkwardly, "Yesterday when I was taking a shower, I accidentally tossed it in the dirty laundry bin. Luckily I got it back before my sister realized, but it was so close&"

Hey, can you be a bit more serious? You're making my heart jump even more than when I was a human pack mule. If your sister found out I was making you wear women's underwear, she would first take out her gun and shatter my kneecaps.

"Hey, if your sister finds out, don't tell her I was the one who made you wear it." I took some preventative measures.

"Then what should I say?"

"Um& just say it's your hobby."

"I don't have those hobbies, I'm only doing it for money."

For some reason, Shu Zhe's face was slightly red. I thought you had no qualms about your greed for money, why is your face turning red?

Soon after, two girls with bandaged knees came out of the room talking and laughing with each other.

I'm not sure if Xiao Qin was still carrying out her 'I'm innocent and foolish' plan, but she was acting really lovable in front of the class leader. It was like she was her long lost sister, well she was at least more lovable than Shu Zhe.

But I knew, if you let Xiao Qin and Shu Zhe swap places and have Xiao Qin live with the class leader every day, the class leader's life span will definitely mysteriously be cut short.

Since Xiao Qin was also injured, the class leader would find it embarrassing to ask her to cook, so she suggested to order takeout.

"Okay." Shu Zhe raised his hand in approval, "Let's order pizza from Pizza Hut."

All you think about is pizza, are you a teenage mutant ninja turtle?

Xiao Qin shook her head and showed her perfect hands to the class leader.

"It's fine, I'm happy I could cook for the class leader. Ye Lin classmate will also help me out."

"Okay&" the class leader felt her forehead with her hand as if the exhaustion hit her all at once, then she sat powerlessly on the sofa.

"I'm sorry, I suddenly feel a bit tired. If Xiao Qin is willing to help us, then I'll have to shamelessly wait for dinner."

"No problem, leave it to me."

Xiao Qin seemed to have completely forgotten about her knee pain. She tied on the class leader's sky blue apron (it was a bit too big for her) and pulled me towards the kitchen by my hand.

Then, it was like Xiao Qin just noticed a boy of similar age standing near her.

I thought Xiao Qin, who had androphobia, would scream and wake up the class leader, but instead, she tilted her head and looked at Shu Zhe strangely.

It was the same as last time at the movies when Xiao Qin mistook Shu Zhe with a wig as a girl.

Xiao Qin reached out her hand and placed it on Shu Zhe's flat chest.

"Sis Xiao Qin, what are you doing?" Shu Zhe felt awkward.

Xiao Qin ignored Shu Zhe's question, then reached out and held his chin.

Shu Zhe wanted to resist, but Xiao Qin gripped his chin tight. Then she forced him to turn his head to the left, then to the right. It made me think of old slave auctions, where the buyer has to inspect his goods.

After measuring him up and down, Xiao Qin patted his shoulder happily.

"Younger sis Xiao Zhe, please take care of me~?"

Shu Zhe's face was flushed with anger, "Sis Xiao Qin, stop joking around. I'm a boy."

Xiao Qin continued to pat Shu Zhe's shoulders with a lot of force. Every pat would force Shu Zhe to lower himself a bit.

"Let's not care about the small details. As for my little sister Shu Zhe who has even smaller breasts than me, I'll definitely protect you."

It seems like the class leader was too exhausted, so she fell asleep and didn't really hear our conversation.

Shu Zhe tried multiple times to break free from Xiao Qin to no avail. Xiao Qin pressed Shu Zhe's shoulder cavity, I wasn't sure if it was a joint lock technique, but it caused Shu Zhe to grimace in pain and plead to Xiao Qin:

"Sis Xiao Qin, why& are you so strong? Didn't you have a weak body? Bro Ye Lin, hurry and tell sis Xiao Qin to let go of me&"

"Huh~? I'm not strong at all." Xiao Qin grinned, "It's because my younger sister is too weak."

"I& I'm not your sister, I'm a boy."

"Stop joking, where can you find such a cute boy? You'll be punished if you lie, admit that you're a girl."

Xiao Qin said as she increased the amount of force she used.

Shu Zhe wanted to scream for help, but I glared at him because I was worried he would wake up the class leader.

Two large tears rolled down Shu Zhe's eyes and he could only admit:

"I& I'm a girl&"

Xiao Qin then let go of her hands and beckoned me:

"Come cook with me. Sis Xiao Zhe should be familiar with the situation at home, so she can come and help."

I don't think Shu Zhe would even know where the pots and pans are kept, but why is Xiao Qin suddenly not afraid of Shu Zhe anymore. Androphobia is not something you can throw away at will.

Now that I think about it, I remember how Xiao Qin said she would be flustered when she saw pictures of bro Chun and bro Zeng. Thus, I can conclude her 'androphobia' is triggered by what she sees, their actual gender is not important. The important thing is if the other person looks like a boy or a girl.

Is it possible Shu Zhe became more and more feminine after being my rope model and wearing women's clothing for a period of time? Did he already pass the line in Xiao Qin's mind where he would be considered a girl even if he doesn't wear a wig?

In addition, I heard your actions would appear more feminine when wearing women's underwear. Shu Zhe was currently wearing the sexy white rose underwear, so he's still in a crossdressing state.

Uh& not bad. If Xiao Qin's androphobia is this muddled, I can use Shu Zhe as an opportunity and might be able to cure her androphobia. That way, she wouldn't have to stick with me.

Shu Zhe sent me a glance for help as he was made to help and was being called a little sister.

I'm not saving you since you've always expected your sister to do everything for you. Now you can have a taste of how much hard word it is to cook.

After about ten minutes, the class leader abruptly woke up. She felt it was disrespectful to fall asleep when she had guests over, so she ran into the kitchen to apologize and ask if we needed help.

"No, it's okay." I pointed to the crowded kitchen, the class leader was shocked to find her younger brother washing the mushrooms diligently.

"If sis Xiao Zhe doesn't know how to cook, then you won't be able to get married."

That's what Xiao Qin said as she ordered Shu Zhe to wash the mushrooms.

Shu Zhe was more afraid of her joint locks rather than not being able to get married. He sent his sister looks of help when he saw her come in the kitchen.

"Class leader, Shu Zhe won't die if he does a little work." I stopped her before she said anything, "We won't tell him to use a knife, only wash some vegetables. You can go back to the sofa and rest."

The class leader could only nod and set the napkins down on the dinner table. She also made a small box with old magazines to throw away the chicken bones later.

Xiao Qin was the head chef, after three or four times of oil splashes, water boiling over, and flames shooting towards the ceiling, she was finally able to make braised chicken with mushrooms.

Xiao Qin leaned against the tiled kitchen wall with an exhausted expression and a blackened face from the smoke. It made her look more clumsy and adorable.

I tasted some of the chicken braised with mushrooms after Xiao Qin carried it onto the dining table. I felt it was a bit bland and lacked either salt or MSG. It would only get at most 6 points out of 10.

But it was the result of hard work for Xiao Qin who has been a boy for many years.

I felt a strange feeling of warmth as the four of us sat around the dining table.

There was space for exactly four people. It was probably prepared so they could eat with their parents.

But the class leader's parents are never around, and Xiao Qin and I are from single-parent families. Doesn't it sort of feel like fate when four kids who lack love come together for a meal?

Shu Zhe muttered "Didn't add salt" after he took a sip of the soup, then Xiao Qin stamped on his foot and he was afraid to make any more remarks, so he obediently finished his meal.

He left the table before even eating one bowl of food, what a small appetite.

The class leader made some polite praises to Xiao Qin's culinary skills. But Xiao Qin straight out admitted her food tastes bad and hopes she can get pointers from the class leader.

Even if Xiao Qin pretended she had a good relationship with the class leader on the outside, she was definitely harboring all sorts of malicious intent in her mind. But when you look at Xiao Qin's intimate actions, you would actually believe she's a natural ditz, someone who would help count the money even if the class leader sold her off to someone else.

Xiao Qin, your acting skills are amazing. You should hurry up and go film with Auntie Ren since you know martial arts and have amazing acting skills.

Since the class leader used her bandaged hands to do a lot of tasks she wasn't supposed to do, the bandages on her right hand came loose in the middle of the meal. The class leader wanted to head back to her room to redo the bandages, but Xiao Qin moved her chair right beside her and made a suggestion:

"Don't worry about the bandages, you should finish eating first."

"But&" the class leader felt embarrassed, "I can't hold cutlery in my left hand and my right-hand kind of hurts&"

If the class leader says it 'kind of hurts', then it means it hurts a lot.

"Don't worry." Xiao Qin picked up the class leader's soup spoon, "All you have to do is move your mouth, I'll feed you."

Then she scooped a spoonful of chicken soup and moved it towards the class leader's mouth without even asking for approval.

But the soup is still really hot, are you not going to at least blow on it before giving it to the class leader? Clearly, she wants to burn the class leader but is acting innocent as usual.

Although the class leader knew the soup was burning hot, she could only brace herself and drink it when she saw Xiao Qin's naive and innocent smile.

Your whole face is red, it wasn't even that red when I was carrying you! Xiao Qin, I can't believe you would do this right after the class leader helped you treat your injuries.

"Class leader, is my soup good?"

Xiao Qin asked dimwitted as if she completely didn't notice the class leader's uncomfortable expression.

"It's& it's good&." in order to not destroy Xiao Qin's zeal, the class leader forced herself to speak with a burned tongue.

"Then you should have another spoonful." Xiao Qin said as she went to get more soup. The expression on the class leader's face was fear of being tortured again.

"Enough." I stopped her, "The class leader won't fill up on soup. If you really want to help her, you should carve some chicken meat for her to eat. If you won't feed her properly, then I will."

The class leader rolled her eyes at me as if to say 'I don't want you to feed me'.

Xiao Qin realized I saw through her plans, so she quickly changed her tactics.

She borrowed a table knife from the kitchen and nimbly carved the chicken meat onto a plate. Then she fed spoonfuls of rice and chicken meat to the class leader.

Hey, your culinary skills aren't amazing, but why are you so skilled at carving meat? Don't tell me you will also carve my meat in the same way once you kill me?

Other than the thoughts about my uncertain future, the scene of Xiao Qin feeding the class leader was pretty heartwarming.

The class leader usually wouldn't accept this kind of care, but she didn't want to refuse Xiao Qin's good intentions, and she was pretty tired.

Thus she slowly chewed and swallowed each spoonful of food Xiao Qin fed her like a sick patient.

I thought Xiao Qin would sneak in a bone once the class leader loosens her vigilance, but I was wrong.

Did the class leader influence Xiao Qin to turn over a new leaf? It was a nice scene of one girl feeding another girl. I could almost see roses and hearts appearing in the background.

It took the class leader a lot of effort to swallow the last spoonful of food. She denied the next spoonful and said apologetically:

"Sorry Xiao Qin, I can't eat anymore."

Xiao Qin pleaded sincerely: "C'mon have another bite~? Just one more."

The class leader was helpless and could only finish off this spoon of food, but Xiao Qin immediately refilled the empty spoon.

"Class leader, eating more will help you recover faster, you need more protein. One more bite, just one more."

The class leader clenched her teeth and ate that spoonful of food too.

Xiao Qin scooped the third scoop of food.

"Do your best class leader, eat this one too&."

The class leader waved her hand weakly: "Xiao Qin, I really can't eat anymore&"

Xiao Qin said with a hundred percent sincerity and shimmering eyes.

"Try to eat some more, or is it because my food tastes bad?"

It does taste bad, didn't you say it yourself earlier?

The class leader turned her face away awkwardly, "Xiao Qin, your food tastes good, but I'm already full&"

Xiao Qin suddenly raised her voice:

"You have to eat more even if your full, otherwise, how would you get fatter?"

The class leader was stupefied and stared. Xiao Qin knew she misspoke, so she scratched her head and tried to feign innocence:

"Haha& I was only joking, you don't have to eat anymore if you're full&"

So she was planning on force-feeding the class leader to make her fat and I would no longer like her.

I wasn't sure if Xiao Qin was smart or stupid. You can't change someone's figure in one meal, or was she planning to stuff her to death with food?

After dinner, the class leader sat still at the table with indigestion. Every three seconds, she would make a loud burp.

I pulled out Shu Zhe, who was hiding in his room, to help me wash the dishes. Xiao Qin went to enthusiastically ask the class leader:

"Do you want any desserts or snacks? I could help you go buy some right now."

The class leader pressed down on her chest to temporarily stop the burps, then she instructed Shu Zhe to pour some Suanmeitang for us from the fridge. She couldn't control herself and burped once more before she was able to finish her sentence, her slightly panicked expression was quite cute.

The lazy Shu Zhe had just finished washing the dishes, then he opened the fridge unwillingly. He first poured a cup for me, then he poured another cup for Xiao Qin.

Xiao Qin initially accepted the drink happily, but after drinking half, she put down the cup as if she had just woken from a dream and muttered to herself:

"Damn, sis Xiao Zhe could be on woman number two's side. I made a grave mistake accepting drinks from the enemy."

The class leader couldn't understand who was 'woman number two' or 'sis Xiao Zhe', but she saw Xiao Qin suddenly clutch her own stomach and fall onto the carpet. Then Xiao Qin began rolling left and right while yelling:

"There's poison, there's poison."

What poison. Didn't you see me drink it too? It's all in your head.

When Shu Zhe saw Xiao Qin rolling around on the floor, he was scared witless and said to me in a quiet voice:

"Bro Ye Lin, so your childhood friend is a moron&"

I don't need you to tell me that. It's so hot today, go somewhere else.

After Xiao Qin's scene, the class leader's burps were already gone.

The class leader invited us to stay for some fruits, but I didn't want Xiao Qin to cause more trouble, so I used homework as an excuse to bid farewell.

"Um, you guys, don't forget to do the problems on the back of the language papers."

The class leader said a farewell fitting of her stature, but I felt she placed more of an emphasis on us rather than the 'language papers'.

Does she care more about our actions after we leave?

Even though he was unwilling, Shu Zhe still followed us down the stairs in place of his sister to send us off. I thought about it for a second and handed him three hundred bucks, then he immediately became lively.

"Um& is this a bonus?"

"You can consider it a bonus." I said, "But it's not for you, it's to buy your sister a new pair of running shoes&"

Shu Zhe lost all interest again, "How is it a bonus if I'm using it for my sister."

I hit him on the head, "Aren't you guys family? If you are, then shut up and use the money to help your sister buy a good pair of running shoes. But don't tell her the money is from me, just say it's from your allowance. That way it will make her a bit happy, understand?"

"Tsk." Shu Zhe clutched the bump on his head, "You can't buy a good pair of shoes for three hundred, and I have to go out with Xiao Li on Saturday&"

"Then spend Sunday with your sister." I decided for him, "If three hundred is not enough, then you pay the rest for now. Basically, you have to buy her a comfortable pair of shoes, is it that hard to repay your sister's affection for you once in a while?"

After being threatened, Shu Zhe finally agreed to go take his sister shopping and try to persuade her to buy a new pair of shoes.

I planned to head straight home and let Xiao Qin head to the subway station herself, but Xiao Qin eavesdropped on our conversation and she grabbed onto my arm right after Shu Zhe left.

"I also want shoes. If Ye Lin classmate is buying a pair for the class leader, right in front of his girlfriend& I don't care, even if you think I'm cheap or petty, but I want to wear the shoes given by Ye Lin classmate today, at least one day before the class leader."

"How is it one day earlier." I laughed, "Today's Friday and Shu Zhe is taking the class leader on Sunday, so that means you would be wearing it two days earlier."

"Huh?" Xiao Qin smiled, "So that means you're agreeing to buy me a new pair of shoes? Do& you have enough money? If you don't, I have some here&"

I still have enough capital from the thousands of dollars of profit from 'Cilantro Buns'. Since the main contributor was Shu Zhe, I don't think I'm giving the class leader a new pair of shoes, but rather, teaching Shu Zhe to respect his sister.

As I looked at the bandages on Xiao Qin's knees, I sighed at her intelligence and also felt I would be concerned if she wasn't by my side. I have no idea if she would do something stupid.

It would be better to buy her a new pair of shoes. Better quality shoes will at least lower her chances of falling down.

I said to her while walking towards the subway station:

"I'll also buy you a pair of running shoes."

Xiao Qin studied me closely to make sure I wasn't being sarcastic and I actually wanted to buy her a pair, then she giggled and said:

"I don't want running shoes. They say girls run too fast with running shoes and their boyfriends can't catch up. Buy me a pair of shoes that's inconvenient to walk in."

What kind of shoe is that? Shoes are made for walking, a pair of shoes that's inconvenient to walk in is putting the cart before the horse.

Or are you referring to high heels? I don't think high heels are a good fit for your childish nature, also what if you fell again because of the heels.

Thus I ignored Xiao Qin's protests and bought her a pair of running shoes.

As we walked out of the store, Xiao Qin stared blankly at the new shoes in the bag. It was as if she already forgot how awkward she made the shop owner when she asked if they could add heels to her shoes.

She used the back of her hand to rub her eyes and see if the shoes will dissipate into a mist, then she happily held the bag in her arms.

"It's a hard to come by chance where Ye Lin classmate would buy me running shoes&" Xiao Qin said with unease, "Even though I've been frail since birth, I might try my best to participate in PE class from now on."

Frail my ass! You should have already been participating in gym class. You could use your 'instant step' to break the record of the hundred meter in 28 Middle. Then, you can throw the shot put ball and break through earth's atmosphere so it could go visit some aliens.

On Saturday morning, I went to Dong Shan lake to practice with gramps. I saw from afar that gramps' back was facing me, he had both hands on the bench and was completely still like he was practicing a strange martial art.

Is& this the trick for learning Fa Jin? Is this a good chance for me to secretly learn the offensive aspect of Yin Yang Sanshou that gramps refuses to teach me?

According to gramps, Chinese martial arts were only composed of two aspects, 'Fa Jin' and 'Hua Jin', where the former is for offense and the latter for defense. Yin Yang Sanshou shouldn't even be taught to outsiders in the first place, so I'm already lucky enough he is teaching me 'Hua Jin'.

But humans are greedy and are never satisfied. I don't learn martial arts to only defend and excel at getting beaten, I still want to win in fights.

So when I saw gramps supporting himself on the bench in a weird posture, I thought of secretly learning his techniques.

But his posture was too strange.

The gramps had both his hands on the bench with his head lowered. His shoulders were tight and his back was exactly parallel to the ground. He was completely motionless and he had sweat dripping down his bright red face.

Does this skill take that much effort? It seems gramps can barely handle it.

I waited for the gramps to change a position, but he stayed completely still even after ten minutes.

I suddenly came to a realization.

Ye Lin& don't waste gramps' efforts. He's purposely trying to pass off Fa Jin to you so you can learn it.

Normally around this time, I would already be practicing with gramps. Even though I was hiding in the shrubbery around twenty feet away, gramps should already know I had arrived.

He doesn't want to go against the wishes of his ancestors, but he also wants to be able to pass on Yin Yang Sanshou. That's why he's purposely showing me so I can learn on my own.

What a noble act.

Don't worry gramps, I understand. I'll open my eyes wide and ingrain the posture of Fa Jin in my mind.

But, this posture seems a bit graceless.

It kind of seems like where someone lifts their ass when they want to fart. Does it really help with hurting your enemies?

Whatever, it's a once-in-a-lifetime opportunity and I should take the chance to learn.

So, I grabbed a tree trunk and also lifted my ass up.

Um& it's a bit embarrassing. Hopefully, no one sees me.

I tried to exert a bit of strength on the tree trunk while maintaining the position, but it felt awkward and I couldn't even use thirty percent of my power.

& I understand. It's not a posture used for fighting, but for training. It's kind of like how Master Roshi makes his disciples wear turtle shells. If you train under unfavorable conditions, you'll be able to get a hundred times stronger when you actually fight!

I struck the trunk of the tree again in excitement. But no matter how hard I tried, I could never turn my face purple like gramps with sweat pouring down my face.

I clenched my teeth to try and change the color of my face, but I didn't even need a mirror to know it was fruitless.

I was lifting my butt while looking constipated, the level of embarrassment increased once again.

No, I can't be rushed. Gramps only got to where he is today through years of hard work. I have to persevere every day to reach gramps' height in this amazing martial arts.

Once I reach that point, I'll be able to topple this tree with a single strike.

Haha, the time when I'll be invincible is just around the corner! I will follow the level up route of "Boxer ' Giant Boxer ' Super Boxer ' Saint Boxer ' God Boxer"!

Perhaps I was too excited and gramps saw the tree shake.

I think he saw it, but his eyes were really focused. It was as if an inner force insider his body was making disturbing him such that he wouldn't recognize me even if he was looking towards my direction.

How considerate, he's pretending to not notice me.

I felt my talent was lacking as I watched gramps use a lot of energy on his amazing martial arts. I might not even understand the trick even if I watched longer, so I walked near him to tell him to rest.

When gramps saw me walk out slowly from behind a tree with admiration on my face, his face became even more purplish, his eyes bulged, and he cursed at me:

"Fuck, Xiao Ye Zi, if you were already here, why didn't you help me when you saw I pulled my back!"

Ha& pulled his back& isn't it supposed to be a martial arts move& wasn't your face turning red because of your neigong& I imitated him for nothing&

I helped gramps change a posture so he could lie down on the bench. He was finally able to take a breath of relief, his face was no longer purple and he was no longer sweating, then he snorted:

"My body can't take it anymore. Looks like I could bite the dust anytime."

I respected gramps a lot, so in order to not look down at him, I kneeled down beside him and laughed:

"Don't worry, you only pulled your back. Based on your physique, you'll be able to dominate Jianghu for a while."

Gramps spat on the ground.

"Jianghu? Where? The old generation is gone, and the new generation won't do their duties. Martial arts are all going to become extinct sooner or later."

I wanted to say "You should make an exception and pass on Yin Yang Sanshou to me so it wouldn't be lost.", but it wasn't the right time or place so I held it in.

Gramps pressed on his back and sighed:

"I'm 81 this year. I married late and gave birth to a son when I was 24&"

Well, 24 is considered late for back then, but currently, it's not even old enough to level up to a wizard.

"Once I had a son, I headed out to travel across the country and learn with martial art masters&"

It was probably fighting instead of learning, otherwise, why would you only leave after you had a son.

"There are a lot of cunning and sly people who use tricks on the Jianghu and there aren't many actual masters. But I learned a lot from those few masters, those twenty years were well worth it."

Twenty years, did you not go home for twenty years? What about your wife? Wow, woman back then really abided by their roles. If it was now, your wife probably would have had a lover after you left for two months.

"We didn't have good communication back then, so a lot of the folks back home thought I was dead. Everyone was really happy when I came back and our village celebrated for three days, it was great&"

It looks as if gramps was submerged in his memories.

"Then, my wife gave me a daughter. But she wasn't able to have a good life and passed away from sickness soon after giving birth&"

"A lot of the masters I met when I traveled around the world were as crazy for martial arts as I was, but many were not able to make it to the end. There were some who fell at the hands of petty men; there were some who went mad with power and got struck by lightning; there were some who were tricked by bad men and were eventually executed by the law; there were some who protected the people during the Cultural Revolution and were shot to death; but it was the one who was the weakest, the one who everyone ignored, who changed his name and became an abbot at a monastery, who is trading stocks every day and living a good life&"

Gramps sighed:

"Sigh, I have more friends and family in the netherworld than the world of the living. Perhaps they might be beckoning for me soon."

This scene is too sad and doesn't really fit you. Weren't you just happily scamming the dude a couple of days ago?

Thus I ignored my legs becoming numb and continued to speak to gramps while kneeling:

"Master&"

"Don't call me master." gramps got angry, "I already said you're not my disciple."

"Fine, fine." I said, "Gramps, your martial arts skills are unrivaled, what's the big deal with pulling your back once in a while? We youngsters sometimes even pull our backs when playing basketball. You'll be better after two days of rest."

"How about this. I'll still come to the lake to run for the following two days, but I won't practice with you anymore, you should stay home and rest& it's actually more tiring practicing with you than running, so I could also take two days of rest&"

Gramps said in a fit of anger: "Bastard, martial artists can't be lazy. I could rest, but you can't."

Then he stuck his hand into his bosom and pulled out an egg.

I accepted it and thanked gramps in a hurry.

"Gramps, you're too kind, you even bought an egg for me as breakfast&"

"You idiot." Gramps hit me on my head, "It's raw."

"Huh?" I had a dumb look on my face, "How would I eat it raw?"

"It's not for eating, it's for practice." gramps snorted lividly, "I already felt my back was feeling a bit off when I left the house this morning, so I took the egg with me& listen closely, I have to rest for a few days, but in these few days, you have to keep it on you whether you're going to school or taking a shit, and you can't break it."

"Do I put it in my pocket?"

"It can be anywhere, but you can keep it in your pocket. After my back is healed, you better return the egg to me intact."

"Um& how would carrying an egg with me help with Yin Yang Sanshou?"

Gramps glared at me to 'shut up' and I stopped talking.

"Let me tell you, it's said that practicing martial arts is not about a person training martial arts, but martial arts training the person. If you want to train your body to do as you like, then you must develop the habit of moving your body purely out of muscle memory, without thinking too much. In short, the egg is good for you, treat it with care, but if you break it & "

My face filled with fear.

"Huh, are you saying I can't practice Yin Yang Sanshou if I break the egg?"

Gramps glared at me, "If you break the egg, then& you'll have to buy me a new one. Right now, eggs cost nine dollars and forty per kilo."

I unexpectedly received a call from Su Qiao as I was carrying my egg back home.

Strange, how did she get my phone number? Although she did give me her phone number, I never gave mine to her. Did she get it from Auntie Ren?

Just like before, the first things that came out of Su Qiao's mouth were words of gratitude.

However, she did make some progress and began to call me 'Xiao Ye' instead of 'Mr. Ye'.

After she confirmed I was free, Su Qiao began chatting with me. I quietly listened to her while protecting the egg in my pocket, it's not like I had anything better to do.

Su Qiao told me two things which were both good news for her.

First, the role of the blood prince's maid she played in the 'Magic Cauldron' had more lines than martial arts scenes, but since she had a background in acrobatics, she played her martial arts scenes to its fullest and performed better than people who actually knew martial arts.

Naturally, the director praised her and discussed with the screenwriters to expand the depth of her role. Basically, it would be giving her more scenes and upping her role in the show.

She went from a minor character in season one, to a 'recurring character' who may appear over three seasons. Su Qiao still couldn't believe her eyes even when a new contract with a huge increase in pay was placed right in front of her.

Afterward, a reporter from a TV station interviewed her and invited her to be a guest on the series 'Little People, Big Dreams', so she could tell the audience her journey which started as a background character.

For an actor, being able to go on TV and increase their popularity is a great opportunity. But according to Su Qiao, there was another reporter called Zhao Yao who wasn't really friendly. Zhao Yao kept chatting around to see if Su Qiao only got her role due to the 'unspoken rules'.

Damn, wasn't this the same reporter who wrote the story about how Auntie Ren became a call girl after MMA because she couldn't make a living? You can't go around creating rumors (TN: creating rumors is Zao Yao) simply because you're name is Zhao Yao&

But to be honest, Su Qiao did indeed have thoughts about performing 'unspoken rules', but I don't have any power in the crew. At most, I could only ask Ai Mi to not give you any trouble.

Besides, I still don't know who gave you the role as the blood prince's maid. Perhaps it was Auntie Ren? I guess it's possible she did a good thing but doesn't want to admit it&

The second thing was that she was suddenly signed on by a Taiwanese management company.

Her manager was a thirty-six-year-old man with the surname of Fu who was affiliated with 'Tianmu Starlight Ltd Co'. Although it was an unknown company, there were rumors that say it was started by an experienced insider of the industry. It has a lot of capital and backings and will make some huge movements in Southeast Asia in the upcoming years.

Happiness came too quickly and Su Qiao signed the contract which exceeded twenty-six pages without much consideration.

I have some slight understanding of management companies due to my past interest in the film and television industry. It sounds like Su Qiao signed a fully binding contract with the company and became one of their actors. Basically, it means you have to give a share of your earnings to the company for all activities, including advertisements. That alone makes it not as good as a stand-alone contract.

But you can't really blame Su Qiao because she was too desperate to make her mark in the world of performing arts.

The length of the contract was ten years. During those ten years, she can't date, can't get married, and can't get sick for personal reasons. You have zero personal freedom.

In contrast, the company provided a base salary to Su Qiao, which could be considered as good. Furthermore, they guarantee they would do their utmost to provide work immediately after her job at the 'Magic Cauldron' ends.

Overall, I guess it's a good thing. I congratulated her over the phone while I carefully avoided a cyclist to avoid breaking my egg.

The funny part was Su Qiao actually said her manager was interested in me and asked if I wanted to meet him.

Do I even have any talent worth being discovered by a management company? Do they want me to play the villain again? If I wanted to play a villain, Director Cao has a role waiting for me. I would never sign a contract where I would sign away my life.

"But Xiao Ye, Mr. Fu is very interested in you."

Su Qiao urged me.

"No, it's okay." I said, "They're a brand new company, so they shouldn't get too greedy and sign too many people at once. Besides, I already played too many villain roles recently, they should look for someone else."

Even when Su Qiao says they guarantee they would only give me positive roles, I still don't believe good things simply fall from the sky. Instead, I recommended Su Qiao to look up the company's qualifications to make sure they aren't frauds. It would be terrible if they use the contract to force their actors to film AVs.

Seeing she couldn't change my mind, Su Qiao changed the topic. She asked if I was still living alone and if I had anyone cooking for me.

"Huh? How did you know I lived alone?"

"Um& I accidentally overheard a conversation between the martial arts director and Xiao Qin. I actually have a few dishes I excel at, so I can come over to cook for you as thanks if that's okay."

Uh& that would be unnecessary. My house is pretty far from the film city and the crew is pretty busy all the time. It was also hard for you to find a place to rent, so why would you travel such a far distance to cook for me?

I told her that her good intentions were enough, but I had no set rules on meals, I might not even go home straight away after school. I let her know she should spend her free time at home resting to avoid getting sick. Otherwise, it would void the clause on her contract where it states she can't get sick because of personal reasons.

Su Qiao was disappointed she couldn't convince me to meet with Mr. Fu or use her cooking to express her thanks. But she still respectfully said farewell and also told me we should talk some more if I'm heading to film city today.

I'm not sure if I am heading to film city today. If I go to the film city, then I can see Ai Mi, and Ai Mi's panties&

Damn, don't twist your thoughts. Why did I already decide I'm going to make money selling her underwear? Am I really not going to earn twenty thousand dollars through normal means anymore?

When I passed some stalls, I asked for the price of eggs. The vendor told me it was nine dollars per kilo, it was cheaper because of the bird flu going around.

Oh, so that means it won't cost more if I break my egg at Film City.

When I was eating breakfast at a wonton vendor, a police car slowly split the crowd and parked next to me.

The vendors originally wanted to make an unnecessary racket, but they quieted down and continued to operate their business as usual when they notice the police car didn't have 'city management' written on the sides.

The one driving was a police officer I didn't recognize, but constable Ma was sitting on the passenger seat. He got off the car and handed me a blue backpack with a stern expression.

Huh, wasn't this the backpack that was confiscated when someone planted weed on me. Why is the half-empty bottle of drink still here?

"The evidence technicians have already carefully inspected it and haven't found anything suspicious, so I'm returning it to you."

Constable Ma said in a businesslike manner without emotions.

If you weren't obsessed with arresting me, then you would be a model policeman.

It's fine returning the bag, but why keep the half-empty bottle? It will definitely go bad in the summer heat, there's already suspicious elements floating on top. If you took the lab to investigate now, you will probably find toxins!

I poured the toxic liquid into the sewers and handed the bottle to an old granny nearby who was collecting recyclables, then I put on my backpack. (TN: For those who don't know, you can sell plastic bottles in China. Not sure what the price is at now, maybe ¥0.10 a bottle?)

Constable Ma squeezed a few words out his mouth after he saw me finish those actions:

"I can still see through your true personality even if you pretend to be a good person."

Who's pretending? Am I a good person simply because I gave an empty bottle to an old granny?

"I'm not pretending." I said, "Since you can see everything with your eyes, what's the point of pretending to be a good person? It would be nice if all police were like you and could distinguish who was a criminal at a glance, then they wouldn't catch the wrong person&"

Constable Ma snorted when he heard I was ridiculing him.

"Kid, there's a gang made up of teens in Dong Shan City recently stirring up a lot of trouble, you're not involved, right?"

"I am." I said as I pointed to myself with my thumb, "I'm their boss. I even tell them to offer a beautiful girl to me every day as a tribute."

Then constable Ma's phone rang. His face turned gravely serious after he picked up.

"Stay calm, don't alert the enemies." he said, "I'll be there soon."

"Also, tell chubby to wear his bulletproof vest. Even if it's hot, the blubber on his stomach can't save him twice."

Constable Ma pointed at me and wanted to say some parting remarks, but he couldn't think of anything and left with a tragic expression.

Were they going to fight organized crime or to stop drug traffickers? Although Constable Ma was detestable, I still wished him success. Captain Zhao was a good person, it was a shame he passed away. If everyone on the front lines eventually all passes away and get replaced with cowards who are afraid of death, then the crime in Dong Shan city would be as crazy as Mexico.

After I arrived at Film City and reached Ai Mi's RV. I saw her bodyguards standing in a circle and Ai Mi was in the middle wearing her costume for the film. She had a stethoscope around her neck and was listening to Obama's heartbeat for fun.

"Lie down, patients aren't supposed to get up."

Every time Obama wanted to leap up, Ai Mi would press down on his neck. Even though she had no strength, Obama was obedient to his owner and cooperated by playing dead.

When Ai Mi saw me walking over, she seemed pleased with my unexpected appearance. She patted Obama's butt to tell him to leave, then she pointed at where the dog was previously lying.

"Manservant, come here. Let me see if your heartbeat is healthy."

What a childish doctor game. Did you ask your bodyguards to form a circle so no one would see?

But since the grass wasn't dirty and especially since Obama hadn't done his business, I listened to my younger sister's request and carefully laid down.

I had to be careful to protect the egg in my pocket.

Ai Mi was extremely satisfied when she saw me lie down obediently. She leaned over and pressed the stethoscope on my chest.

"Huh? Why can't I hear clearly? Is it because the manservant is already dead?"

You're the zombie. You obviously can't hear clearly because you're doing it over clothes and it's not even directly over my heart.

Ai Mi ordered me to unbutton my top and reveal my chest, but I said:

"Why would a patient have the strength to do that? You should be the one to do it as a doctor."

"I& I'm an advanced doctor who doesn't handle these miscellaneous tasks." Ai Mi argued, then she beckoned Peng TouSi: "Come help the manservant unbutton."

Peng TouSi had a red glow on his face as he accepted the order, it scared me half to death and I quickly unbuttoned myself.

Ai Mi covered her mouth and laughed when she saw me reveal my sturdy chest.

Then she put the cold stethoscope directly over my heart. Damn, it's cold. I wouldn't be playing this game if she wasn't my younger sister.

"Ba-dum, ba-dum", the sound of my heartbeat was carried through the stethoscope into Ai Mi's ears. At one point in time, it was like her mind began to wander.

I then became aware of a serious problem.

She was kneeling on the ground while leaning towards me. From my angle, I could see under her skirt.

The costume's skirt was very short. Although there were magic inscriptions of restriction embroidered on the skirt, it couldn't stop the gaze of a pervert!

She shouldn't be doing this on purpose. Since she was just listening to a dog's heartbeat, she didn't care if she was exposed, but when she changed to me, she didn't notice she was exposing herself.

Or is it because Obama and I were on the same level in Ai Mi's mind?

Don't compare your brother to a dog! We share the same DNA.

"Why did the patient's heartbeat get faster?" Ai Mi was puzzled, "He might be dying. Peng TouSi, get the taser."

I would never tell you my heart started beating faster because I saw your laced panties. Besides, aren't tasers for defense, not for saving someone?

Soon, Ai Mi was called to the scene. She handed the stethoscope to Peng TouSi unhappily, "You could play with the manservant", then she stormed on set.

I was on guard against Peng TouSi coming over while thinking to myself with indignation:

I can't believe she's wearing sexy underwear at such a young age. Is it because she doesn't want to be laughed at in case she gets exposed on camera? Lolis should wear loli underwear, the one she's wearing right now doesn't suit her at all& she might as well hand it over to me so I could sell it.

t

A single scene of the 'female protagonist storming the imperial palace' took up the entire morning. Most of the actions were completed with Ai Mi attached to steel rope. No matter how much Auntie Ren instructed her, Ai Mi couldn't really improve her positioning. She also lost her balance multiple times and had to be untied like a fish suspended with a fishing rod.

But Ai Mi still criticized the other members of the crew. For example, she felt the lights were too glaring, the sound of the rail camera was too loud, or the makeup artist had too many freckles on her face&. it was like she was born to quarrel with everyone.

When it was break time, I asked Auntie Ren why Xiao Qin wasn't here. Auntie Ren told me in a bad mood that she locked Xiao Qin at home to learn from a new art teacher she hired.

Since Xiao Qin decided she wanted to become a great shoujo mangaka, it seems she went and bought tons of manga goods and filled her room.

In order to support her daughter's hobby and so she doesn't think about me all day, Auntie Ren invited the scene artist's best friend. She was an avant-garde artist at a fine arts institution and was suitable to be Ai Mi's art teacher. Starting from this week, she would teach Xiao Qin how to draw for at least 8 hours a week. Xiao Qin is not allowed to leave the house or even use her cellphone before she completes the request.

No wonder she didn't bother me today, so it's because she went to learn how to draw. I guess it's good, since it would take a burden off me if she focuses more on drawing.

"Also.." Auntie Ren said, "Were you the one who gave Xiao Qin the pair of running shoes she brought home last night?"

"Eh? How did you know?"

"It's obvious because she put it on her desk and stared at it all night without sleeping. I had to force her to go to sleep, but when I woke up, I found out she went to sleep while wearing the shoes."

Ah& I could kind of understand Auntie Ren's anger. A pair of shoes could cause her daughter to be out of her mind, which meant Xiao Qin felt her boyfriend was more important than 14 years of upbringing. If I had a daughter like her, I would also lock her up at home.

I remembered Xiao Qin had a habit of not wearing clothes when she went to sleep. She also only bought her first bra two months ago, so she might not even wear it when she goes to sleep.

That means, when Auntie Ren went to wake up her daughter this morning, this was the scene she saw: Xiao Qin was only wearing panties and running shoes and she might have even been sleep talking about me while hugging her pillow.

Of course she would get really angry. Her own daughter being smitten in love would only remind Auntie Ren of her past self.

Shifting the focus back to Ai Mi, since she offended the crew today, the director finally reminded Ai Mi through the makeup artist to maintain his prestige: the underwear she wore today was too trendy, even though they won't take shots under the skirt, but in high-speed shots, it will affect the overall effect. He recommended her to change into a simpler one, at least one that matches the color of the costume.

That's why Ai Mi was inside the RV taking a shower and changing her underwear while I was outside freeloading a meal.

"What a perverted director." Ai Mi complained before she went to take a shower, "He should have told me sooner if he already realized, instead I had to be eye-raped for so long."

Huh, the last time I heard the word 'eye-rape' was from Eunuch Cao's mouth, does Ai Mi meet a lot of fans who eye-rapes her? Or is it that all female idols can't avoid being eye-raped by their fans?

I was at a loss after eating the "Provence Chicken Pasta" made by a French chef. I was slightly shaken by the claim that China had the best food in the world. At the same time, my blood flowed to my stomach to digest the food and I lacked brainpower.

I wiped my mouth and asked Peng TouSi:

"Where are Ai Mi's used underwear usually kept&"

All the bodyguards who understood Chinese (such as 004 and 005) all looked at me in alarm.

I cursed my low intelligence and quickly put on a serious expression and spoke with a concerned tone:

"Weren't there a couple of stalkers who went overboard when she was in America? I was worried they would try to get her underwear if it wasn't kept in a safe place."

I spoke and waved my arms while my words also hinted as if to say: "You guys dare suspect me."

Peng TouSi took my words as a brother's concern for his sister, so he nodded and said:

"Miss Ai Mi'er's worn clothes will be dropped through a specialized tube into a sealed laundry basket. Then it will be taken to the hotel where it would be washed by a specialist."

Peng TouSi took the QingZi Academy VIP building as a hotel, but I guess he's right since the decor definitely looks like a hotel. I haven't been there in a while.

"After the clothes are washed, it will then be brought to Miss Ai Mi'er. The ones she likes will be put into the closet and the ones she doesn't will be thrown into a pulverizer."

Well, I could understand why you throw the clothes into a pulverizer, but why do you wash it before you decide? Don't you know the earth has a limited water supply?

I said I saw a giant cricket as an excuse to get away from the bodyguards and ran to the other side of the RV to scope it out.

This side was closer to the forest and was much cooler. I calmed myself and began to look for the twenty thousand dollar treasure placed in the two protruding 'detachable areas' from the RV.

You could hear the faint sound of trickling water from one of the detachable areas with a curtain.

That should be where Ai Mi is taking a shower. I can't peak on my sister showering as a brother, but I can estimate the position of the specialized tube based on the position of the shower.

I strolled next to the window of the shower. Usually, Peng TouSi would be keeping guard outside when Ai Mi showers, but did Peng TouSi not come because he trusted me to guard her?

It's embarrassing I couldn't live up to Peng TouSi's expectations. I grabbed the bottom trims of the windows with both my hands and peeked in on my tiptoes. I wanted to find any clues I could about her underwear.

I swear I'm not trying to peek at my sister shower. Even though I saw a glimpse of her toe, my goal is only my sister's underwear.

I suddenly realized there were many more hands grabbing the trims of the window.

One, two, three, four&. why are there four hands?

I turned my head and saw Kyle in the same posture as me, then he spoke in broken Chinese while winking:

"Shhh, let's fight fairly. We should not expose each other."

When the hell did you get here? Are you a ninja instead of a warrior? Why would I not expose you?

Don't peek at my sister. I'll beat you to death&

I grabbed onto Kyle's clothes and pulled him into the forest. He didn't resist because he didn't want to make any loud sounds.

Once he determined we were at a safe distance, he freed himself, put up his fists and his eyes were burning with fervor.

"Fight, who wins, who peeks."

Shut up, hemorrhoid warrior. (sorry, Xiao Qin's nickname suits him too well) That's not why I'm fighting, I have to beat you up since you were going to peek on my sister.

Right when I was about to fight, I remembered I had an egg in my pocket.

Not only was Kyle older than me, he also had muscles developed from working out at a gym. He's not an opponent I could beat easily.

If I broke my egg half-way through the fight, I might not lose much money, but it will affect my spirit.

If an unidentified sticky liquid appears on my pants, then I would have to tell Kyle to pause the fight.

"Wait, my egg broke."

Kyle will definitely stop attacking and even look at me with sympathy.

I don't need you to sympathize with me, I'm talking about chicken eggs, not my balls.

Or I could take the egg out and leave it on the ground before I fight.

But that would go against gramps' order. Even though gramps doesn't have clairvoyance, I would still have a guilty conscience.

"Wait, I can't fight you with eggs." Would I have to say that to Kyle?

Kyle would definitely laugh out loud: "I also have eggs. Don't worry I won't hit your eggs."

"My eggs are not the same as yours, I have to take it out and put it on the ground&"

Then Kyle will make a (™o™) face for sure.

Peng TouSi came over in a hurry when my imagination was still running wild.

When he saw we were about to fight, he picked us up like chicks, one in each hand. We couldn't do anything regardless of how hard we struggled.

"Please don't interrupt Miss Ai Mi'er's bath time." Peng TouSi said, "It's the only time she can relax and it's even more important to her than sleep."

"I didn't interrupt& Ai Mi's bath time." I explained, "It's him, he came here to peek. Aren't you a bodyguard? Take out your gun and shoot him, then bury him."

After Kyle heard I wanted to turn him into fertilizer, he panicked and spoke a lot of English. I couldn't understand anything he said.

In order to convey his anger, Kyle kicked me while he was suspended in the air. I didn't want to suffer any losses, so I reached my leg out, but&

Damn it, my legs are too short. The hemorrhoid warrior deserves the death penalty!

Perhaps it was in consideration that Kyle was the protagonist and burying him in a ditch would affect the filming progress, so Peng TouSi put Kyle down and told him to "Go", then he pretended to pull a gun out from his waist.

Kyle immediately ran away without even looking back.

Peng TouSi then put me down, patted my shoulders, and said:

"Lin, good job keeping watch. I'm at ease if you're here."

Don't feel relieved yet! I was actually looking through the window along with Kyle and we saw the same things. I'm ashamed that I'm not even as loyal as a bodyguard who has no blood relations with Ai Mi.

I criticized myself while feeding Obama next to the RV. Ai Mi's bath time already exceeded forty minutes, why does she take so long.

I was holding a bag of Natural Balance premium dog food that 005 gave me and feeding it piece by piece to Obama. I couldn't help feeling a bit envious when I saw him eating it so happily.

No, I'm not envious because of the food, if that was the case, I could just put some in my mouth. I'm envious because an animal doesn't have any worries at all. They could eat and sleep whenever they want, they basically live like gods.

As soon as my mind wavered, I tightened the bag and didn't feed him anymore.

Obama still sat in front of me with eyes of expectation.

I rebuked Obama like a kindergartner teacher educating kids:

"Do you only know how to eat? Can't you do anything to make your owner happy, even doing a roll works."

As a pure-blooded and noble Husky, Obama was initially aloof, then he rolled his eyes to express his discontent.

I remain unmoved and continued to say:

"What are you looking at?"

Obama grumbled since he couldn't get any more food, so he went back into the RV with his head drooped.

Huh, is he finding a cool place to sleep or is he going to get some food from the French chef? How impatient, he could get some food if he did a simple trick.

Soon after, Obama came out of the RV with a completely different look. He was bursting with vigor and wagging his tail as if he deserved the dog food in my hands.

I was baffled and took a closer look: it seems Obama was holding something in his mouth.

Damn, isn't that Ai Mi's laced underwear.

Where did you find it, isn't the laundry bin sealed? You traitor, why do you think you can trade Ai Mi's panties with food?

Obama ran near me and stood up on his hind legs. He put his front paws on my shoulder and was going to pass the underwear into my hands.

His eyes were full of understanding as if he wanted to say:

"Brother, I could only help you up to here."

Who's your brother? I don't need a dog to sympathize with me!

Should I accept this pair of underwear? Even though it's only a piece of cloth that's been on my sister's body, it's worth twenty thousand dollars! I can't lose this chance!

But it's stained with dog saliva. Even if it's an 'original' pair of underwear, there's more dog than Ai Mi. As an honest businessman, I kind of feel guilty giving underwear that's been in a dog's mouth to Director Cao.

But it's fine if I wash it. It's not like Director Cao said he had to have a pair of 'original' underwear. If it was a fresh original one, he said he would pay thirty thousand dollars!

Right when I was about to take it, 004 and 005 came over. 004 took the panties from Obama's mouth, and 005 scolded him:

"Again? Can you not give out Miss Ai Mi'er's panties to everyone?"

Huh, so this wasn't the first time Obama used Ai Mi's underwear in exchange for food? So, he doesn't have super intelligence, but rather he was conditioned by a stalker?

Regardless of the truth, the international lolicon association (ILA) would give you a medal.

Although Obama held on and wouldn't let go (since it's something he could exchange for food), he was eventually subdued by Peng TouSi who came over because of the sound.

"Throw it in the pulverizer." Peng TouSi handed the underwear to 005 and gave him a command.

What a waste. Space is limited in a RV, but they still brought along a pulverizer. No, I can't go and look and the pulverizer. My heart bleeds simply thinking about the twenty thousand dollars that's going to be shredded.

Even though I failed at obtaining my sister's underwear, I've still obtained some valuable information. Once I find a more suitable time, dog food and a tooth cover, I might be able to obtain a pair of underwear not drenched in saliva.

Where would I get large tooth covers, but tooth covers won't work either. The main problem is the saliva from the tongue, I would have to use a 'tongue cover'& being a human is so worrisome&

In the afternoon, Su Qiao gave me another call and told me her manager wanted to meet at a nearby cafe. I thought he definitely wanted to scam me if he was this enthusiastic, so I said I had hemorrhoids and couldn't drink coffee to refuse Su Qiao's good intentions.

I circled around the RV multiple times to see if I could deduce the inner layout of the RV, but it was fruitless.

It's not like Ai Mi forbid me from entering, but she was in a bad mood and didn't let me in her personal area. I was only allowed to sit with the bodyguards in the rear cabin area.

Is the rear cabin even a suitable place for people to stay? It's even worse than economy class on airplanes! Seven or eight bodyguards with large figures have to squeeze into two tight rows of seats without a chance to even stretch your limbs. Their eyes are wide open as if they're going to embark on the beaches of Normandy.

Is it so they can leave the RV quickly to deal with urgent matters? Stop making a big deal over minor issues, which lolicon needs eight muscular bodyguards armed to the teeth with weapons?

The worst part is there's a hole the size of a volleyball in the middle of the floor. You guys won't even believe me if I told you its use. It's used for peeing, if your bladder is full, then just empty it into the hole. Even though there's a washroom specifically for bodyguards, you can't use it unless it's urgent.

It's awful, what kind of lives are American bodyguards living? Why don't they raise their pitchforks and revolt against the evil capitalists who exploit them?

Wait, it seems Ai ShuQiao would be the evil capitalist. Usually, only antagonists would tell other people to beat their own mother.

But it's fine, I don't have any relationship with Ai ShuQiao. You can safely overthrow her while I'll give you support. Then we can share her wealth equally.

But now that I think about it, Ai Mi is a ruthless capitalist.

She actually told her brother to stay in the narrow rear cabin. Even though it had a great air filtration system, it still couldn't beat the strong smell of men! Also, I had to urinate in front of these foreigners, who knew if any of them were gay like Peng TouSi.

Besides, if I stayed too long, the egg in my pocket might turn spoiled. It seems gramps was still planning on taking the egg back from me to eat. If the egg was ingrained with the flavors of European and American men, gramps might give me a death strike in a fit of anger.

That's why I never got on Ai Mi's RV. I waited until the sky got dark and prepared to ride the subway home.

Ai Mi had just finished filming and she was cooling off her tired body on her personal water bed. She used a remote control to open the automatic window of the

RV a third of the way, then she rested her chin on her arms and stared at me without any energy.

"Manservant, when are you breaking up with that violent woman?"

It's useless asking me since even if I break up with Xiao Qin, it has nothing to do with you. I should be the one asking you when you would be taking a shower and changing your underwear.

"It's all because of you& I think mom found out about us cheating& now she hired a writing teacher to monitor me every day. It's so annoying. Hurry up and take responsibility by knocking the teacher out on his way home!"

Why do I have to take responsibility? This was only caused by your own laziness. What crimes did the writing teacher commit? I, on the other hand, want to hire some terrorists to knock out Ai ShuQiao.

Seeing as I didn't reply energetically, Ai Mi angrily shut the windows and told the driver to drive away. I was left standing alone in the exhaust of the RV.

An old man dressed in a suit, who I didn't recognize, placed his hand on my shoulder and tried to comfort me:

"Don't lose hope. There will be more chances."

Damn, who are you? Don't just jump out and scare people!

Wait, isn't he Kyle's personal translator? Kyle was standing in the distance while sticking up his thumb& Is this what he means by a fair fight? Did he send a translator to boost my morale when I failed to pick up Ai Mi? I don't need it, I wasn't even trying to pick up my sister. As for someone like you who's full of evil desires, you should get as far away from here as possible.

After I chased Kyle away, Auntie Ren drove next to me, but she had no intention of giving me a ride.

She rolled down her window and I saw an envelope filled with money in the passenger seat.

Perhaps& is it the second batch of payments for playing the role of the evil monk? (It's probably also the final payment) Based on Auntie Ren's expression, it looks like she's planning to head to the hotel where my dad is staying and hand the money to my guardian.

It's really a waste of effort since my dad will transfer the money to my account once he gets it. Auntie Ren, you're so stubborn. Or are you afraid I'll buy Xiao Qin more things once I get the cash, and Xiao Qin will throw herself into my arms?

Auntie Ren, you're intelligence is out of date. Xiao Qin already threw herself in my arms ages ago. Also, I would never spend money to win Xiao Qin's favor, it's more likely I would spend money to annoy her. The running shoes are a special exception.

I didn't want Auntie Ren to waste her time, so I urged her to not go.

"Auntie Ren, you already had some bad luck the last time you went to deliver money, are you not afraid of meeting the anti-pornography brigade again?"

Auntie Ren glared at me, "I can't believe he would tell it to kids, how shameless&"

I laughed and said: "It's better to be safe than sorry&"

Auntie Ren looked at me like I was trash and snorted:

"Last time, I already ran into the anti-pornography brigade, if I run into them again& do you think your family runs the anti-pornography brigade?"

Then she slammed the gas and sped away, leaving me in the exhaust of the yellow bumblebee.

Kyle's translator came over and patted my shoulders again:

"Don't lose hope. There will be more chances."

Screw you, get the hell out of here! Why are you still here when Kyle already left? How does it even look like I failed at trying to pick up Auntie Ren? How perverted would I have to be to make a move on my mother-in-law!

I didn't respect the elderly and raised my fist. He turned away like a gentleman and walked away energetically.

It looks like there are no normal people around Kyle. I should stay away from him in the future.

In addition, the stubborn Auntie Ren who had to deliver the money to my father had even worse luck than last time.

Five minutes after Auntie Ren walked into the hotel, before she could even finish a conversation with my dad, she noticed a lot of special police outside wearing NBC suits.

They surrounded the hotel and their leader made a loud announcement on the megaphone.

It seems in the afternoon, there was a tourist living in the hotel who was tested positive for the H7N9 virus. In order to prevent the virus from spreading, the leader made an order that everyone in the hotel will be forcibly quarantined for a week. No one can leave until they determine the crisis has been cleared.

What kind of development is this? Auntie Ren must have looked pale at the time.

Since it has to do with the public's safety, even Auntie Ren's brother or father wouldn't be able to get her out. It seems the 'Magic Cauldron' would be missing the crucial martial arts director for the next week of filming.

Even if Auntie Ren told my dad to contact the president of the HHH Enthusiasts Club, Director Cao would say the president was busy with some sort of experiment and didn't have time for anything else.

Thus, Auntie Ren was forced to stay in the same hotel as my father for at least a week without any personal belongings.

Auntie Ren must have had tears in her eyes, and I, as her junior, can only feel sad for her&

Ai Mi was the happiest when Auntie Ren was placed into a forced quarantine.

She was the first one to call me to share her joy.

"Hahahahaha, she deserved it. She was always so mean to me, so it's her karma."

Ai Mi was holding her stomach and rolling on her bed while laughing. I could imagine it even if we were speaking on the phone.

"Hahahha& she's even closed together with the manservant's father." Ai Mi's laugh became more and more evil, "A man and a woman sharing a room together, maybe Ren HongLi would be pregnant with your little brother or sister when she gets released. I want to see how she would even demonstrate the moves with a large belly."

"Keep dreaming." I said, "Auntie Ren would never be interested in my dad. Also, even if my dad watches too many AVs and goes wild, he wouldn't be able to beat Auntie Ren even with three of him."

"What do you mean by three of him?" Ai mi asked, "Do you have three fathers?"

It's a metaphor, do you not understand metaphors? Looks like she exaggerated when she said she was at grade 10 Chinese. She knows a lot of internet slangs, but doesn't know other common phrases.

"What I mean is Auntie Ren could fight against three people equal to my father. By the way, you don't have to worry, Auntie Ren would never live in the same room as my father even when they're closed in the same hotel."

"Huh, then where would she live?"

"Um& even though my dad is in a room with two single beds, he occasionally had friends over to stay the night& but when Auntie Ren learned she couldn't escape from the quarantine, she immediately chased my dad out of his room."

"A turtledove takes over the nest of a magpie? No wonder she's the violent girl's mother, how barbaric&"

"Oh, that's a nice use of the idiom&"

"Of course, I don't need you to praise me. What happened next?"

"Then she split apart a couple who came to the hotel to celebrate their wedding anniversary. She was living with the woman and sent my dad to live with the man&"

"Split apart& did she force them to get a divorce? So Ren HongLi can't stand looking at a successful marriage because her own was a failure? How awful."

"No, she never forced them to get a divorce, she only made them live apart from each other& it's because the couple had a fight on their anniversary and they didn't want to live together anyway&."

"So that's what happened, how boring&"

When my dad told me what happened, he admitted he actually hoped Auntie Ren would live in the same room as him, but his wish burst like a soap bubble.

After being sent to the other guy's room, he couldn't focus on editing his teaching materials and the other guy was always complaining:

"Did your wife also kick you out? I guess we're both the same."

"Sigh, they all say marriage is the grave of love. It was way better before we got married."

"Huh, are you a teacher? Which university should my son attend?"

Damn, my dad really wanted to hit him, but he endured it since the other guy was a fatty over 200 pounds.

The fatty also snored loudly at night, so I guess it must have been hard on his wife too.

Basically, even though Auntie Ren and my father was stuck in the same hotel, they never shared the same room.

Every time they met, Auntie Ren was always in a bad mood as if it was my dad's fault she was stuck in the hotel.

But it wasn't like she couldn't participate in the filming process at all. She commandeered my dad's laptop to video chat with the directors in film city and also to verbally direct their actions. Even though it was a bit awkward, it was still better than being completely absent.

Auntie Ren was able to protect her job, but my dad's work was delayed. But his old classmate was entirely reasonable and understood the bird flu was uncontrollable, so it didn't matter if he took a bit longer to make the teaching materials.

Well, it's not like bird flu actually affects his work even if my dad was trapped in the hotel everyday. The uncontrollable one was Auntie Ren who kicked him out of his own room and took his laptop. Auntie Ren was the main cause of why my dad couldn't do his work.

But regardless of how hard Auntie Ren worked, filming progress slowed down and Ai Mi was able to get a bit of rest.

"Manservant, I want to go to Henderson Mall again Sunday, come with me." Then she lowered her voice, "Remember to buy me coke. For some reason Peng TouSi always drops his vigilance around Henderson Mall, it might be because he's gay&"

Henderson isn't the same words as homosexual! (TN: Because Henderson and homosexual in Chinese share the same character, she thinks the two are related) Peng TouSi thinks you're under a lot of pressure, so he gives you a chance to drink coke once a week on purpose. I guess I could go with her to Henderson tomorrow and act like an actual brother, I've been spending too much time recently thinking about underwear.

Ai Mi couldn't sleep after she hung up the phone, so she actually told her subordinate to find out Auntie Ren's room number and give her a prank call.

"Hello, is this Madam Ren HongLi? The original owner of this room is cursing you in your dreams, we are helpful spirits who wanted to notify you&"

Auntie Ren thought the call was from my dad, so she threw down the phone and rushed into his room. When she saw someone under the covers with their hand near the phone, she gave the person under the covers a beating.

When my dad came out of the washroom, he shockingly discovered the fatty had fainted. The fatty was actually still snoring and it was even louder than usual.

Xiao Qin didn't find out about the quarantine until a bit later on. Maybe Auntie Ren only gave her a call when she was positive she had no chance of leaving the hotel.

She probably told Xiao Qin to take care of herself and don't act stupid. She would tell a friend to take care (keep a close watch) on Xiao Qin or something along those lines.

It was clear Xiao Qin didn't think it was serious when she spoke to me over the phone.

"It's a pity they didn't live in the same room&"

It's inappropriate for a girl to say that&

"If they lived in the same room, then they could discuss our marriage all night!"

I guess you still only think about things from your perspective. Did you already decide my dad would be your father-in-law? Keep dreaming, they are both still a mature man and woman. Luckily, they didn't live in the same room, or they might be doing something else all night long.

I managed the online store a bit before I went to sleep. 'Uncle Fireball' sent me a message to confirm if the sexy white rose panties would be shipped out tomorrow.

Tomorrow is Sunday, but even if Shu Zhe already wore it for a full 72 hours, there's no need to retrieve it right away. Also, Shu Zhe promised he would take his sister shopping for a pair of running shoes.

Thus I apologized to Uncle Fireball and told him the model had some personal affairs, so I could only ship it out on Monday.

Uncle Fireball didn't complain since he was able to have the model wear it for four days by paying only ¥300.

The other orders were all ordinary like vibrators, dildos, figurines of Maria Takagi, a real life model of Obama's penis (It's sad how these are considered normal in our store). I packaged all the orders and planned to ship them all out at the same time.

On Sunday morning, I took a cold shower, put on some casual clothes, and ran three laps around Dong Shan Lake.

Gramps never came, so he was probably still at home resting, which meant I still had to keep carrying the egg on me.

But it wasn't a big deal if I was only going with Ai Mi to the mall. It's not like I was getting into a fight, so the egg won't break.

The schedule was the same as last time. Peng TouSi would stand at the entrance while I took Ai Mi up to the 6th floor on the elevator. (She had her eyes close for the entire ride up) She ordered a bunch of food from the food court and, of course, she didn't forget the coke.

Ai Mi drank every last drop of coke in the bottle, then she used her tiny tongue to greedily lick the bottle opening. She looked up at me and wanted to say something.

Does she still want more? Even if she's my sister, I can't let her have her way all the time, since coke isn't exactly healthy for you.

Thus I shook my head, then I lied and told her Peng TouSi had snipers on the building across from us and if she bought more than one bottle of coke&

"They would shoot the person who sold me the coke." Ai Mi said seriously.

"What does the person who sold you the coke have anything to do with it? They would shoot the bottle in your hand, then the coke would spill all over the floor. Please don't tell me you're thinking about licking the floor&"

"Hmph, don't look down on me. I'll only lick the coke that sprayed on my body."

What's there to be proud of? It's still embarrassing licking coke off your body. Also, why did you believe my lie so easily. Do you actually have a sniper in your bodyguard division, why didn't I ever meet them?

Ai Mi asked me to buy two banana splits from DQ when we passed by the ice cream booths. We sat down at a seat and finished our own shares.

I'm not sure why Ai Mi likes DQ more than Häagen-Dazs. It might be because she sees no difference in ¥30 and ¥60, they both might as well be free.

The DQ saleswoman looked at the Häagen-Dazs booth across from her with a smile of contempt like how a victor looks at a loser.

The Häagen-Dazs across didn't have a single customer and the salesman felt uncomfortable and began to draw something on the glass of the freezer.

Don't tell me he's drawing something to curse the DQ customers?

That's enough. Why do you guys have to fight to the death when you're only selling ice cream? Also, you guys face each other every day, why not take some time after work and go on a date, stop always trying to curse the customers.

Later on, Ai Mi and I unwittingly walked onto the level of the mall with a video game arcade.

Ai Mi looked through the glass and exclaimed:

"Hey, Winnie's in there."

I took a quick glance and saw Xiong YaoYue sitting in front of the Street Fighter 4 machine. She was currently in the middle of a decisive battle with a middle-aged man with long hair, earrings, and a stubble beard.

Ai Mi grabbed my wrist and pulled me into the arcade. The female cashier behind the counter excitedly paid her respect to the God of Wealth as Ai Mi passed by. Last time, Ai Mi gave her quite a generous tip after she had her buy some ice cream.

The middle-aged man in a battle with Xiong YaoYue whole-heartedly admitted his loss before we got closer. He stood up from the stool and lowered his head to Xiong YaoYue:

"You're incredible. I've never met someone as skilled as you in a long time. I originally thought if I don't make it in music, I can still do well in fighting games& who knew my worldview was so small."

Xiong YaoYue was wearing short-sleeves and hot pants as usual. But this time, she didn't have the superman S logo on her shirt, instead, the word 'Show Off' was written in the front.

I can't believe you would wear that shirt. Although I've seen many young men wearing these kinds of shirts recently, it's the first time I've seen a young girl wearing one.

Even though the words 'Show Off' was written on her clothes, Xiong YaoYue did not show off in front of the middle-aged man.

"Oh, mister, you don't have to be that polite~"

Xiong YaoYue scratched her head and giggled.

"Mister, it seems you lost miserably, but your attacks were really strong. I got nervous and actually exceeded my normal abilities and won on a fluke."

Hah, usually most people would be negatively influenced by nervousness, but you exceed normal capabilities when you're nervous? It's a waste playing video games if you can defy the natural order.

"Miss Xiong, you really know how to comfort people&"

"Don't call me Miss Xiong, call me Yue Yue." Xiong YaoYue emphasized her statement while knocking on the machine, "I didn't lie. If I lied, then let me never be able to get married."

The middle-aged man made a bitter smile: "Miss Yue Yue is beautiful and spirited, how can you never get married? But for an old man like me, I might not be able to find a wife&"

"Don't be discouraged." The energetic Xiong YaoYue didn't want to see other people feeling dejected, "If you continue with your music, you'll make it one day. One of my classmates went to one of the restaurants you sang at and they really appreciated your music. She said your music was filled was sadness and was great to listen to when in a bad mood&"

The middle-aged man had an awkward expression, but then he quickly became relieved.

"Haha, I can't help it, it's my style. Other people all feel sad when they hear my music& I won't bother you anymore. I still have to perform at three different restaurants with my band in the afternoon."

He spotted Ai Mi immediately when he turned around to leave.

Ai Mi was wearing a relatively plain gown for her, and her two ponytails were tied up with a red string. She wasn't wearing sunglasses, but she should still appear different than her image as an idol.

The long-haired middle-aged man grabbed his stubble with an expression of disbelief. His gaze was concentrated on Ai Mi even after he left the arcade when he looked through the glass at her one last time.

Damn, is he a lolicon like Director Cao? It looks like I have to stay alert even inside the mall. If Ai Mi was molested because I couldn't watch properly, then I'll have to punish myself.

But the man's eyes had a bit of sadness and it wasn't filled with lust like Director Cao. Maybe he's not a lolicon, but a musician, perhaps he recognized Ai Mi.

Then the sadness in his eyes could be explained. Ai Mi was able to obtain numerous fans purely based on her appearance and sweet voice, even when she sang songs she didn't even like. Yet diligent artists are forced to be always on the move because they can't obtain the appreciation of the masses. There's too much difference in destiny.

But I don't care if you're sad or jealous. Even if you're a hidden lolicon, I'll protect my sister. So please don't do anything that would make me go berserk.

After I warned the long-haired man, I saw Ai Mi and Xiong YaoYue already playing together.

"Winnie, do you come here every week?"

Xiong YaoYue was really happy because AI Mi didn't call her 'Miss Xiong'.

"Pretty much. I can get some free AC on hot days and you can play a long time with one token, so it's worth it."

The cashier lady looked at Xiong YaoYue with scorn. The arcade usually doesn't welcome high-level players.

Xiong YaoYue waved at me, "Ye Lin, as expected, you came with Ai Mi! How about let's play a round?"

"Play with me first." Ai Mi took the second player seat of the machine, then she ordered me to buy arcade tokens for her.

When I returned with 50 tokens, Ai Mi didn't want to carry them because it was too heavy, so she told me to carry all of it.

She didn't even bring a handbag today, so she couldn't carry it on her even if she wanted to.

I thought it would be boring just watching the two girls so I went to play hoops. Before I left, I left 25 of the tokens with Xiong YaoYue and asked her to accompany Ai Mi.

"No problem." Xiong YaoYue replied, "If you're paying, I can even purposely lose a few games, because I'm the 'if I pay I would never lose, but if someone else pays, I don't mind throwing a few games' person!"

Can you please not bring up that nickname again? Also, why would you mention you're going to throw games in from of Ai Mi? She might be small, but she has a lot of pride, actually, she's already frowning at you.

"Winnie, you don't have to throw games. I can easily master these simple games."

"Huh, are you an expert? If you're even better than Ye Lin, then I'm looking forward to it."

"Of course, the manservant is on a much lower level& which key do I press to throw bombs."

"&.."

I threw 50 consecutive shots at the basketball machine. I wanted to maintain my skill and I tried to deceive myself: my skill wouldn't drop even if I haven't touched a basketball recently.

I could hear the Fu Yan Jie advertisement ringing next to my year: "Regardless if it's now or the future, let's maintain our love."

The future is near. If I lose the basketball game, then I would have to drink Fu Yan Jie in front of the class.

"Ye Lin, Ye Lin, come over here."

Xiong YaoYue suddenly called me. It seems they already went to play on the boxing machine.

Every time you use a token, the target would rise. You can punch it as hard as you can to determine the power of your punch.

I thought Xiong YaoYue called me because she wanted to know my strength. I was eager to give it a try, but Ai Mi told me she called me over so I could get a picture and become the target on the screen. Then they would have more enthusiasm when they play.

Why are you guys making evil grins? Do you really want to put my face on the screen and give me a beating?

I couldn't change their minds, so I stood in front of the camera and got my picture taken. I'm actually pretty photogenic, some people might think I'm a dedicated villain for the game.

Ai Mi raised her fist and said: "I'll go first."

She mustered her strength and punched the target.

"Oof~" I made a sound effect to accompany her punch.

The target didn't move at all. You can see a slight indentation on the corner of my mouth on the picture, but there was virtually no difference from the original. A score was displayed in the top right corner: 18

Regardless if the unit of power was pounds or kilograms, the attack power was shockingly low. The jaws of a polar can exert over 1800 kilos of force, so even if there were a hundred of you, they can't open a polar bear's jaws.

I guess you would only be around half of Gong CaiCai's strength. How embarrassing. If you're this weak, how would you protect yourself against lolicons. No wonder you can't leave your bodyguards.

Ai Mi looked at her unprecedented low score with shame. Fortunately, Xiong YaoYue came up from behind and ruthlessly punched the target.

299 points. Although the unit of power was unclear, my face on the screen began to swell up like a pig and Ai Mi cheered. Are you that happy with your brother being hit?

In order to teach them a lesson, I rushed forward and struck the rising target ferociously.

550 points. It seems the unit of measurement is pounds. I read on a boxing magazine that the power of Tyson's left hook was 500 kilograms, so if I was able to hit 550 kilos, wouldn't I be insane?

Before I pulled out my phone to use a unit converter, my picture had a completely sunken nose, and his face was already unrecognizable.

Wow, it really looks like I have nothing better to do, I actually beat myself up.

I got a high score of 550 on the punching machine.

"Damn." Xiong YaoYue was stunned by my score, "Did you take Viagra?"

Don't be so vulgar in front of my sister.

Xiong YaoYue tried to teach Ai Mi multiple times how to throw a punch, but it didn't raise her score at all. Her score actually began to deteriorate and she experienced a record low score of 9.

Xiong YaoYue thought for a moment before she picked up Ai Mi from behind so she could use her legs to kick the target. Since the cashier lady already received a tip from Ai Mi previously, she turned a blind eye.

It's fine you girls are playing around, but don't forget Ai Mi is wearing a one-piece dress. Her underwear was revealed when she did a high kick. Today, she was wearing pure white panties with a bow knot befitting of a loli. Can you please stop tempting me with your underwear, I really want to act properly as an older brother for once.

I suddenly remembered the egg in my pocket. Did the egg break because of the punch I threw earlier?

I felt it and it was still whole. Just in case, I wrapped the egg in a napkin as an extra layer of insulation.

Sorry gramps, you only said I have to carry it everywhere, but you never said I can't wrap it. I think it's already good enough I didn't wrap it in cotton.

Ai Mi was finally satisfied and stopped playing after she scored 101 with the assistance of Xiong YaoYue and the stool.

"What does 'show off' mean?" Ai Mi pointed to the words on Xiong YaoYue's T-shirt.

"Um&" Xiong YaoYue racked her brains for a bit, "It's a saying from the northeast. Have you seen Zhao Benshan's skits?"

Ai Mi shook her head with a vacant expression.

Thus Xiong YaoYue sent me a request for help with her eyes. As Mencius once said, "The trouble with people is that they are too eager to assume the role of a teacher". Personally, I love to lecture others, so I went over to explain:

"To show off basically means to flaunt. For example, a wealthy person would flaunt their wealth or a good looking person would flaunt their appearance& basically do things they shouldn't, so they're labeled as show-offs."

Ai Mi pouted with discontent.

"Manservant, are you mocking me? When did I flaunt my money or looks? I don't care about other people's opinions!"

Hey, I wasn't talking about you. I thought I was making a common example, but was I subconsciously telling Ai Mi to restrain her actions?

Xiong YaoYue stepped out to mediate: "Siblings shouldn't fight."

I turned pale: "How& did you know&"

Xiong YaoYue paused: "Didn't you say she was a relative's child, then wouldn't you guys be cousins?"

Ai Mi clicked her tongue, "Who's his cousin&"

Damn, why are you looking down on me with those eyes? Once the truth gets revealed, I'll make you lower your head and call me brother a hundred times.

Ai Mi purposely gave me the cold shoulder and began chatting with Xiong YaoYue.

They talked about things like whether PSY has any relations with Zhao Benshan, or if the Chinese or American government got their hands on alien corpses.

While they were chatting, Xiong YaoYue complained about how her underwear was stolen off her balcony the day before yesterday.

"Dong Shan City is full of perverts. It was sportswear, it didn't even have any patterns, and they could still use it to rub one out?"

"It's that damn underwear thief again. I thought he died since we didn't hear any news about him for a couple of weeks. I heard he always wears an outdoor jacket and can scale buildings with his bare hands& I really don't understand the allure of women's underwear, he should just go get a girlfriend."

When Xiong YaoYue was criticizing how men love women's underwear, Ai Mi looked at me with a strange smile.

Why are you smiling at me? Did you learn how to read minds like Obama? I'm not the same as the underwear thief. The thief is doing it to jack off while I'm doing it for money. He can steal anyone's underwear, but I can only steal my sister's underwear!

Xiong YaoYue would have never been able to guess that the underwear thief was the boss of, Tang Jiang, the taekwondo member she almost got into a fight with.

He's a boss and the young master of the Taekwondo dojo, people often call him master Xu Shao.

But I don't any evidence, so it's only a speculation. I'll arouse the police if I go over there and try to catch him, and Constable Ma is just waiting for the day when I cause trouble.

By the way, did this underwear thief already steal Ai Mi's underwear?

No, he couldn't have. Peng TouSi already said Ai Mi's underwear was watched closely and destroyed when it wasn't needed. There's no way the thief could get past that many bodyguards.

But I can't underestimate him. As an underwear collector, he will probably do anything to get his hands on underwear he's laid his eyes on.

Does that mean I have a competitor to fight for the prized underwear?

It makes me angry when he's causing me so much trouble.

Just you wait, I won't lose. I'm betting on my dignity as an older brother, I will never let my sister's underwear fall into the hands of others&

When Xiong YaoYue said someone broke onto her balcony and stole her underwear, Ai Mi asked:

"Why didn't you shoot him?"

Xiong YaoYue didn't know whether to cry or laugh: "Where would I get a gun? Chinese citizens don't carry guns."

Ai Mi exclaimed, "Oh, I forgot you guys lived in a dictatorship, how pitiful."

Don't randomly denounce us as a dictatorship! I don't think America is superior to China in terms of gun control. Do you really want China to have as many school shootings as America?

Speaking of school shootings, I thought of the class leader. Xiong YaoYue was wrong about Chinese people not owning guns, I mean the class leader has one. What's the point of keeping that old gun, is she going to use it to shoot a disloyal boyfriend?

When they were speaking about underwear, Ai Mi made a suggestion to visit the fourth floor's clothing area. She even said, "Winnie, I'll help you buy any underwear you like."

"Eh." Xiong YaoYue was still surprised even when she knew Ai Mi came from a rich family, "How could I let a child buy things for me?"

Ai Mi immediately frowned, "Who's a child! I'm already an adult! I'm giving you a tip because you spent time with me, are you looking down on me?"

"No, no." Xiong YaoYue waved both her hands with a smile, "I like taking advantage of others. If you're giving me a tip, then I'll willingly be your dog."

Ai Mi looked at me complacently after she heard Xiong YaoYue's words of devotion. It probably meant "This is how you act as a qualified subordinate".

Thus, Ai Mi led her two subordinates (Xiong YaoYue and me), as if she was leading a thousand man army, arrogantly to the fourth floor.

When we passed by the Häagen-Dazs counter, Xiong YaoYue sent a few glances at it, and Ai Mi immediately bought her three scoops to eat.

"Ah, it's embarrassing being treated by Miss Ai Mi."

Xiong YaoYue said as she scratched her head while eating the ice cream.

If it was embarrassing, why did you keep staring at the store from a distance? If it was embarrassing, why did your order three scoops? Also, Ai Mi didn't bring her wallet today, so I'm the one who had to pay.

But I can't resent Ai Mi, she probably thinks I could still use the American Express black card.

"Hehe, I love three scoops, because there's three balls, one more than you&"

Enough, the joke's already overused, and it's not even funny. Besides, I could also say: I won't lose to your three scoops, I also have three balls on me since I brought an egg.

Everyone probably already guessed that the female salesperson behind the DQ counter was staring daggers towards the Häagen-Dazs counter.

After we arrived in the clothing section, the first thing to catch my eye was the dazzling lineup of shoes for men and women.

I unexpectedly saw two familiar figures.

Oh, it's the class leader and Shu Zhe. What a coincidence, they came to Henderson mall to buy shoes.

But the class leader didn't even notice me, she wasn't sitting on one of the in-store seats to try on shoes. Instead, she was standing in a ceramic tile corridor while talking on the phone with a grave expression.

"I'm not making a fuss over a small issue. You guys aren't aware of the importance of the problem."

"You'll take care of it later? How long would that take? As long as you take care of it, I'll even send you an award."

"&your manager wants to speak to me? Then, put him on."

Huh, it looks like the class leader got into an argument, is something wrong with the mall's service? I thought the class leader wasn't one to be picky about attitude. They must have done something really rude for her to be this angry.

Damn it, it wasn't easy trying to get the class leader to buy a new pair of shoes. I should teach the person who made her angry a lesson.

The class leader continued to argue on the phone. When she got excited, her long hair was also shaking all over the place.

"No, I'm not trying to cause trouble on purpose. You guys were the ones who got the tiles wrong."

Tile? I couldn't make any sense of the problem at hand, Henderson mall doesn't even sell ceramic tiles. Was the class leader calling a contractor because she wants to renovate her house or something?

"What do you mean it's too late? It's not a complex procedure, it's pretty simple&"

"It will cause trouble for the customers."

"Hurry and fix it or I'll never return to this mall."

The class leader said angrily as she stamped the ground.

This was when I realized there was a tile out of place next to the class leader's feet.

The corridor was supposed to be tiled with alternating black and white tiles along any straight line of tiles.

However, there was an out of place tile. Basically, the white and black tile had their correct positions swapped.

It would be unbearable for someone who had OCD like the class leader.

So, that's the problem. No wonder Shu Zhe was standing far away with a bitter face and pretending he doesn't know you. It's indeed a bit embarrassing for your sister to get into a heated argument over an out of place tile. But you guys look similar and you're both wearing jeans and a white shirt, almost everyone would know you guys are siblings.

Some passersby heard the class leader's conversation. Some covered their mouths and laughed while others began to whisper to each other.

"She's a good-looking girl, but gets pretty awful on the phone. Her boyfriend is going to have it tough."

"It's not like it's the tiles in her house, it's fine if there's a mistake. Does she get paid for being nosy?"

"It's called OCD. Nowadays, you can't leave your house without some kind of mental illness like depression, enochlophobia, agoraphobia, or acrophobia&"

"Look, the boy over there is probably her younger brother. He looks a lot more normal than his sister and he's cute, if only I was ten years younger&"

Stop, how is Shu Zhe more normal than his sister? I reckon he's currently still wearing the sexy white rose panties! He keeps rubbing his legs together when he's standing, is it going to fall because he didn't tie it properly? Stop causing more trouble, how will I help you explain if the underwear falls out?

Shu Zhe changed to a posture to reflect his youthfulness and believed he was the focus point of the crows when he heard praise. It was as if he was surrounded by camera flashes and he wanted his handsome figure to be recorded into the pictures.

Some men even sneaked a few glances at him.

Shu Zhe interpreted the men's gazes as envy and he became more arrogant. He even considered the shoe store as a model walkway as he paced back and forth.

When we were on the elevator, Ai Mi was telling Xiong YaoYue about 'the three laws you must know for a subordinate' and Xiong YaoYue was listening earnestly while licking her ice cream. That's why she was a bit slow at recognizing the class leader and her brother.

When Xiong YaoYue saw the class leader, she wanted to go and give her a passionate hug, but she gave up when she saw her panting with rage while speaking on the phone.

Ai Mi was the first one who saw Shu Zhe showing off. Perhaps it was because she was used to acting in front of a camera, so she could easily recognize when someone wanted to show off.

"I know how to use that word now." Ai Mi said suddenly.

Huh, which word?

Ai Mi beckoned Xiong YaoYue to keep up, so she could act as her bodyguard. Then, the two of them approached Shu Zhe.

Shu Zhe met Xiong YaoYue before, so he already knew she was class 2-3 PE committee member who always causes trouble for his sister. But he didn't recognize Ai Mi who looked like a flawless Barbie doll.

Shu Zhe stopped his walkway performance and wanted to ask something, but Ai Mi beat him to the punch and pointed to his nose and said:

"What are you trying to show off by walking back and forth?"

Initially, Shu Zhe was worried if he would be able to hold a simple conversation in English when he saw the blonde and blue-eyed Ai Mi walking towards him. He never expected Ai Mi to quote something Zhao Benshan said in one of his skits.

"What are you trying to show off by walking back and forth?"

"I&" Shu Zhe wasn't sure how to respond to Ai Mi's sudden question.

Xiong YaoYue was still focused on eating ice cream, watching the event unfold while standing behind Ai Mi.

"Sis Yue Yue." Shu Zhe pleaded for help from Xiong YaoYue, "Who is this child?"

"You're a child! Your entire family is all children!" Ai Mi yelled.

Actually, Ai Mi was twelve this year, so she was only younger than Shu Zhe by one year. But she does appear to be more childish than Shu Zhe, and she's only about 140cm (~42 73) tall. It's possible people could even mistake her as an elementary school student.

After the class leader finished her conversation with the mall's manager, she heard someone insulting another person's family as children. Because she was still upset about the tiles, she glanced towards us like a hawk.

Ai Mi quivered and immediately hid behind Xiong YaoYue.

Xiong YaoYue was still focused on eating ice cream.

The class leader's anger dissipated slightly when she saw it was only a little girl. She put away her phone and walked towards her brother.

Ai Mi thought the class leader was coming to take care of her, so she immediately jumped behind my back.

"What's wrong?" I asked, "I thought you said you weren't afraid of anything other than lightning, getting lost, UV rays, and ball sports?"

I didn't include acrophobia because I also suffer from it to an extent.

Ai Mi didn't rebut me, instead, she grabbed the side of my body and only peeked her eyes out while trembling.

"I've seen these eyes before&"

Huh, the class leader's eyes? She does have piercing eyes, but there's no need to be this scared.

"When I was about 6 years old, right around the time before I won the California kid's beauty pageant, my mom hired a Russian sniper who serviced in the army, his name was Vasya&"

Another person from Russia. I remember Peng TouSi was also an underground Russian fighter before he came to America. Ai ShuQiao might have no interest in China, but it seems she really fancies Russia.

"Vasya was young and beautiful. At the time, I liked him a lot and thought it would be fine if I married him in the future&"

Wow, don't decide to get married that easily! Even if he's young, he's at least 20 years older than you. Why do loli's always long for cool, older brother types? I'm also older than you, why don't you look up to your real older brother?

"But Vasya didn't get along well with others and often got into arguments with the other bodyguards. I don't know who insulted him, but he actually pulled out a gun and killed six bodyguards, then he pointed the gun at me&"

Damn, what a scary development. Ai ShuQiao, stop hiring untrustworthy people to protect your daughter.

Then, Ai Mi timidly pointed at the class leader.

"Vasya's eyes at the time were very similar to hers."

"If Peng TouSi didn't block the bullet for me, I would already be dead&"

"That's why you can't get close to people with these eyes, they are dangerous. Manservant, are you acquainted with her? Hurry up and end your relationship with her, because she will either kill you or break your heart."

It seems that Vasya didn't get a happy ending. It was also sad that Ai Mi had to witness the end of a person she once liked.

But it's ridiculous to shift your childhood shadows on to the class leader. Even though the class leader does have sharp eyes and the ability of a sniper, she would never pull a gun without at least trying to use reason. Even if she did want to blast off someone's head, she would aim at someone like me who would feel her legs in secret rather than a loli like you.

But no matter what I said to Ai Mi, she refused to get closer to the class leader. Afterward, whenever Ai Mi would meet the class leader by chance, Ai Mi would always hide behind shelter, and that shelter would usually be me.

At this point, the class leader had already chatted with Xiong YaoYue and was able to find out that she was my relative's child and was able to speak two languages fluently because she was mixed-race.

The class leader switched to her usual genial expression but it was already too late.

She took a step towards Ai Mi and Ai Mi took a step back while pulling me with her.

The class leader bent down slightly to lower her height and greeted Ai Mi:

"Hey there, don't be scared. Can I pat your head, I can also help you braid your hair."

"No way." Ai Mi stuck out her tongue at the class leader, "You'll beat me to death."

"Eh." The class leader inspected her body with shock and didn't feel like she was dressed ferociously.

She came to a realization when she saw me standing between them.

"Did Ye Lin say something bad about me? Don't believe him, I'm a good person."

Ai Mi snorted, "Liar, Ye Lin is the good person. You're a bad guy, a super-bad guy."

I should really take a picture of the class leader's current expression and hang it up on a wall as a souvenir. I would laugh every time I see it.

Hahahaha, class leader, now you know how it feels to be wrongly accused! Good job, Ai Mi, no wonder you're my sister! I've never experienced a world where I'm the good guy and the class leader is the bad guy even in my dreams!

The class leader bit her lips with resentment when she saw me burst out laughing. But it made Ai Mi think the class leader was angry at her, so she hid her entire body behind me with fear and trepidation, it's not something that could be easily faked.

The class leader didn't give up easily when she was rejected by animals, so she came over and wanted to hold Ai Mi's hands. Ai Mi didn't want to be touched, so she started running around me while the class leader chased from behind.

Stop running around, I'm going to get dizzy. Go play tag somewhere else.

The class leader wanted to try her best and get in good terms with Ai Mi, but Ai Mi was too fast and the class leader couldn't catch her.

Perhaps the class leader thought I was an obstacle, so she tried to push me aside, but she hit right near my pant pockets.

"Class leader, you hit my egg." I blurted.

The class leader couldn't look at me with any more contempt, she wanted to say something but swallowed her words when she saw Ai Mi hiding behind me with vigilance.

"Sister, let's buy shoes first." Shu Zhe yelled at his sister, "You should try this pair of shoes the salesperson brought."

"Coming." The class leader replied with embarrassment and walked towards her younger brother.

The class leader's attitude towards her brother was even better than usual. It's probably because she's touched that her demanding brother would use his own allowance to buy her a pair of shoes.

Sigh, let's hope Shu Zhe will care for her sister from now on. Look at how touched your sister is when you offered her to buy a pair of shoes. You should cherish your sister and stop always thinking about money.

As I was deep in thought, Shu Zhe walked behind me and whispered:

"Bro Ye Lin, fortunately, I bumped into you. I found a good pair of shoes for ¥366, please give me another hundred."

I can't believe the first thing you did was come ask for money. Even if it's all an act, at least be more cautious in front of your sister, I don't want her to know it was me who paid.

Xiong YaoYue finally finished eating, then she held her sticky hands in front of Shu Zhe and asked:

"Do you have any tissues? I forgot to bring some, lend me one."

Shu Zhe handed over a tissue with a hint of revulsion. I remember he once emphasized to me that Xiong YaoYue was not his type. He said he wouldn't have a sense of security going out with a girl stronger than him.

I think any girl who goes out with you doesn't feel a sense of security. Gong CaiCai is the only person in class 2-3 who fits your standards.

"Let me use the tissue too." I said.

I took the tissue from Xiong YaoYue, but I stuffed a hundred bill inside and handed it back to Shu Zhe. Shu Zhe sent me a smile as if he understood.

"Give me the ¥34 back later." I told Shu Zhe.

Shu Zhe became unhappy when he heard, "I'm not returning it, let's consider it my errand fee."

The class leader was currently trying on shoes, so I could only endure it because I didn't want her to hear me arguing with Shu Zhe.

Shu Zhe, who knew how to take advantage of the situation, stuck his hands in his pockets and walked to his sister with a smile.

"Is it a good fit? Let's buy it if it's a good fit."

"I think it's a bit too expensive& the other pair that was ¥185 was already pretty good, there's also one on sale for ¥99 by the elevator&"

"No, you can't wear those cheap shoes or it would be embarrassing for me if someone else sees. I'm not going to eat dinner tonight if you buy the ¥99 shoes."

"Okay, you can make the decisions today&" Even though she was rebuked by her own brother, she had a joyous look because her brother was buying her shoes with his own allowance.

Xiong YaoYue didn't notice when I passed the money to Shu Zhe with the tissues, but Ai Mi was able to see it from a lower angle.

"What's going on." Ai Mi hid behind me and asked, "Manservant, did they threaten you? Did Katyusha say she'll shoot you if you don't give them money?"

Don't give the class leader a weird nickname, her name is Shu Sha, not Katyusha. Don't give a Russian nickname simply because she has similar eyes to Vasya!

"No one's threatening me. I'm just returning some money."

I explained to Ai Mi and I also told her some general information on the class leader and Shu Zhe.

"It's still suspicious."

Ai Mi posed like a detective and followed me around while monitoring the class leader and her brother.

The first thing the class leader did after buying the shoes was to get as far away from the incorrect tile as possible.

"I'm never coming back to this mall again." The class leader said, "If they even make these basic mistakes, there might even be problems with the blueprints and foundation. This place could immediately collapse once an earthquake hits."

"Class leader, don't scare me." Xiong YaoYue said anxiously, "I come here almost every week, it would be really unlucky for me to be buried in an earthquake."

"& if I was buried, you have to come and save me. Don't forget to bring me a cold coca-cola."

Xiong YaoYue said and then began to laugh out loud. She said the words of the famous 'Coke Boy' from the Sichuan earthquake and probably thought she was funny.

Other than Ai Mi who began to recollect about the taste of coke, none of us laughed, but Xiong YaoYue kept laughing loudly without any regard for the people around her.

It's embarrassing how easily she laughs& or should I say brave?

After the chance encounter with the class leader, Xiong YaoYue completely forgot about the fact Ai Mi was going to buy her underwear. When Ai Mi didn't let the class leader pat her head, the thick-skinned Xiong YaoYue went over to be patted by the class leader.

"Sob sob ~~~ class leader, the sports underwear I was drying on my balcony was stolen, you should comfort me." Xiong YaoYue was fake crying with exaggerated movements.

"I thought you can't expose sportswear to strong sunlight." The class leader was expressionless, "Wouldn't the wire change shape if you left it on the balcony on such a hot day?"

"Ah, right." Xiong YaoYue came to a realization but she began to wipe her fake tears again, "Even if that's the case, I don't think the panty thief came to help put away my clothes. I'm so unlucky, sob sob sob~~~"

The class leader felt she was pitiful for faking her tears, so she could only helplessly pat her head, "There, there, don't cry. Just be more careful in the future."

Xiong YaoYue raised her head all of a sudden and it pushed back the class leader's hand.

"Right, class leader, I remember your underwear was also stolen once. If I think about the thief using our underwear to jack off, I just want to tear him apart."

The class leader had a slightly red face, "Don't say that in front of everyone&"

Xiong YaoYue was full of righteous indignation, but I wanted to tell her: The panty thief wasn't the one who stole the class leader's underwear. Shu Zhe was the one who stole it and he even tried to sell it to me, it's a shame the class leader is still in the dark.

"Winnie, Winnie." Ai Mi beckoned Xiong YaoYue while hiding behind me and Xiong YaoYue quickly cane over in response.

"Miss Ai Mi, what are your orders?" Xiong YaoYue acted as if she was a captain of the Schutzstaffel and did a salute.

"Don't get too close to that person, it's dangerous&"

"Huh, who?"

"Katyusha& the one you guys call class leader. She might kill all of us."

"No way." Xiong YaoYue laughed, "Even though the class leader keeps a gun hidden at home, she would never point it at us."

"So she does have a gun?" Ai Mi's complexion worsened, "I also never thought Vasya would point a gun at us before he killed the bodyguards."

"Who's Vasya? Is it a character from a TV show?"

The group underwent pointless chatter as we wandered aimlessly towards the washroom.

"I have to use the washroom." Ai Mi, who drank a lot of coke, said, "Winnie, come with me."

"Alright." Xiong YaoYue cleared the path in front of them and escorted Ai Mi inside the washroom.

I thought it would be advantageous for Ai Mi's security to have Xiong YaoYue as a new subordinate, at least she can act as a guard in the female's washroom in my stead.

Shu Zhe also entered the men's washroom with an embarrassed expression. It probably wasn't to urinate, but to adjust his underwear because it was straddling him too tightly.

The class leader and I were the only ones left standing outside. She was holding a shopping bag with her running shoes while I leaned against the wall. It seems we didn't really have a topic we could talk about.

"Xiao Qin& are her knees better?"

The class leader hesitated before she asked a question.

"I don't know." I replied, "I haven't seen her for a few days."

A faint sense of relief was shown on the class leader's face, but it soon disappeared behind the aloof expression of the top student.

No, instead of aloof, it would be more accurate to say self-disciplined.

At this point, Shu Zhe came out of the washroom with a dark expression.

"Bro Ye Lin." He walked in front of me and said quietly, "Come with me for a sec."

The class leader seemed to be concerned, but Shu Zhe made an appearance as if to say he had something to discuss with me between men. He led me to a bench near some railings and made sure his sister didn't follow us.

Shu Zhe reckoned my body could block his sister's field of view, then he carefully took something out of his pockets.

Isn't this the sexy white rose underwear? Why did you take it off? Even though it's already been 72 hours, it's not the right time to worry about how long it has been worn! If the class leader found out, then Ai Mi's prediction would become true!

Also, don't hand it to me. Didn't I already tell you to keep it in a Ziploc bag, I don't want to touch your worn panties.

"Bro Ye Lin, the straps&"

This was when I realized that one of the straps had ripped.

Shu Zhe seems to be scared because he damaged the merchandise.

"It wasn't on purpose. I just wanted to adjust, then it snapped, would I have to repay it?"

He looked at me tearfully.

Why are you trying to act cute? Do you always beg for forgiveness every time you make a mistake, why can't you take responsibility like a man?

But, I guess there's no reason to use a man's criteria as judgment for a person who wears women's underwear.

Right when I was worrying about how to handle the underwear, Xiong YaoYue ran over like a whirlwind.

She separated the two of us and asked with a smile:

"Ha, what are you guys doing so secretively?"

Shu Zhe's hand trembled and he was scared, so he threw the underwear off the railings.

Thus the sexy white rose underwear floated like a butterfly and fell towards the central lobby, on top of a man's head.

The underwear landed on a middle-aged bald man. From far away, he looks like, Le Jia, one of the speakers on 'If You Are the One'. (My aunt likes him) The man raised his head with surprise and exclaimed:

"Huh? It's raining panties in the middle of the day, and it's still warm! Whose is it? I'm a conservative man, so I'm afraid we won't get along."

His shouted alerted the security and a couple (more than one) of guards came over and began to investigate the mystery of the panties.

Shu Zhe was scared to the point where he bit his fingers and shrunk his head back so he wouldn't be seen by the people in the lobby.

But it was too late since Xiong YaoYue had witnessed the entire event.

Xiong YaoYue's body trembled and her face flushed with anger.

"So that's what's going on."

She widened her eyes.

What? Can you not make it a big deal? Last time, you already scared me half to death when you suddenly said 'siblings shouldn't fight'. What new realizations have you made this time?

Don't tell me you made a connection to the time when you saw me carrying the black lace panties and you realized the truth about the 'original panties"?!

No, that's impossible, there weren't enough clues. Besides, there's no way she could make a deduction like Conan with her brain.

Or, since she always mistook me as a homosexual, she could speculate I had a gay relationship with Shu Zhe?

Damn, I'll really be angry if you said that. In order to express my rage, I'll straight out grab your tits in front of everyone.

I couldn't predict Xiong YaoYue's train of thought no matter how hard I tried.

Then, Xiong YaoYue grabbed Shu Zhe's collar and shouted:

"So& you're the underwear thief. Hurry up and return my underwear!"

Wow, your guess is completely wrong. Even though Shu Zhe once impersonated the panty thief (stole his sister's underwear), he doesn't meet any of the requirements to be the thief. The main requirement is he has to be able to scale buildings with his bare hands. Shu Zhe can't even scale the school gates, how can he be the panty thief?

"Yue Yue, you're mistaken." I tried to explain.

Xiong YaoYue shook Shu Zhe with all her strength hoping the underwear he hid on his body would all fall out.

I think you watched too many cartoons. What kind of thieves carries their stolen goods with them?

Shu Zhe's voice when he was trying to explain the situation was laughable.

"Sis Yue Yue~~ stop shaking me, I never stole any underwear~ Ye Lin gave them to me~~~"

Shit, don't sell me out. Didn't I already tell you that if you get caught, just say it's a personal hobby?

Xiong YaoYue cast her gaze of doubt towards me.

"Ah, so you're the panty thief. No wonder you had a pair of underwear with you last time&"

"I'm not." I denied it in a hurry, "The panty thief can scale buildings with his bare hands, but I have acrophobia, so how could it be me?"

Ah, I accidentally admitted it, how embarrassing. Men shouldn't admit their own weaknesses, they should keep it all bottled up.

I get a bit nervous just thinking about the time I was riding on the elevator with Ai Mi.

"Then.." She turned and stared at Shu Zhe, "You're still the panty thief."

"Sis Yue Yue, I already said it's not me." Xiong YaoYue didn't believe him regardless of how hard he tried to plead innocence.

At this moment, Ai Mi hopped behind Xiong YaoYue and poked her back.

"Winnie, what are you playing?"

Xiong YaoYue hugged Ai Mi with vigilance and distanced her from Shu Zhe.

"Miss Ai Mi, be careful. This guy might look innocent, but he specializes in stealing women's underwear."

Ai Mi glanced at Shu Zhe with scorn then looked at me.

"It doesn't matter. He's not the only one who wants to get my underwear&"

Huh, what do you mean? Why are you looking at me? Did you already realize I was coveting your underwear? What an amazing sixth sense, no wonder she's my sister&

No wait, this is not the right time to be proud. If Ai Mi increases security, then I have even less chance to succeed. If I knew this was going to happen, I wouldn't have spent money willy-nilly and instead saved it.

Then the class leader finally walked over. Ai Mi immediately hid behind Xiong YaoYue, Shu Zhe and I also stood up from the bench.

"Did something happen?" The class leader asked with suspicions.

"No.." I sent a meaningful glance to Xiong YaoYue, "We're just fooling around."

The class leader was in a rush to leave as she felt Henderson mall wasn't amicable towards people with OCD. The remainder of us all followed behind the bellwether.

The class leader and Shu Zhe walked in front, Xiong YaoYue and I walked behind them, and Ai Mi hid behind the two of us. She would occasionally monitor the siblings from between the spaces in our arms.

"Hmph, eyes are the windows to the soul. You can read people from their eyes."

Ai Mi mumbled to herself.

"Even though they look similar and the brother can easily pass off as the sister with a wig, the spirit in their eyes are completely different."

"The sister would be the type to be the last one standing in a war. If she gets humiliated, then she will retaliate without any hesitation!"

Hey, are you talking about Vasya? But you do have some good insight, since it's true Shu Zhe could pass off as his sister with a wig. It's probably because you always deal with makeup artists and the like so you can easily imagine someone with a wig.

"Then, do you think her brother can survive a war?" I asked with curiosity.

"Him&" Ai Mi wasn't really interested, "He's useless and will probably be captured by the enemy and used as a male prostitute&"

Xiong YaoYue abruptly cut into our conversation.

"Stop talking about wars, Shu Zhe&" In consideration for the class leader, Xiong YaoYue lowered her voice, "Shu Zhe is the panty thief. A lot more girls will become victims if we leave him alone."

"Especially the class leader. I was wondering how the class leader would get her underwear stolen when she's so cautious, but it's because she was living with the thief! I can't believe he would even steal his sister's underwear, we should hang him up and flick his dick off!"

Shu Zhe shuddered even when he couldn't hear our conversation clearly.

I laughed: "Yue Yue, think about it for a second. Shu Zhe is a weakling, there's no way he could be the thief. Even if he had the courage, he wouldn't even have the strength to climb onto a balcony."

Xiong YaoYue's face was serious, "Ye Lin, don't be naive. Chang Wei also said he didn't know martial arts."

Isn't Chang Wei a character from 'Hail the Judge'? He raped a woman, then killed their entire family of thirteen including their guard dog. Then in order to evade his crime, he said 'I don't know martial arts'.

But it seems like you know a lot of obscure things! Although Chang Wei has a fan base on the web, not many people know about him. I'm begging you, can you please use more well-known references?

"I know it!" Ai Mi happily raised her hands and said, "There are a lot of Chinese comments on Facebook that mention Chang Wei on White House related pages any time children of government members cause a ruckus in China!"

"The people on the internet say Chang Wei is a real portrayal of children of government officials running wild because Chang Wei is the son of Chiang Kai-shek&"

My god, you were completely misguided by internet trolls. The president of the Republic of China was Jiang Jieshi. Westerners called him Chiang Kai-shek because of the Cantonese pronunciation. (TN: Then there are some more long-winded references to Chiang Kai-shek and references that's unimportant)

When we reached the first floor, Xiong YaoYue suddenly remembered the important task at hand was to expose the panty thief.

So, she picked up a wad up ball of paper from underneath a broom of a nearby janitor, then she aimed it at the back of Shu Zhe's head:

"Let me test if he knows martial arts."

"BUMP." "OW."

Shu Zhe turned around with resentment. Xiong YaoYue put her hands behind her head and whistled to feign innocence while Ai Mi hid behind me and stuck her tongue.

"Sis." Shu Zhe complained to the class leader, "That mixed-race child threw a wad of paper at me."

"It's okay." The class leader tried to mediate, "You don't need to fight with a child. It's not like paper would hurt."

"But the paper looks really dirty."

Shu Zhe pulled out some more tissues and wiped his head.

"Hmph, looks like he's a good faker." Xiong YaoYue spat, "I don't believe he doesn't know martial arts."

He doesn't. Not only does he not know martial arts, but he also doesn't even reach the class standard for physical education. He might get injured one day if you keep trying to test him.

When we exited the mall from the revolving doors, Xiong YaoYue purposely pushed against it to trap Shu Zhe inside one of the sections. He couldn't enter or exit and was on display like a monkey at a zoo, but she still wasn't able to determine if he knew martial arts.

"Sis Yue Yue, so you were playing with me to your amusement." Shu Zhe protested, "What did I do? I already said I had nothing to do with that pair of&"

Shu Zhe decided to swallow the rest of his words since the class leader had amazing hearing.

This time, Peng TouSi had parked Ai Mi's car in front of the mall's entrance. He opened up an UV umbrella and went to welcome her after he saw her exit.

"Did you have fun today?" Peng TouSi asked gently.

Everyone's faces, other than me and AI Mi, were filled with alarm when a black iron tower suddenly blocked the sun.

"Even though I knew Miss Ai Mi was rich, I never expected her to have a bodyguard."

Xiong YaoYue's mouth was wide open.

The class leader was the first one to calm down among the three of them. She prudently swept her gaze across Peng TouSi's face, but I could still see her tightly clenching the bag in her hand.

Peng TouSi bent down to apologize for scaring the girls. The expression on his face was even more gentle than before. If you looked in his eyes, you would feel like he's someone who could never hurt anyone even if he had a scary scar under his eye.

Peng TouSi saw the class leader and said with a hint of sadness:

"Excuse me for saying, but your eyes reminds me an old friend of mine&"

Huh, are you talking about Vasya? Are you saying the class leader's eyes are similar to a sniper's even when she's not angry? Vasya shot a bullet at you! Even if you already had a lot of bullet wounds, why do you need to refer to him as a friend? Did you already reach nirvana and will never hate anyone anymore?

The class leader hesitated and thought about how to answer, but Xiong YaoYue was the first one to go up and pat Peng TouSi on his abs.

"Hahaha, that's such an outdated pickup line! What do you mean she seems like an old friend, you're almost 50 years old!"

Peng TouSi's face reddened, "I'm not 50, I only look a bit older&"

Xiong YaoYue continued to laugh, "Hahaha, I never expected a black guy to be this fluent in Chinese! Oh, don't get mad, I'm not discriminating, I'm pretty black myself!"

The class leader pulled Xiong YaoYue back because she kept on being rude.

Shu Zhe, who hasn't said a word, had his attention focused on the luxury car behind Peng TouSi.

Last time when the Five Tiger Punishment Squad kidnapped Shu Zhe, he was mesmerized by the Mercedes-Benz SUV. I've mentioned it before that their SUV looks like a tricycle in comparison to Ai Mi's personal 'Batmobile'.

That's why Shu Zhe's eyes weren't able to leave the luxury car and he became much more polite towards Ai Mi.

"So& you were from a rich family. Please excuse my prior offensive remarks. I apologize."

"No problem." Ai Mi said with despise, "I don't remember the words of trash."

The class leader immediately scowled at Ai Mi when she heard her call her brother trash. Ai Mi quickly jumped into the car as if she was targeted with laser sights.

"Drive." Ai Mi commanded, "We have to leave the range of the sniper."

Peng TouSi gave us a courtesy smile (but it was ambiguous towards me), got into the drivers seat, and stepped on the gas.

Ai Mi stuck out her head from the back seat and called out to me and Xiong YaoYue:

"Come to my place to play when you have time. Manservant knows the way, so you guys can come together."

Then she stuck out her tongue at the siblings.

"Katyusha and trash don't need to come. If you guys get near Qing Zi academy, then I'll tell my bodyguard to mow you guys down!"

Because Ai Mi stuck her head out without paying attention, there was a kid who couldn't hold onto an empty coke bottle. It was blown up by the wind and coincidentally hit Ai Mi on her head.

"Ah (gt;_lt;)"

Ai Mi clutched her head and glared at the child who committed a serious crime.

"Damn fool, you dare hit my head? The worst part is you used an empty coke bottle& did you want to taunt me with the fact you already drank all the coke?"

"Peng TouSi, steer to the right and crush them!"

Of course, Peng TouSi didn't listen and drove away slowly after some persuasion.

Their car slowed down due to traffic. Ai Mi leaned at the window and stared at the child who threw the bottle at her head.

The child was holding hands with his mom and was planning on crossing the road. He timidly looked at the older sister who had an evil smile on her face.

Ai Mi turned around to find a weapon but only found a stack of bills.

She didn't even think about it and picked up the stack and threw it at the child's face.

"Eat this."

Due to the face Ai Mi was too weak, it only pushed the child back a little bit, he didn't even fall down.

Yet Ai Mi thought she was victorious. She laughed out loud as she was taken away on the speeding car.

The little boy had a red nose and he picked up the wad of cash and asked his mom:

"Is this fake money?"

His mother was originally upset someone hit her child, but her mood changed when she took a closer look at the money. She pulled the child onto the sidewalk and immediately pulled out her phone to make a call:

"Honey, you won't believe what happened, today&"

Xiong YaoYue who saw the entire event, said:

"I also want to be hit in the face with cash."

She grabbed my wrist and asked me:

"Tell me the truth, how much money does Miss Ai Mi have? Tell me the secrets of being a lackey, I also want to receive a lot of money. Once I have money, I can hire my own lackeys!"

But the class leader was not satisfied with how Ai Mi used money to hit people.

"Even if you have an enormous amount of money, you should at least donate it to people who need it! Ye Lin, why do you have relatives who don't know how to conserve at all&"

Don't ask me, she was raised by Ai ShuQiao. I barely had any influence on her yet as her older brother.

Shu Zhe, on the other hand, seemed to be immersed in his thoughts.

"Bro Ye Lin, is Ai Mi your second aunts child?"

Nonsense, my second aunt only likes bald people like Le Jia. If it was her child, she might have forced them to be bald.

"No, don't make guesses, Ai Mi is& a child of a distant relative. So distant I don't even know how to refer to them&"

It's actually not a distant relative, but it's true I don't know how to refer to Ai ShuQiao as I would never call her my mother.

"Is that so& although she doesn't have a good personality, she still looks pretty good. I think she'll be good-looking when she gets older&"

Huh, what the hell are you thinking about? Are you trying to hit on my sister? Don't you already have a girlfriend or did you have change of heart when you realized Ai Mi was loaded?

Keep dreaming. Do you want to stay home all day while my sister raises you? You're even worse than Kyle! If you dare lay your hands on my sister, I& I'll castrate you.

Even if you use your sister as trade& I won't agree. If you ask me why, I'll give you a reply used by Goda from Doraemon:

Because my sister's mine and your sister is also mine.

The four of us were preparing to return home, while Xiong YaoYue was fretting:

"I still haven't finished my language class homework."

Ah, I haven't finished either, so I shamelessly asked the class leader:

"Class leader, did you finish? Can I borrow it&"

"No." The class leader said with a cold face, "There's no point if you don't do the homework yourself."

Shu Zhe then said enthusiastically: "Bro Ye Lin, I might be able to help you, but you have to tell me more about Ai Mi&"

"No one's allowed to help him." The class leader ordered, "Aren't you embarrassed having a junior help you finish your homework?"

I never said I would let a junior write my homework. And I would never tell Shu Zhe anything about Ai Mi.

Xiong YaoYue suddenly said loudly: "Okay, I'll tell you everything about Ai Mi if you help me finish my homework."

Wow, she has no integrity since she admitted she was worse than her junior. Also, what do you even know about Ai Mi that Shu Zhe doesn't know?

The class leader looked at the excited Xiong YaoYue and wasn't sure how to evaluate her.

Xiong YaoYue said: "Class leader, I won't just eat for free at your house, I'll guard your underwear in return."

Huh, when did the class leader agree to feed you? It seems like you're now a master at getting free food. And you're still suspecting Shu Zhe as the panty thief, so do you want to test his martial arts again? I don't really care if you break him, but I also want to eat at the class leader's house&

"Class leader." I then spoke without shame, "I heard if more people eat together, you can reduce global carbon emissions&"

"Save it." The class leader saw through my crafty plan, "Whether or not Xiao Xiong goes to my house has nothing to do with you, so hurry and go home and finish your homework."

So I returned home with low spirits. I also called the delivery service and sent out the prepared packages.

t

After I sent out the orders, I remembered the pair of underwear Shu Zhe was wearing fell into the hands of Le Jia (that's what I will tentatively call him). There was no way I could deliver the goods to Uncle Fireball on time, so I had to notify him.

I turned on the computer and coincidentally, he was also online. I sent him a crying emoji:

"Dear customer, I'm very sorry. Miss model got the white underwear dirty during a party. Since washing the underwear defeats the whole purpose, I could tell her to wear a new pair for three days and send it out as soon as possible."

"If you feel you have suffered any damages, we can also offer a full refund&"

Uncle Fireball sent an okay emoji, which I assumed meant don't worry about it.

"Hm, it's hard to find many honest sellers like you these days."

"You guys don't try to make excuses or push the blame onto someone else."

Please stop, I already feel ashamed. I'm actually not honest at all since the underwear I'm selling is not worn by a 'miss' but by a 'mister'.

Uncle Fireball pushed his imagination to the limits when he heard miss model got her underwear dirty in a party:

"Maybe she wasn't able to make it to the washroom in time because she drank too much? If that's the case, you don't need to change it for a new pair, send it over as is, I don't mind."

No, based on your words, it's not you 'don't mind' but rather you 'like it'. I can't believe you would even be interested in urine-soaked underwear.

"Who cares if it's soaked with urine. A lot of mammals choose their partners through the scent of urine. Urine contains a lot of precious pheromones!"

Uncle Fireball stated his ideas with conviction.

"Female urine is a common item sold in Japanese perverted goods stores. There also blood-stained tampons, imouto juice& "

Stop, I'm going to barf. If you like Japan, you should just move there. I'll introduce you to Director Cao so you guys can go together.

After I was able to handle the delayed product, I was at a loss of whether I should order the ¥13 eggplant with rice or the ¥15 twice-cooked pork and rice. I was no less depressed than an emperor deciding on which concubine he should copulate with for the night.

All of a sudden, I received a one line text from Ai Mi:

"Do you want my underwear?"

Shit, so she still found out! When did I reveal it? (Or was it that obvious?) What should I do, what should I do&? If I answer 'yes', will she give her underwear to me?

No, I can't admit it. I can't let my little sister look down on me. Even if I want to exchange her underwear for money, I have to steal it, otherwise, I wouldn't feel any sense of accomplishment.

Huh, why does my train of thought seem similar to that of the panty thief? I don't want to have the same thoughts as a pervert! I'm not a pervert, I just don't want to embarrass myself in front of my sister!

So I replied: "Are you joking? Who wants something that dirty."

I couldn't help but think: "Ai Mi always takes 40 minutes to shower, so her body should be even cleaner than Shu Zhe's, that means her underwear&"

Ai Mi didn't reply immediately. After a while, when I thought she already forgot about me, she sent me a ('_') emoji.

Is that supposed to mean doubt? Do you not trust your own brother?!

Even though people always say to ask older people for advice when you run into trouble, I only call my dad to ask if he ate or not. I would never ask him how to get my hands on Ai Mi's underwear.

In addition, my dad must have complex feelings towards Ai Mi since she is my little sister but has a different father. He can't even bring himself to hate Ai ShuQiao, so I doubt he would hate his daughter. But I can't let them meet before our sibling relationship is revealed.

The weather was too hot and it affected my brain, I actually forgot Auntie Ren took over my dad's hotel room and I still called the same number.

Auntie Ren picked up the phone in a fit of anger: "Who is it?"

I was shocked to the point I almost fell off my chair, then I spoke hesitantly: "Uhhhh&."

Auntie Ren wasn't able to recognize it was me and she said angrily: "There are no males living in this room so stop asking if we need escorts. We don't need any female or male escorts!"

Then she slammed the phone down.

It's worrying that Auntie Ren mistook me as a prostitute.

And the sex workers are too unprofessional. I mean, they are already under quarantine so you wouldn't be able to get in even if they called you.

This time, I called the right number. My dad was eating a meal provided by the hotel and apparently they added the root of the Isatis tinctoria to strengthen your immune system.

My dad told me he was living pretty well these past couple of days. Even though the fatty snores a lot, he found out they had the same hobby and could chat when they were bored.

I asked what hobby they had in common.

Apparently the fatty was a moderator in a certain erotic forum. He once posted one of my dad's AV reviews and complimented him.

"I never expected there was such a talented professor." The fatty said.

The compliment is completely wrong. When is writing AV reviews a criterion to become a university professor?

The fatty gave my dad an internal account to the forums and my dad shed tears of gratitude. In order to express his thanks, he told the fatty about the existence of the HHH enthusiasts club. The fatty expressed regret for not having met earlier, then said he would work hard to get into the club so he can become a member with my dad.

Damn, they a got another new member! Are they working as a MLM or something?

That night, my dad and the fatty got together to discuss female AV actresses over alcohol. They never expected out of the two AV films they downloaded, one was a cartoon, and the other one was a bunch of men doing gay wrestling. The fatty's wife came into the room to retrieve something and caught them right when they were stunned.

"I can't believe I didn't know about your tastes even after we've been married for so many years&"

The broken-hearted wife complained to Auntie Ren.

I heard later on that in order to resolve the misunderstanding, my dad went to apologize in the fatty's stead and was finally able to make them bury the hatchet and sleep in the same room together again.

But then my dad didn't have a place to stay.

He paced back and forth in the hallway until midnight. Auntie Ren finally opened the door because she was annoyed by the sounds of his footsteps.

"Stop acting pathetic, are you here to remind me you were the one who rented this room?"

"No& if you think I'm noisy, I'll go somewhere else&"

"Why are you going somewhere else? Are you trying to make everyone know I took your room?"

"No, I don't have the guts&."

"That's what I thought. I'll let you stay here for the night, but let me make something clear, if you make any moves&."

"You're a MMA champion, how could I do anything to you?"

According to my dad, they each slept on their bed that night and nothing happened.

I hope that's the case.

It would be terrible for me if something happened.

It was cloudy and foggy on Monday morning. I almost fell into a gutter when I ran to Dong Shan lake. Shit, they should at least put up a warning sign when they removed the grate cover for repairs!

When I took a closer look, even though there was a red sign, I couldn't see anything through the fog. Hurry up and change it into a flashing sign, otherwise, if I fall down, there will be no one there to manage my gigantic harem!

I originally thought gramps wouldn't come in this weather, but when I arrived at the usual spot, I saw him sitting on the bench and waiting for me.

I pulled out the egg and handed it to gramps with devotion.

Gramps inspected the egg and put it into his lap with satisfaction when he didn't find any cracks.

I was puzzled and asked: "Gramps, even though I carried the egg on me, why didn't it help with my martial arts skills?"

"It didn't?" Gramps feigned a shocked look, "Uh& I was able to prove through experimentation that what they write in martial arts novels have no basis."

So you were trying to make fun of me?

Seeing my dissatisfaction, he said: "Xiao Ye Zi, did you think I only told you to carry the egg because I wanted to prove martial arts novels were all nonsense?"

"Then why did you make me carry it?"

"Um& while it was indeed one of the reasons, the other reason was because my back hurts, so I couldn't let you be comfortable too&."

You& you're awful! No wonder you're the one who survived the longest out of all your martial art companions. No wonder they say 'Whom the gods love die young'!

It began to drizzle when it was time for school. Everyone was happy because the flag-raising ceremony was cancelled as a result.

I noticed the class leader brought a navy blue raincoat to school instead of an umbrella. I guess this means she started to bike to school again.

Unexpectedly, she took over a week to recover after I spanked her butt. The class leader's skin is softer than I imagined.

As she walked into the school building and removed the hood of her raincoat, she had the atmosphere of a general. Her resounding footsteps split apart the crowd and numerous boys sent her longing gazes.

I felt an inexplicable sense of superiority.

Haha, even if she's actually a general, she's a general that's been spanked by me! It's something that will always be recorded in history! Even if you killed me to cover it up, your brother still knows the truth, or will you kill him too!

Xiao Qin, who brought her running shoes to school on purpose, stared anxiously out the window at the rain.

"It's annoying, will the weather clear up before PE class in the afternoon&"

She was wearing the springautumn school sportswear, but there were quite a few people wearing it in this weather.

I focused on finishing Friday's language homework, I hope I could finish it on time.

"We haven't spoken at all over the weekends, don't you miss me?"

Xiao Qin asked bitterly.

"Nope." I glanced at her knees, but I couldn't see her injury through her sports pants.

Xiao Qin pouted.

"By the way, since my mom was quarantined, her classmate and art instructor came to accompany me and it's really annoying."

"What's wrong with having more people around, Auntie Ren is afraid you would be lonely. Did your art skills get any better?"

"My art skills are already amazing, they don't need to be improved (g3f)."

"The art instructor advised me to start from the basics, for example drawing an egg& but who has the time. Eileen Chang once said: You have to start early to become famous!"

Ah, I could have gave you some assistance yesterday if you wanted to draw an egg, but my hands are tied today.

"In order to let a large number of readers appreciate my masterpiece as soon as possible, and be moved by my romance manga to the point where their souls are touched and they wish they were dead&"

Do you really want them to wish they were dead? Are you drawing manga or giving them arsenic?

"I registered as an author on u17 and applied to post my manga, 'Love at Zhoukoudian'&."

Why is it 'Love on Zhoukoudian'? Is the main protagonist the Peking Man of Zhoukoudian? If it's a romance between cavemen, then that means it's even more ancient than Jay Chou's 'Love Before BC'! Do you guys think whoever unearths the oldest relic is the winner?

"The worst part is I wasn't able to qualify because the editor said he couldn't tell what I was drawing."

No, he was already being polite. You can only draw shapes like potatoes and eggplants, instead of calling it 'Love at Zhoukoudian', it should be 'Love at a Vegetable Garden'!

"Hmph, I can't believe I was treated unfairly even though I'm a genius, they must be jealous of me. Just like how Van Gogh received the envy of the painters around him, they must be planning to unite and oppress me. Didn't Lu Xun once say that in order for a genius to exist, there must be soil to create a genius, but why's the soil under my feet so unwilling?"

Hey, wake up, you're a genius of the killing fist, not a genius at drawing. Also, Lu Xun was referring to the soil to be used for growth, not for stepping under your feet&

"Nowadays, it doesn't matter if you're good at drawing. As long as your story has romance, you can leave it to the readers to use their imagination (gt;ã-)~~~~"

If that's the case, why are you making a manga, just go and write a novel! It will definitely sell as long as you're willing to post a sexy picture of yourself on the back cover and write some nonsense about relationships in your autobiography! A lot of people will come to your signings to shake your hand and get your signature, but I can't guarantee what things they did with their hand right before the signing&

"m(o^p)n It's not like all the other manga that were approved have good drawings&"

"Especially 'Uncle Shu drawn at 5 years old'. They will approve a 5-year-old, but they won't approve a 14-year-old?"

The author chose the name as a joke& Eunuch Cao showed me the manga once and it was actually pretty interesting.

"That manga only has shitty drawings, shitty scenes, shitty plot, shitty characters, I can't believe people read it&"

The author wrote about himself intending for it to be self-deprecating. Do you not understand self-deprecating humor? It's like when some people say my dog son is incompetent, do you think their son is actually a dog?

"I laughed at the first page. It's clearly an elementary school student's doodle~"

You will understand if you read a bit more, the drawings are actually pretty decent.

"I get angry just thinking about how this shitty work can get on the recommended list while my works won't even be approved. So, I used the roast function on u17 and left comments on every page saying 'super shit manga, it can't be compared to Celery Sensei's' Love at Zhoukoudian!"

So you're the type of 'mangaka' who only attacks other authors instead of improving your own works. Also, who's Celery Sensei? Did you already create a pen name for yourself? Also, in Japan, only published authors can refer to themselves as sensei, please get off your high horse.

"I discovered: The authors who get on the recommended list all have connections behind the scenes. I only left 500 roasts, but I was banned saying I was spreading trash messages&"

You deserved it, besides 500 is already a lot! For something like 'Love at Zhoukoudian', I could tell it's trash without even reading it!

"Hmph, I'm not getting recognized because there's too much competition in China. I already sent a draft of 'Love at Zhoukoudian' to the editing department of Hana to Yume. They specialize in publishing shoujo manga, so even if they don't understand Chinese, they will still bow down in front of my ultra-realistic art!"

Damn& The magazine is called Flowers and Dreams, not Potatoes and Eggplants! Stop wasting Auntie Ren's hard-earned money for this stupid shit!

"Uh& Ye Lin classmate, I didn't make an international postal delivery. I asked my art instructor who often visits Japan and Hong Kong to help me drop it off&"

"But the art instructor also envies my talent since she recommended me to not deliver it. In the end, I was still able to convince her, but she said once my mom leaves quarantine, she would quit as my art teacher&"

"Hehe (ã6ã) is she at a loss for what to teach because I'm too talented? It looks like she's pretty self-aware!"

But it seems like you have zero self-awareness! She's simply giving up on someone as hopeless as you. I'm begging you, PLEASE. STOP. EMBARRASSING. Chinese manga.

In order to save time, the language homework was collected by both Gong CaiCai and the language class representative. When Gong CaiCai came to me, she wanted to say something, but she shrank away from Xiao Qin's hostile gaze at her breasts.

After class, Xiong YaoYue was sitting on top of Gong CaiCai's table. Gong CaiCai said sadly: the underwear she was hanging on her balcony was stolen on Sunday.

"WHAT!" Xiong YaoYue's loud voice nearly broke the ceiling, "But I was at the class leader's house yesterday, I don't think Shu Zhe had the time to do it."

"Why would it be the class leader's brother?"

Xiong YaoYue clutched her chin and made a puzzled expression.

"Does he have an accomplice? I kicked him under the table, stepped on his shoes, pulled his ear when the class leader wasn't looking, stole his wallet, but he still wasn't able to show he knows martial arts, of course, I returned his wallet&"

Damn, not only did you freeload a meal off the class leader, you even hit her brother! No wonder Shu Zhe doesn't like girls stronger than him, he's already treated like this before they are even in a relationship!

"Xiao, Xiao Xiong&" Gong CaiCai said hesitantly, "I don't think the thief is the class leader's brother. Actually, when I went to collect my underwear, I met the thief&"

"Ah, did he do anything to you?!" Xiong YaoYue's voice changed due to her worry.

"No& but even though he was wearing a face mask, his eyes were upright, and he even greeted me&"

Upright my ass, what kind of upright person would steal underwear! But I did hear young master Xu had a good appearance. If I had his appearance, then I would never be mistaken as a bad guy!

So he only stole underwear and didn't harass you? I guess he has his principles as a thief.

Even if that's the case, he doesn't deserve praise. If I caught him in the act, I would probably give him a beating.

This reminds me of that battle we had under the bridge. He was the first one who pulled out a knife like a coward but wasn't even able to land a single hit. He's not even as good as Tang Jiang. If we meet again, he will lose miserably again.

As Xiao Qin had hoped, the weather cleared up before PE class.

After consulting with teacher Yu, Xiao Qin came to PE class wearing her new running shoes and observing from the sidelines.

She didn't participate, but only stood behind a pole and stared at me with a (^__^) look on her face. I was able to experience a peculiar feeling of being raped by her burning gaze.

I guess this is what people mean when they refer to a perverted gaze.

Today was one of the rare occurrences where gym class was right after the break, so we ended up having an extra hour of free time.

The weather became clear after the rain. There were some uneven ground on the field where you could see small puddles of water.

The sun wasn't very bright and a cool breeze would blow by once in a while. It was a perfect day for exercise.

I played a bit of 3v3 with our class' basketball team. I was shocked by Niu ShiLi's improvement, he was almost able to do a layup over me.

Sun Yu had the worst performance out of all the team members. I have suspicions that he's wasting all his energy playing taboo games with the school doctor.

Xiao Qin stood next to the basketball court throughout the entire game. She was standing cautiously with her hands on her thighs while looking at me with affection.

Due to intense movements when I was trying to grab the rebound, my shirt lifted a bit and exposed a portion of my abs. Xiao Qin was like a beast who caught a whiff of some wild game and she had ?!?!?!?!?! in her eyes.

Stop acting love-struck near me, you're distracting me. That's why Niu ShiLi was able to take the ball away from me!

I also noticed Xiao Qin cherished her running shoes and she avoided all of the puddles. Every time someone would run by spraying flecks of mud towards her, she would move slower and carefully evade it.

That's why her running shoes still looked brand new even after wearing it for an hour after it rained.

That's enough, are you trying to advertise those running shoes? The point of running shoes is for exercise, it will start crying in its sleep if you only wear it for display.

I wasn't able to concentrate when Xiao Qin was a spectator, so I stopped after playing a few rounds.

I left the basketball court to stroll around leisurely and Xiao Qin followed behind me like she was my tail, something I couldn't shake off no matter how hard I tried.

"Hey, didn't I say you can't let anyone know you're my girlfriend at school?"

"Um& I'm a fragile girl trying to ask the strongest boy in our class how to improve my physical health&."

I'm not the strongest in our class, that's Niu ShiLi. Besides, calling yourself fragile is the furthest from the truth since you can run, jump, and even fly.

When we passed by a puddle, I wanted to mess around with her so I stamped in the puddle sending dirty water flying everywhere.

Hahaha, now it looks like your running shoes will get dirty.

Xiao Qin immediately recognized the danger. In order to protect the running shoes I gave her, she rushed forward to catch all the mud with her jacket and hair.

Are& you dumb? Shoes will always get dirty. Even if you were able to preserve it indefinitely in its current state, you will grow out of it one day because of puberty. Or are you saying you don't mind staying at your current height for the rest of your life as long as your chest can get a little bigger?

Xiao Qin smiled even though she had specks of mud on her face:

"It's a good thing the running shoes Ye Lin classmate gave me are fine&"

"Did you bring napkins?" I asked.

"Yup." Xiao Qin quickly took out her pack of napkins and handed it to me.

I looked out to see if anyone was paying attention to us, then I pulled out two napkins to wipe the mud off on Xiao Qin's face.

Xiao Qin was well-behaved and stood still like she was in front of a dentist.

But her face gradually turned red. She placed her hands coyly in front of her and pointed the tips of her feet towards each other.

"It seems Ye Lin classmate is treating me better because you discovered my talents."

"What? I was only taking responsibility for my actions. What talents do you even have?"

"The talent for manga! As expected, do you like talented girls?"

Damn, how are you not embarrassed? I think it's more accurate to say you have the talent to piss off manga editors instead of talent for drawing manga. Besides, how are you a 'talented' girl? Recently, the girls have been playing a 'Chambers of

Imperial Concubines QQ Group Game'. There's an announcement in the group which states all new palace maids must display their talents such as poetry writing, or singing, but they don't want any girls who know martial arts.

Did you hear that? You're the type even concubine groups don't want. They will worry you would assassinate the emperor if they let you join!

There was a piece of mud stuck on the bridge of Xiao Qin's nose that was hard to remove. Even though Xiao Qin had already shut her eyes so I could use some force, I feel like I would damage her skin if I rubbed too hard.

Ah, I'm so kind. I still remember the past when the Little Tyrant would constantly injure my skin and I would always return home riddled in scars and bruises. The worst part was when she would sometimes catch me in excitement and tell me she wanted to 'treat' my injuries.

She would directly put things like orange juice, hot spicy soup, and leftover Popsicle sticks straight onto my wounds. It's a miracle I haven't died from an infection. The worst time was when she used superglue to close a wound I had on my eyebrow. *You shouldn't use superglue on living things, please don't imitate this at home.* It hurt like hell. I remember when I was rolling on the ground in pain and she actually told me to endure it because 'good medicine tastes bitter'.

I suddenly recalled recent news about failed plastic surgeries where they would inject silica gel into people's faces& did I turn from a cute shota into my current state because of the superglue Xiao Qin put on me? Damn it, you ruined my face, how are you going to repay me? What if I can't find a wife?

Ah, wait, it seems Xiao Qin was ready to offer herself as an apology, so it's not like I can say her apology isn't sincere.

I should make it clear: the reason why I didn't want to use too much strength was not because I was worried about damaging my future wife's skin, but because I know girts protect their own skin like how boys protect their balls. (Sorry for the vulgar comparison, but I feel it's accurate) That's why even if it's the Little Tyrant, I won't hit her face in retaliation for the things she did to me in the past.

Right when I was worried about how to remove the mud, Xiao Qin opened her eyes and made a suggestion:

"Ye, Ye Lin classmate, if the mud is too dry, all you have to do is add some spit onto the napkin&"

She said as the corners of her lips lifted into an uncontrollable smile and her shoulders also began to tremble in excitement.

Do I have to rub my spit on your face? Keep dreaming. There's no need for us to play around with indirect kisses when we've already had a French kiss before.

I said in a sour mood: "My spit is too valuable, so you should use your own."

Then I pulled out a new napkin and moved it next to Xiao Qin's lips.

My intention was for her to lick the napkin, so I can use the wet napkin to wipe away the mud on her face.

I didn't expect her to completely ignore the napkin. She suddenly clamped onto my index finger and held it in her mouth.

She began sucking on it while looking at me with large innocent eyes.

Please don't make my imagination go wild. I was wearing thin and loose shorts in order to play basketball. If there were any changes at all inside, it would stick out!

We were in the middle of the playground in a public place. There were a couple of girls playing badminton near us, but if they saw us, I would never be able to clear my guilt.

However, I didn't immediately pull my finger out because as my finger met her tongue in her warm and wet mouth, it reminded me of a cat's tongue and gave me an illusion of playing with a small animal.

Xiao Qin's goal was to give me the illusion that she was cute and not dangerous at all, that I could spend the day petting her head& keep dreaming, felines are all hidden killers. I've personally seen the cat in my grandparent's house kill a bunch of sparrows. Who knows when your sharp claws will attack certain parts of my body when I turn my back on you&

Thus I pulled my finger from out between Xiao Qin's lips with a pop.

It seems as if she still wanted to continue.

"Ye Lin classmate tastes a bit salty&"

No shit, of course I'm salty. I'm covered in sweat since I just finished playing basketball.

In any case, I finally had some spit, so I rubbed it on her nose and used the napkin to wipe away the mud.

I also wiped away the mud on her hair. I left the mud on her clothes because most of them were on her chest.

Even if Xiao Qin had a pathetically flat chest, I still didn't want to rub a girl's chest in public.

I was still dissatisfied with how Xiao Qin's running shoes were like new. I had to think of a different way to make them dirty.

I looked around and noticed the two girls was tried of playing badminton and they were planning on returning it.

Wait, isn't that Loud Mouth and Little Smart? One's way too fat and the other's way too skinny, you guys should get more exercise.

I suddenly had a bright idea and took their rackets and planned to play with Xiao Qin.

Loud Mouth wanted to tease us a bit, but she was panting like crazy, so she went to rest by the flower gardens with Little Smart supporting her.

I handed one of the rackets to Xiao Qin, then I told her to back up and purposely told her to stop near a puddle.

"Hmph, you should play some badminton to exercise because you're fragile. Get ready to receive my hit."

I threw the birdie high in the air and took a deep breath. I exerted all my strength and smashed it towards Xiao Qin.

The birdie I smashed with all my strength hit Xiao Qin on her stomach.

It was impossible she wasn't able to either avoid or catch the birdie with her martial arts background. The only possibility was that she was only concerned with keeping the running shoes clean and she completely ignored the birdie.

She had a pained expression when she was hit.

I felt like it was karma. Do you think I would forget your past brutal nature simply because you pretend to be fragile? Keep dreaming, I'll rather be friends with the straightforward Little Tyrant than someone like you who's always full of false pretenses!

In order to not make me wait, Xiao Qin picked up the birdie and hit it back to me weakly.

Did you not eat breakfast? Even Little Smart was able to hit it further than you! You're clearly a fierce tiger, yet you pretend to be a feeble kitten. I detest fake people and I'm definitely going to make you show off your true strength in this game!

Thus I sent another smash to force Xiao Qin to move. It would be good if her shoes get dirty, but I also want her to counterattack.

Come, show off the Little Tyrant's true powers. Let's determine the victor with a game of badminton!

I never expected she would surrender herself and remain in place. She pretended she couldn't see the high speed birdie and was struck again in the stomach. It hurt to the point where she dropped her racket, then she clutched her stomach and squatted down.

It should be fake since when we fought as kids, she wouldn't even budge when I repeatedly hit her stomach. It was to the point where I had doubts hard Qigong was a technique passed down from her ancestors. So, there's no way a birdie will be able to injure you.

Xiao Qin would always only make weak hits. If I also hit it back gently, she would be pleased and play a few rounds with me as if we were a young couple.

Stop kidding me, who's a couple! A Spartan's badminton game should feel spartan! Shouldn't I be yelling 'Bankai' while you yell 'Kaio-ken' and we'll have a battle that shakes 28 Middle down to its core?!

Every time I have these thoughts, I would smash the birdie as hard as I could. Then, Xiao Qin would immediately give up and use her arms, legs, or chest, as a cushion to receive the birdie.

I can't believe she didn't have a single speck of mud on her shoes even though there were three puddles between the two of us. I just don't believe you would be able to beat me in terms of persistence.

Thus I sent another smash at Xiao Qin's stomach, but this time I heard a dissatisfied female voice:

"Ye Lin, do you find it fun bullying Xiao Qin?"

The class leader had just finished volleyball practice. She was wearing a skin-tight sports uniform with a towel over her shoulder, and she was currently looking at me with an overbearing gaze.

Don't interrupt a Spartan game! Be careful to not get swept away by our strong fighting spirits!

The class leader went to support Xiao Qin.

"Xiao Qin has a weak body, so why are you forcing her to play badminton. Does it feel good bullying a weaker person?"

Who are you calling weak? Did you already forget the time when Xiao Qin pressed you down on the sofa and forced you to show your breasts? If the Little Tyrant was a boy, you would have been raped. You're the weak one here, I can't believe you were easily tricked by Xiao Qin's acts.

The class leader led Xiao Qin to the side, while she picked up the racket and said to me:

"If you like badminton that much, I'll be your opponent."

Eh, I don't really want to play with you. Why do you keep trying to get involved?

The class leader was about to serve when she noticed there were three puddles near her.

"So, not only did you want to bully her, you also made her stand in a terrible spot. Ye Lin, it seems like you're rotten to the core!"

You're not allowed to call me bad! Aren't you wearing the new shoes you bought on Sunday? Although I can't be considered a good person by giving you shoes through Shu Zhe, but at least don't call me rotten!

I explained: "I told Xiao Qin to stand near the puddles& for her own good. It was to bring out her potential in the face of adversity!"

"Is that right?" The class leader looked at me mischievously, "If that's the case, let's change spots and you can come 'show off your potential'."

"Uh&."

I couldn't really say anything, so I could only change spots.

The class leader stood on the dry and even ground and took a deep breath. The birdie was tossed high up in the air, then it sped towards me like lightning.

The first thing she aimed at was my left foot. These shots are hard to hit back for right handed people. And I could only barely make out the birdie with how fast it's going.

But there's no a way a seven foot man like me can't hit back a girl's serve.

I shouted and took a small step to reach the spot where the birdie would land. I did everything I could and was able to hit it back.

Hahaha, I'm not easy to deal with. Even if you're an expert, I&.

Ah, what's stuck on my shorts and shoes! Isn't it mud? If I try to recollect what happened, didn't I step into a puddle just to reach the birdie?

Ah, I fell into my own trap. I might even have some mud on my face, Xiao Qin, come and help me wipe it.

The class leader smashed the birdie back without giving me a chance to rest. Her jet-black hair rose into the air and was filled with a youthful energy.

It looks like you're pretty handy since you even used the towel to wrap around the handles for more grip. Why did you have to hit it towards a puddle again!

The class leader couldn't help but laugh when she saw my sorry figure as I dived into puddles to desperately return the birdie.

What are you laughing at? Does a Justice Devil like you even have bad intentions or do you consider this as proper punishment for me?

"Class leader." Xiao Qin finally spoke, "Ye Lin classmate isn't your opponent, so please stop bullying him."

How am I not her opponent? Who says she even has the ability to bully me? Let's play for three hundred more rounds, I don't think you have more stamina than me. Once all your limbs are sore, I'll be able to use my amazing techniques to defeat you!

Xiong YaoYue passed by holding a volleyball in each hand. When she saw the class leader's lively figure and my sorry figure, she laughed and said:

"Class leader, stop teasing Ye Lin, she's already taken."

"Who&. who's teasing him." The class leader blushed and wasn't able to return the birdie I hit to her.

"Oh yeah!" I jumped in the air for joy as I was able to score against the class leader for the first time. Then, I accidentally landed in the largest puddle.

My appearance looks as if I just finished a survival game.

By the way, why did Xiong YaoYue say 'she was taken'! Even if Xiao Qin was my girlfriend, I'm a guy! Or did you say 'she' because I'm a homosexual!

The class leader also seemed to object to Xiong YaoYue:

"The school prohibits early relationships, but you say Ye Lin's already taken&"

Xiong YaoYue replied carelessly: "Oh, you want to know who he's taken by, it looks like you're pretty nosy& hm..hm.. well it's that person&"

She unintentionally swept her gaze across the field, which meant my gay partner was in the school, but I had no idea who she was referring to.

The class leader misunderstood that Xiong YaoYue was looking at Xiao Qin. When Xiao Qin saw the class leader looking at her, she straightened her back hoping everyone would realize that she was my girlfriend.

I'm not sure why but the class leader lost all interest in badminton. She returned the racket to me and went with Xiong YaoYue to return the volleyballs.

Since I was standing down wind, I could slightly hear their conversation.

The class leader said: "I don't know who you heard it from, but Xiao Qin definitely doesn't have normal feelings for Ye Lin."

Eh, is the class leader referring to how Xiao Qin caused my little brother to get lost, so she feels guilty and wants to repay me with marriage?

While it's true that she feels guilty and wants to marry me, but I never had a little brother! That's just something Xiao Qin made up on the spot! The class leader still believes it because she saw my cute shota pictures, plus the lies Xiao Qin made up with the plots she read in manga!

After the class leader mentioned 'unusual feelings', Xiong YaoYue didn't know she was talking about Xiao Qin, so she thought the class leader was discriminating against homosexuals. Then she turned serious and began to lecture the class leader:

"Class leader, I was wrong about you -?, I never expected you would be this reluctant to accept new ideas."

"I& I don't think it's a new idea?"

"Oh, did they have it in ancient times too? Anyway& you can't call their feelings abnormal. In the beginning, it might seem a bit weird, but you'll get used to it."

The class leader turned around and glanced at me and Xiao Qin.

"But& are those feelings& really love?"

"How is it not love? It doesn't matter what other people think as long as the two of them love each other. Class leader, don't interfere with Ye Lin's relationship or I'll cut ties with you!"

"I& I'm not interfering&."

The class leader lowered her head as if she did something wrong. Her voice became quieter as she moved further away and I couldn't hear the rest of her sentence.

Xiao Qin clutched her stomach, it seems she still had abdominal pains.

I walked over and spoke impatiently:

"Stop pretending, they already left. With your indestructible body&"

Xiao Qin suddenly grabbed the lapels of my jacket and it seemed she was about to cry.

"I, I'm bleeding."

"Stop joking. It was only a birdie, not an armor-piercing round, how would you bleed&"

"No, no." Xiao Qin shook her head feebly, "It's an internal injury, not an external one&"

"Hahahaha." I laughed louder, "It's not like I'm Zhang Sanfeng, how did I give you an internal injury&."

Xiao Qin clenched her fist and hit me once on my chest.

Sigh, a weak punch isn't enough to display your anger. Let me have a taste of the Little Tyrant's iron fist&

Xiao Qin said anxiously:

"My, my place down there is bleeding!"

What. The. Hell. Are you saying it's your period? No wonder you kept holding your legs together. Why are you in gym class if you're having your period, just stay in class and sleep like before!

Xiao Qin said with grievance: "It wasn't supposed to come this early, but after I was hit by the birdie&"

Fuck that, are you saying your period came early because I hit you in the stomach with a birdie?

I passed the rackets to two passing students in a hurry and carried Xiao Qin to the infirmary.

The girls in our class pointed behind my back and whispered:

"What's going on? Is Ye Lin in charge of sending all injured girls to the infirmary?"

"Then we should be careful when exercising or Ye Lin will get to take advantage of us."

"Why doesn't the teacher do anything?"

"Stop joking. I heard Ye Lin is high up in the triads, there's no way the teacher could do anything."

It was the second time Xiao Qin was princess carried to the infirmary, but she couldn't enjoy it like the last time. She spoke nervously:

"Ye Lin classmate, I thought it wouldn't come this soon, so I didn't bring tampons. Now& I think my pants are a bit wet&"

No need to say anymore. I could tell it's wet without even looking, I mean it's rubbing on my damn arm! It's blood! It's blood from Xiao Qin's secret area. In ancient times, this blood was considered to have great powers. Not only can it cause misfortune to men, but it can also be used in sorcery and curses.

Damn, do I have to get rid of my arm now? I mean, if it's stained with Xiao Qin's poisonous blood, I might be cursed to fail at anything I do later on in life. Should I just suck it up and hack off my arm?

When we reached the infirmary, it was one of those rare days where Chen YingRan wasn't messing around with a shota. I placed Xiao Qin on the bed, but Chen YingRan saw the bloodstains between Xiao Qin's legs before I spoke.

"Oh, so you guys did it!"

Chen YingRan applauded us as congratulations.

Stop clapping. Even if we did it, I wouldn't come here so you could laugh at us. Hurry up and take out your tampons.

I left Xiao Qin behind and returned to class 2-3 to borrow a pair of pants from Xiong YaoYue (since she always wears shorts and keeps a pair of pants as backup).

"Hehe, why do you need a girl's pants?" Xiong YaoYue grinned evilly, "Does 'he' want you to wear girl's clothing to set the mood?"

"Stop joking around, it's for Xiao Qin."

"Okay, fine, let's just say it's for Xiao Qin." Xiong YaoYue passed me a bag with her pants, "But& you have to wash it cleanly before you return it! I don't want to lend a boy a pair of pants and get pregnant when I wear it later&"

How dirty do you think I am? If you're afraid of getting pregnant, then please stay 100m away from me at all times.

As you could imagine, Xiao Qin told everything to Chen YingRan. and soon the fact I made a girl have an earlier period while playing badminton spread through the entire school.

It wasn't a big deal being looked down upon by my classmates and the class leader, but the crucial point was when it was spread outside of the school, the details were reduced maliciously.

'Badminton' was the first word cut out, so it made it seem like 'I made a girl get an earlier period after I hit her'. There were also multiple variations such as 'I used a metal pipe to hit a girl until she had an earlier period', or 'I kicked a girl until she had an earlier period', or 'I kicked a girl until she had a miscarriage', etc&

Damn, who hates me to this extent where they would fabricate and spread all these rumors about me? Even the punks and hoodlums I beat up before denounced me while appearing to be upright gentlemen.

Before school was over, I called Shu Zhe out to give him a new pair of sexy white underwear. I told him to wear it for another 72 hours to make the smell last.

He couldn't help but smile when he saw me, then he asked:

"Bro Ye Lin, I heard&"

"If it's about me kicking someone until they had a miscarriage, don't say anything&"

Shu Zhe disappointingly said 'okay'.

After a while, he said: "Bro Ye Lin, can you think of a way to catch the panty thief?"

I was curious: "Why? Did you start worrying about the well-being of girls after wearing women's clothing?"

"No." Shu Zhe shook his head, "It's because sis Yue Yue always suspects that I'm the panty thief, so she keeps trying to test my martial arts. She really messed with me a lot on Sunday, and she even threatened me by saying if I told my sister, she would say I molested her."

"Who would even molest her? I heard even some thugs avoid her. Bro Ye Lin, if you don't help, she'll probably drive me to death!"

If Shu Zhe died, then that would be a huge loss for our adult goods store. So I agreed to help him explain to Xiong YaoYue, but I didn't guarantee I would be able to catch the thief.

Xiao Qin still had a full head of sweat from menstrual pain and she laid gasping at her desk.

She said she could stay in class because she doesn't want to split apart from me every time she had menstrual pains. I didn't listen to her and called two of Auntie Ren's friends to come to pick her up.

The two of them looked like young married women and one of them seemed to be Xiao Qin's art instructor (the one who will quit at the end of the week). When she saw me, she stopped as if she was struck by lightning, then she asked:

"Kid, do you have any interest being a model for our art college?"

Did you get drawn in by my physique? It seems you have good eyes, but I can't since I'm not used to being naked in front of strangers.

"You don't need to take off your clothes." She said in a hurry, "We're hosting a drawing session related to the communist party, but we're missing people for the Kuomintang party&"

Damn, so you want me to play the bad guy again? Have you seen a Kuomintang member as young as me? Even if they aren't good people, they wouldn't recruit minors!

"Ye Lin classmate can't be your model."

Xiao Qin, who was already sitting in their car, stuck her head out the window to stop her.

Eh, are you trying to help me? Am I still a cute shota in your eyes even when all other people call me a bad guy?

"Ye Lin classmate is mine, he will be my personal model in the future!"

Xiao Qin shouted.

"It doesn't matter if he's nude or wearing a Kuomintang uniform, I'm the only one who can draw him!"

Xiao Qin didn't come to school the following day. It has already become a regular pattern for her to be absent every time she has her period.

To be honest, every time it happens, I actually feel like something's missing.

Thus I spent the class managing the online store with my phone.

Although I've never mentioned it before, out 'Happy Valley Love Shop' actually has a few regular female customers.

Since both sides are anonymous on the web, there are no topics that are considered off-limits.

We also had four customer service representatives, 'Donkey Kong', 'Mario', 'Lilac', and 'Southland Red Berries'. The last two nicknames sound like female customer service representatives.

Actually, these four people are all impersonated by me. It was in order to make our shop seem more professional. It's actually pretty common on Taobao, so that's why stop hesitating the next time you're looking for a specific customer service representative.

Some female customers would leave the following reviews:

"Haha, I went on a blind date once with it hidden under my clothes. It felt so good during our meal that I almost couldn't hold it in. He looked at me strangely, maybe he noticed?"

Fuck, why are you even going on a date if you're not serious about it! Just spend the rest of your life with the sex toys from our store. Or do you want to satisfy your weird fetishes by purposely attending a blind date!

Some other female customers commented:

"The seven modes are really amazing. I don't even need a boyfriend anymore, but it uses too much electricity. Does your store sell rechargeable batteries too?"

Go to an electronics store if you want rechargeable batteries! Even though I'm grateful for your patronage, please find a boyfriend. Even if it's for the sake of conserving electricity for the country.

Some other comments left by female customers were even more odd:

"Where did your model get her hair done?"

Shu Zhe is wearing a damn wig! They style of hair was already set when it left the factory, but again I need to reiterate, we're a sex shop, not a barber shop.

After managing the store for a short while, I received a text from Director Cao.

It was a good thing I set my phone to vibrate, otherwise, I would have been caught.

The text said:

"My life force is about to dry up without Miss Ai Mi'er's underwear, please hurry&"

What does your life force have to do with loli underpants? I've heard my dad say that the 'holy water' that often appears in movies and games was made by soaking pages of the Holy Bible in regular water. Perhaps by soaking loli underpants in water, it would create Director Cao's life water?

I'm not sure if it was a misconception, but it seemed like the class leader intentionally kept her distance from me when Xiao Qin was absent. Did it have something to do with what Xiong YaoYue said to her yesterday?

If that's the case, then you're severely mistaken. Xiong YaoYue was referring to my non-existent same-sex partner, not Xiao Qin. Besides, if Xiao Qin and I were in an actual relationship, you shouldn't be avoiding me. You should take out the school rules for 100 ways the school prohibits relationships between boys and girls, then smash it on our heads to stop our relationship and focus on studying.

Or perhaps is there some hidden reasons for why you don't have the confidence to break us apart?

Unlike usual, Xiao Qin came to class after only one day of rest.

On Wednesday morning, Xiao Qin came to class feebly and returned the washed pair of pants to Xiong YaoYue.

"Ah, so it was actually for you!" Xiong YaoYue seemed surprised.

Seeing as Xiao Qin had no energy, I teased her a bit and said:

"What's 'Love at Zhoukoudian' about? Is it a bunch of cavemen beating up dinosaurs while dating?"

Xiao Qin spoke as if she was on her last breath: "Yes& it's about cavewomen checking out which caveman looks the best, then knocking them out with a club and dragging them back to their caves& "

What kind of love story is that! Besides, I think knocking people out with a club is what archaic men did to archaic women. Why was it reversed in your story?

It was not a wise decision for Xiao Qin to force herself to come to school. Even though Loud Mouth and Little Smart came to check up on her, and the class leader helped her make molasses water, it did nothing to help her pain.

She pretty much spent every class sprawled on top of her desk. She would tense up from pain while looking at me with a bitter smile.

"Ye Lin classmates acts as my pain medicine." Xiao Qin said, "It wouldn't hurt if I look at you some more."

"Although the medicine my mom gave me is pretty effective, I heard taking too much pain killers would lower your intelligence. That's why I only took one, and then I'll have to persevere with willpower&"

"Take the medicine if it's effective! You don't have to worry about your intelligence since its already at the minimum level!"

"Ye Lin classmate, Ye Lin classmate&" Xiao Qin called me name weakly.

For a second there, I thought she was about to say her last words.

"Can you let me suck your fingers for a bit?"

"What?"

"My pain isn't really subsiding by only looking, but it might work better if I suck it, even if it's a bit salty&"

Then go suck on yourself if you don't like the taste! Also, how could I let the girl next to me suck my fingers in a scared classroom where people come to learn?

"What a selfish boyfriend&" Xiao Qin lamented, and began sucking on her right index finger.

"Oh, misht tashte sertmms witer dan Ye Lin cwashhmate&" (My taste seems lighter than Ye Lin classmate)

Don't speak with your fingers in your mouth, I couldn't even understand what you said. And it's not like you're a dish, why do you care if it's sour, sweet, bitter, or salty?

After forcing herself to get through lunch, it seems she couldn't hold it in anymore. She asked the teacher for a leave of absence and to help her to the infirmary.

I secretly ran to the infirmary before the first class after lunch began. I wanted to see how Xiao Qin was doing (and this way those noisy girls from our class wouldn't be here).

I never thought Chen YinRan would be absent too. Xiao Qin was lying on the bed by the window, I'm not sure if she took painkillers, but she was in a deep sleep.

I walked next to her quietly and looked at her slightly red face in silence.

Her bangs were a little messy, but it gave off a sense of asymmetric beauty. Between breaths, Xiao Qin's face was like a work of art sculpted from white marble. Especially her slightly opened lips, she was like the dewdrops that accompanies sunrise, or the buds of a flower, spreading a young woman's charm.

I couldn't find any traces of my old nemesis from her current appearance.

How pathetic.

My greatest enemy is right in front of me, but I can't even take my revenge. What's even worse is I had thoughts about secretly kissing her while she was asleep&

As expected, her poison has already infiltrated my body. The Sparta in my heart has also become more taciturn. I tried to visualize the image of the Sparta in my mind. Eh, Sparta, what are you doing, why are you kneeling while facing the wall? Damn, you're kneeling on a washing board, when did you fall to this level?

While feeling sorrow for the fall of Sparta, I heard Xiao Qin chuckle.

I thought she woke up, but she was only talking in her sleep.

"You're mine& you can only look at me&"

Oh, she's actually speaking full sentences. Is she talking about me? Should I go buy some sunflower seeds (TN: popcorn) and enjoy the show?

"Ye&."

I thought she was about to say 'Ye Lin classmate', but she turned in her sleep and said:

"Ye Lu&" (TN: Ye Lu is donkey, her nickname for Ye Lin when they were kids)

So, you weren't dreaming about the current me, but commemorating the good times when you bullied me! Is that why you have a happy smile on your face!

"What should I do& even if I called him donkey as a nickname, he still looks really good&."

Is& is she referring to my shota appearance? So you didn't call me donkey because you thought I was ugly?

"If he still looks really good when he gets older, a lot of girls will like him&"

Then, Xiao Qin had a worried expression.

"It's enough if I'm the only one to like him&"

"That's why& fairy godmother&"

What the fuck are you dreaming about? Why would a 'fairy godmother' appear? Do you think you're Cinderella?

"Fairy godmother& please use your magic to make Donkey ugly& even though I've been hitting his face all the time, it doesn't seem to be working&"

Screw you! Cinderella made a wish to attend the prince's dance, but you wished for your prince to turn ugly? I thought you hit my face to show your strength, but you wanted me to turn ugly? Was that why you also used super glue to close the wounds on my face?

But regardless of your reasons, it seems your wish was fulfilled by the fairy godmother! Where is that old bastard, I'm gonna strangle her!

And you, you black-hearted Cinderella. Actually you're not Cinderella, but Cinderella's step-sisters. Have I been treating you too well lately? Should I carry out my previous plans to thoroughly break her heart, so she would run away?

Xiao Qin was a bit more energetic on Thursday since she was able to endure it for the most painful days.

"Ye Lin classmate, let's go watch a movie together on the weekend."

"What are we watching?" I said in a bad mood, "Are we watching 'Cinderella's Step-sisters' or 'Snow White and the Wicked Queen'?"

"Those movie names sound really strange& and why do you sound angry&"

No shit, I was able to find out that you always wanted me to turn ugly when I heard your sleep talk yesterday! I can't believe you intentionally hit my face to ruin my appearance. Although my appearance doesn't matter as a Spartan, you still reset the handsomeness I inherited from my parents with great difficulty!

I ignored Xiao Qin and played a game I installed on my phone last night. It was called 'Angry Grandma' and it's pretty fun.

Xiao Qin stared at my phone for a while before she shrunk back after being called out by the biology teacher.

I didn't speak to Xiao Qin for over half an hour.

Actually, students shouldn't be talking to each other in class anyway, they should be focused on learning.

After class, I still sat at my spot playing on my phone.

Xiao Qin spoke timidly: "Ye Lin classmate, I&"

I kept tapping on my screen and ignored her.

"Um&."

Tap tap tap tap tap tap&

Xiao Qin couldn't endure it anymore:

"Sob sob~~ (gt;_lt;)~~ Ye Lin classmate would rather play with a grandma than play with me."

Damn, at least use the full name of the app. Niu ShiLi already suffered some severe mental damage! Please don't make other people think I have special interest in old grannies!

I let Xiao Qin borrow my phone for a bit to make her stop talking. It was also in order for her to experience 'Angry Grandma'. I sent a text to meet up with Shu Zhe before I handed the phone to Xiao Qin.

Of course, I wanted to meet up with Shu Zhe to collect the underwear. This time he didn't screw it up, he passed me the underwear in a sealed bag then stuck out his hands.

"Huh, you want money? You're so greedy, I already gave you the payment last time before you took the job."

"No." Shu Zhe feigned a displeased expression, "Bro Ye Lin, I'm asking for a new pair. Didn't you tell me to use my time to its fullest?"

My face stiffened: "Sorry, I was a bit lazy recently, so I didn't contact any clients and I didn't get any new orders."

"What?" Shu Zhe was dissatisfied, "What's wrong with you? I thought I would get a new order right away, so I didn't bring a change of underwear. Now it's all cool and bare down there."

Bare my ass, it's not like you're wearing a skirt. Even if some classmates pulled down your shorts as a prank, it's still better being found naked than wearing women's underwear.

I tapped his head with my fist.

"Are you the boss or am I the boss? If you think I'm not putting in enough effort, then you can contact the clients yourself, since I have four customer service accounts anyway&"

"Bro Ye Lin, are you telling me to be a part of your customer service team?"

"That's right. I'll give you the most effeminate name out of the four, 'Southland Red Berries'. I'll tell our regular customers Miss Model is in charge of that account. Since you're great at talking, you should get more business with your own ability."

Shu Zhe looked down and began to think earnestly.

"Then& will I get paid extra wages for working in customer service?"

He still only cares about money as expected.

"No, you're already earning plenty. In our current arrangement for worn panties, you're already taking a large cut, while I only get a bit. From now on, I'll let you manage the entire 'Original Underwear' operation. I'll only take the profits for the underwear itself, while you take the profits for the 'original' portion& I'll tell you how I set the prices, as for if the customers will be willing to pay higher prices, that will depend on your own abilities."

"Um& since the customers think I'm a girl and they can choose a pair of underwear for me, I think they will be happy if I'm also doing customer service."

"That's true. They might also tease or harass you, so you better not get mad at them."

"No way, how could I offend our wealthy customers? It's not like I'm suffering any losses since I'm a guy. I'll go along with them and flirt a bit then make them pay more money."

Amazing, you already laid out an entire plan. For all of our upright customers out there, please don't pick 'Southland Red Berries' for help when visiting our store. He has a sweet mouth, but he will back stab you.

I helped him install the Taobao app on his phone and told him the login information for the 'Southland Red Berries' account. I also taught him basic operating instructions along with our previous customers and their character traits. He was able to pick up everything pretty quickly, it's no wonder all the teachers think he's a good student.

When I returned to the classroom, Xiao Qin was still playing 'Angry Grandma', it looks like she was pretty mesmerized.

Well, since she acted like a boy for a long time, it's easy for her to get addicted to games.

After I sat back down at my desk, Xiao Qin reluctantly returned my phone, then she suddenly asked:

"Why does Ai Mi think you want her underwear?"

Shit, did you look at my messages?! I was careless, I made the most common mistake for men, you have to clear your chat and text history before handing off your phone to your girlfriend!

My face flashed different colors.

"Um, there are bound to be self-centered people in show business, she's just too sensitive."

Xiao Qin used the English textbook as cover and showed a doubtful expression.

"But, the one sin my QQ group have been talking about siscon anime recently. For example 'My Little Sister Can't Be This Cute', or 'As Long as There's Love, It Doesn't Matter If He Is My Brother, Right', or 'Nakaimo - My Sister Is Among Them!', and more&"

"I told them: having a relationship with blood-related siblings is disgusting. They told me I don't appreciate art and can't accept the new contemporary aesthetic trends. And they said I wasn't a true man&"

"I said I wasn't a man, but a woman, and girl's think that relationship with blood-related siblings is disgusting. They called me a feet-picking uncle and told me to screw off&"

"Ye Lin classmate, I'm not a feet-picking uncle, right?" Xiao Qin asked with tears in the corners of her eyes.

Of course not. Do you even need to ask?

"Then& am I right when I said a relationship with blood-related siblings is disgusting?"

"&.."

"Why are you hesitating? Do you actually have impure thoughts towards your blood-related sister? Is your first step to get her underwear, then gradually move on to obtain her more important things?"

Please, I only want to steal her underwear to make some money, it has nothing to do with incest. Besides, I wasn't even planning on giving Director Cao worn panties. I would wash it clean before I give it to him. But it would be too embarrassing to tell you these things.

"If you want a girl's underwear, I can give it to you at any time& how about after class&."

What are you going to do after class? I don't need your underwear. Ask again when you can sell a pair of your underwear for ¥20,000!

The awkward conversation finally ended when the English called on Xiao Qin to answer a question.

Then, I completely ignored Xiao Qin. I played 'Angry Grandma' until level 36 and didn't even give a chance for her to ask any more questions.

At night, when I was managing orders on the computer, 'Popeye' and 'Uncle Fireball' logged in simultaneously. Popeye told me, he still hasn't gotten his wages for the month, so he can't buy any new treasures and he feels a bit lonely.

I told him to not feel bad and he could have a chat with customer service representative number 4, who was Miss Model, anytime, since it's free anyway.

Popeye was amazed and went to chat with Shu Zhe. It seems Uncle Fireball already knew about it and had a chat with Shu Zhe earlier.

I told him the sexy white rose underwear would be shipped tomorrow night at the latest and he was ecstatic. He also told me he came up with a new line of work for our business.

"I said Ms. Red Berries&."

"Huh?" I then remembered he was referring to Southland Red Berries. Ms. Red Berries is probably a nickname he made for her.

"I was looking at Ms. Red Berries schedule, and it looks like she's still a student."

"Yes, she's a student. She's in high school, but she still has a baby face, hahahahaha&&"

I awkwardly tried to cover it up.

"I had a chat with her earlier and she's great at making me happy. She doesn't even get mad when if I make a perverted joke. My imagination wanders when I chat with her while looking at her photos."

"I was able to choose a pair of underwear while asking for her opinions, it was a great experience. You might have already seen the order for the 'semi-translucent silk underwear'. Please let Ms. Red Berries wear it tomorrow, I spent 500 big ones not including the price of the underwear&"

Wow, Shu Zhe you're pretty incisive if you can make a customer so happy with only a few words. You were even able to raise the price by ¥500, by comparison, I'm barely even making ¥50 of profit on each pair of underwear.

"But original panties are just too expensive, and the smell disappears quickly& I feel like the store can release some other new consumables&"

"Dear customer, what are you referring to?"

"For example, balloons."

"Balloons?"

"That's right. There are definitively people out there who would buy balloons Ms. Red Berries personally blows into. Even if it's not used for smelling, you can still hang it on the ceiling and use it as a mood setter. It will be even more effective when used along with her underwear."

Uncle Fireball was working hard for our store while spitting out ideas:

"I recommend Ms. Red Berries to wear lipstick when blowing up balloons, that way, it's like she intentionally kissed every balloon. Some customers would impatiently untie the balloon, so they could take large gulps of her breath while having an indirect kiss with her!"

When you say 'some customers', you're probably just referring to yourself. But it's not a bad idea. Since I let Shu Zhe manage the 'You Choose What I Wear' service, I should start a new project.

Balloons are very cheap and you can buy them at any supermarket. It doesn't take a lot of effort to blow up a balloon, and we could start work immediately after I buy Shu Zhe a cheap stick of lipstick, but as for how to price it&

"¥20 for balloons without lip marks, and ¥50 for balloons with a mark."

It was if I could see Uncle Fireball slapping a table energetically.

If I could earn ¥50 for a balloon, then I'm going to go buy lipstick tomorrow! Also, you could blow balloons at any time without waiting for a 72 hour cooling period, and the small profits will build up quickly.

Since Gramps was afraid of getting back pain again, he became more cautious when teaching. The time I spent practicing with him on the lakeside was evidently reduced.

As a result, I arrived earlier at school every day. Early Friday morning, I walked passed the school gates and coincidentally bumped into Shu Zhe.

"Bro Ye Lin, are you also on class duty?" Shu Zhe asked me.

I didn't respond and passed him the silk underwear that was stuck in between a notebook.

He knowingly stuffed the notebook in his backpack, then he looked around for people before stick out his hand towards me.

"Please give me the ¥500."

He seemed to be immensely pleased with himself.

What's there to be proud of? Do you think you can show off the fact that you speak with customers while pretending to be a girl? Can you please take a closer look at reality, I mean the silk underwear Uncle Fireball chose has a opening slit in the middle! If you wear it, wouldn't your dick be hanging out? It's way too perverted.

Thus I didn't hand him any money and looked at him with contempt.

"There's nothing to be proud of even if you're a bit good at 'keeping company'. Besides, I'm not carrying a lot of cash with me. I'll give you the money after 72 hours, after you hand the 'goods' to me."

"Why?" Shu Zhe was discontent with my decision, "Didn't you always give me money first?"

"Hmph, that's before, but not anymore. Did you already forget how you messed up the sexy white rose underwear? It's because you became negligent after I gave you the money first, so I decided to postpone the payment to prevent similar events from happening&"

I said as I cracked my fingers.

"Do you have anything else you want to say?"

"N, no&." Shu Zhe mumbled, "It's fine as long as you pay me&"

After two classes, I decided to skip radio calisthenics even though I was the PE committee member. I flipped over the back wall while everyone was displaying their youth and headed off to buy lipstick.

The class leader would be furious when she finds out. Those lackeys from the student council will definitely realize when a student is missing and report it to the teacher, then our class will have points deducted. Plus, Eunuch Cao also made some sort of new boy and girl pairing radio calisthenics and purposely did the wrong movements (for example, when the girl next to him turns to the right with her back facing him, he would purposely make obscene postures towards her back). Our class might even be branded as the worst class at radio calisthenics.

It can't be helped even if I make the class leader mad, since there are the fewest number of students outside the school during radio calisthenics. I definitely don't want to be seen by an acquaintance when buying lipstick.

Especially if I was seen by Xiong YaoYue, then she would be even more confident that I was a 'bottom' homosexual. She might even try to share her lipstick experience with me.

Now that I brought it up, I'm not even sure if Xiong YaoYue has even used lipstick before.

I've said previously that there was a bookstore at the end of the food stall street. It was located halfway underground and had a secret section where you could buy hentai and AV. Recently, they opened up new products towards girls and began to sell simple makeup products.

I slipped into the concealed store entrance and glanced around. Luckily, there were no other customers, and the boss was sitting behind the counter with a full head of sweat and a desk fan in front of him.

"Young man, did you come here to watch films." I never came here many times, yet he still remembers me well.

I remember I came here last time to buy a copy of 'The Holy Bible · The Old Testament' for copying, but he recommended me the hentai, 'Bible Black', and it pissed me off so I left.

"I'm not here to watch films." I said with embarrassment, "I heard you guys are selling makeup, I& I wanted to buy lipstick for my girlfriend."

Ah, so embarrassing. I don't really care much about the boss' vulgar smile, but the main problem is that Shu Zhe isn't my girlfriend! I should have just bought it online.

It would have been fine to bring Xiao Qin too. Even if she still has menstrual pain, she would still follow along happily if I bought two lipsticks and promised to give her one. Then, I could even tell Xiao Qin to help me buy more lipstick in the future.

"No wonder you don't need to watch 'Bible Black', you already have a real person." The boss joked around while recommending a line of light pink lipstick.

"Not these ones." I said, "I want the really really bright red ones."

The boss was surprised, "I never thought you would have such unique tastes for someone so young&"

I already know girls nowadays like lipstick with light colors. Some avant-garde girls use blue, or black, and red was already long out of date. But I need lipstick to leave kiss marks on a balloon. It wouldn't be clear enough if it's a light color. At that time, will you take responsibility if customers leave me negative reviews?

In the end, I didn't really have many options since there were too few red lipsticks. I ended up buying a more expensive one that claims 'keeps your lips moist and lasts a long time'. It contains some sort of honey nectar essence and naturally fights against oxidation.

Damn, I spent fifty big ones! That's enough for me to buy two lunches and have some leftover. I remember there were a lot of ¥20 ones online, what a blunder.

But it's fine if I think about it. If it goes well, I can sell each balloon for ¥50 and make my money back.

I returned to school during break when radio calisthenics had already ended. I walked carefully in the hallway with the lipstick in my pocket, but I didn't expect to meet the class leader when I turned around a corner.

The class leader was standing in the hallway and removing the creases on her skirt.

Because girls might expose themselves during radio calisthenics if they're wearing a skirt, a lot of girls would prepare a backup pair of pants in the summer. They would put on the pants for radio calisthenics, then switch back to a skirt when it's over.

How troublesome.

The class leader saw me walk over, but she didn't interrogate me on why I skipped radio calisthenics. Instead, she was glancing at something on the windowsill on her right side.

Isn't that a kitten? It was a furry kitten that was not much larger than the palm of your hand. How did it even get into the school and on top of the windowsill? 28 Middle prohibits bringing pets inside the school, but it's even worse if it's a wild cat.

If I remember correctly, the head teacher hates cats. The number one thing she hates is student relationships, and the second thing she hates are cats. If she found the kitten, she would definitely kick it onto the roads.

Speak of the devil, right when I was thinking about her, I heard her irritating snarl:

"Where did that cat go? Hurry up and find it! Don't you guys know the vice-principal is allergic to cats? We have to toss it out!"

Then you could hear the footsteps of at least 5 other people. I guess there are at least four members of the student council working as her accomplices.

Based on the sound, they are within 20 feet of us, and they could catch the kitten once they turn around the corner.

The kitten was completely unaware of the nearby dangers. It stretched lazily and called out to the class leader.

"Meow~~~"

The class leader had a surprised and joyous expression.

There's actually a cat that doesn't care about a hunter's aura! If I looked closely, this cat has a similar pattern on its fur similar to the cat overlord who wanders around the monastery.

It's the overlord cat who swatted the class leader with his meaty paws after being stared at for over twenty seconds.

Is this kitten a descendant? Are newborn cats not afraid of tigers?

"Head teacher, can you give the cat to me after we catch it?" One of the student council members asked with bad intentions. Since they were nearby, we could hear their conversation clearly.

"Do you want to bring it home to raise it?" the head teacher spoke with indifference.

"No, my aunt's husband is great at making a snake and cat dish, so I want to provide him with some materials&"

"Alright, you can take it home."

What kind of situation is this? The class leader's Justice Devil aura already shot through the sky. Are you planning on going against the head teacher and the student council for this cat?

As long as you don't mind losing your position as the class leader, I'll stand beside you as long as you give me an order.

I don't typically hit teachers because of my father's previous career, but the head teacher isn't even a teacher in my eyes. The head teacher hasn't taught students anything other than turning on each other.

I thought the class leader would order me to give the head teacher and the four student council members a beating to save the kitten's life. Then, she would have to give up her position as the class leader and become a problem student like me (why do I feel slightly expectant).

Who knew she took an action I never would have expected.

She calmed down in an instant, quickly ran up to the window sill, grabbed the kitten, and& covered it under her skirt.

Damn, you exposed yourself! You didn't even expose yourself during radio calisthenics, but you did in front of me. I was able to see your pure white legs!

At this point, the head teacher and the others have already caught up. They were puzzled because they couldn't find the cat after glancing around.

"I clearly heard a cat&"

The class leader held down the hems of her skirt and made an unconcerned expression. She looked like some of those literature and art girls while gazing out the window.

Actually, she was monitoring the head teacher's group's movements in the window's reflection.

The class leader wanted to clench her legs together, but she was afraid of hurting the kitten. But it would also feel awkward if she didn't clench her legs.

The class leader sat down in the most rational method to hide the kitten that was under her skirt; she crossed her legs.

The advantages are clear, since she can hide the kitten in the triangular space between her legs.

But the disadvantage when a girl takes this posture is that it makes them seems as if they don't want to talk to anyone. It's also extremely disrespectful in front of the head teacher.

"Huh, aren't you class 2-3's class leader, Shu Sha?" The head teacher pushed up her circular oversized glasses.

The class leader used one hand to hold down her skirt and scratched her neck with the other, "Sorry, my throat's a bit hoarse today, so I can't speak loudly."

Even though the head teacher saw me standing nearby, she believes I was only passing by and she continued to question Shu Sha:

"Have you seen a kitten pass by?"

"No&"

A faint meow could be heard from under her skirt before she even finished speaking.

You're definitely going to get caught! I mean, you stuffed a kitten into a hot and unventilated area on a hot summer's day, there's no way it wouldn't meow! Even if it has resistance against your hunter's aura, it would still panic after being embraced by a hunter!

The head teacher was like a fly attracted to the smell of shit and she shifted her gaze towards the class leader's skirt.

The other four student council members, three guys and one girl, all looked at the class leader's skirt.

"Why do I hear meowing coming from your body?" The head teacher asked coldly.

"It's not a cat." The class leader denied it in a hurry, "I said my throat was a bit hoarse, my words just kind of sound like a meow& if you don't believe me, I'll say it again."

"N~oo, me~ow, me~ow~~~~"

The class leader wasn't great at telling lies, but she tried her best to imitate a cat with an innocent expression.

It's too cute. If she raised one hand towards the ceiling, then she would look really similar to a lucky cat! The three male student council members all blushed while the female student council member was going crazy with envy.

The head teacher snorted, "You think you can fool me? Everyone already knows you like cats. The 'cat club' I cracked down on had records of you being a previous member."

The class leader tightened her grip on the skirt as she was exposed, but she still refused to admit the truth:

"I, I didn't join the cat club because I like cats, it was because I& I like to abuse cats, so I was kicked out of the club. I'm really not hiding the cat."

All of a sudden, the class leader groaned with a pained complexion, but she was able to remain composed after she clenched her teeth.

Did the cat scratch her? Did the kitten unleash its weapons at the class leader's thighs because it's being trapped in a tight and hot space?

What an ungrateful beast. It should be happy hiding under a place where many people would line up to take its place.

"Shu Sha, stand up." The head teacher commanded.

The class leader shook her head, "I can't, my leg is injured."

The head teacher sneered.

"How strange. Why is a student who is usually serious and honest keep telling lies? Didn't you say earlier you had a hoarse throat? Then, why are you speaking louder."

The class leader bit her lips in frustration.

Unfortunately, the cat didn't stay still and began to claw randomly under her skirt. Because the class leader pressed down on the sides of her skirt, it kept trying different ways to escape. No, you can't go there!

The class leader gasped in surprise and arched her body forward. Her body was as red as a pomegranate.

In order to hide the cat's sounds, she also forced herself to meow periodically.

I couldn't stand it anymore, so I walked between the class leader and the group of five and I stared at the head teacher.

The four students each took a step back and left the head teacher at the frontier.

"Ye Lin, what& are you doing?" The head teacher asked nervously.

"Yeah, what am I doing?" I scratched behind my ear and replied sloppily.

"I'm trying to have a conversation with Shu Sha, it has nothing to do with you."

"Ah, what a coincidence, I also have to talk to Shu Sha. Can you let me talk to her first?"

"Hmph, Shu Sha is a top student, why would you need to talk to her." The head teacher became a bit upset.

"That's not true." I blew off the earwax I picked off my pinkie, "She might have been a top student for too long, so she's looking for me to do some bad things. Actually, when Shu Sha crosses her legs, she really gives off the impression of a female gang leader, what do you think?"

Shu Sha was angry I made fun of her in this situation, but the kitten was more important and she couldn't move.

We stood in a deadlock for a while, then the head teacher glanced at the four pieces of trash who were backing up and she finally gave up.

She warned me before she left:

"Ye Lin, I'm not afraid of you, I'm letting you go because you're acquainted with Xing Xing."

Stop lying, who are you even trying to scare? I'm the one who held back; if you weren't Xing Xing's aunt, I would have already punched you.

The class leader glanced at me after the cat catching squad left.

"Turn around."

"Why?"

"Do& you even have to ask? I have to take the kitten out."

Now you know how to be embarrassed? I've already seen it when you hid the kitten, it's a shame I couldn't clearly see the color&

I turned around, then the class leader held the kitten in her hand and breathed a sigh of relief.

"Kitty, you dodged a bullet."

The class leader spoke to the puzzled kitten.

"Stop playing around." I said, "Hurry and release the cat outside the school before the head teacher returns. There's a hole in the chain-link fence behind the school, that's probably where it crawled in from."

The class leader reluctantly nodded.

"Why didn't you just grab the cat and run earlier?" I asked.

"Because you can't run in the halls." The class leader answered with a matter-of-fact tone.

So, it was to abide by school rules? I can't believe you even had the time to think about rules in that situation! It's a good thing the school doesn't prohibit hiding cats under your skirt.

I walked in front, while the class leader walked behind me using my body as a cover. She was able to carefully deliver the cat to the chain-link fence, and she nearly wept when they had to part ways.

"Kitty, do you live nearby? I'll come and visit, and be careful of bad guys!"

The kitten immediately jumped into the fields behind the hole in the fence after it was free from the class leader's clutches.

The class leader waved at the back figure of the kitten hoping it would look back once.

The cat raised its tail pridefully and left while ignoring the class leader.

The class leader and I were both squatting in front of the chain-link fence. I was observing the ants cause I had nothing to do while she was frustrated.

"Why are you calling it kitty." I asked, "It might not like being called that."

The class leader gazed sentimentally at the spot where the cat disappeared.

"Because there were five cats at my grandparents' place and each one was called kitty."

Ah, what a coincidence, my grandmother's cats were all called tiggy, even their names sound cooler than cats at the class leader's house. (TN: LOL, I don't think there's a cute word for tigers)

The class leader had a pained expression as she pressed her hands against her thighs when she stood up.

"So you were scratched by the cat." I asked, "Do you want to go to the infirmary to get treated?"

"No." The class leader tided up the creases on her skirt, "There's something wrong with the school's doctor. I think she's done something really bad to the students. I'm going to report her to the police once I have any concrete evidence."

I shrugged and didn't make a comment.

I saw the class leader reach into her pockets to look for a napkin with no luck, so I took out my own and handed it to her: "Use mines."

I accidentally pulled out the lipstick along with it, but I quickly stuffed it back in.

Of course, it didn't escape the class leader's eyes, she hesitated a bit and asked:

"It's still in its packaging& did you buy it as a gift for Xiao Qin?"

It's actually for your brother, but I can't say the truth. If I told you, you would burst my head open, turn me into jerky and feed me to the kitty.

I could only acquiesce the class leader's statement.

The class leader seemed to be as disappointed as when the kitty jumped away into the fields.

"Middle schoolers shouldn't use makeup." The class leader said faintly, "But I'll let you off this once."

Why does the figure of the class leader's back when she's leaving seem even more lonely?

I didn't return home immediately after school. I first went to Wal-mart to buy two large bags of balloons. It should last long enough for Shu Zhe to blow it and train his lung capacity.

When I was teasing the tortoises in the fresh section, I coincidentally bumped into Xiao Ding from the pet hospital. It seems he was out buying some pacific saury for his mother.

He might be silent in front of girls, but he's extremely talkative when speaking with me. He first talked about how Dr. Zhao was careless and had his wallet stolen when he was focused on curing a dog. It was Shu Sha who noticed when she came to do volunteer work, otherwise, it would have become even more troublesome.

He then began to talk about how Shu Sha has been doing more volunteer work the past couple of days, but the animals didn't really have a positive change of attitude towards her. It makes people want to sigh when a beautiful girl would rather stay with a bunch of sick animals after school instead of going shopping with a boyfriend.

Then finally, he talked about the topic that made him the most excited:

It turns out Dota 2 is about to have their open beta.

Towards a noob like me, who has only played Dota, Xiao Ding began talking non-stop about the classic champs of Dota 2, the amount of skill it takes to play, and the items. Even the news outlets are praising the game. Zhe Jiang is recruiting one hundred and eighty universities across the country and more than two hundred associations to participate in the Esports competition, so they could select the future national team for Dota 2.

Then at the end, he criticized LOL like usual. He said it's a game only elementary students would play and he would cut ties with me if I played LOL.

Damn, are you done yet? Are you saying the relationship we've built up is not even worth more than a game? (It probably sounds weird to say it this way&)

Also, who even wants to play LOL? I'm currently playing a real-life version of a school life romance galge, so I can establish a large harem!

I staggered home in the heat after separating from Xiao Ding. Right when I was about to unlock the door, I saw a piece of broken tin foil in the door's lock.

Isn't this the godly trick Peng TouSi displayed last time to pick a lock with tin foil? Since the front door of our house has a lock with the worst security, an expert can easily open it with tin foil!

Since Ai Mi isn't living here, it's someone other than Peng TouSi.

Did my house get robbed?!

I pulled out the tin foil, opened the door, and rushed inside. I quickly scanned around at the objects inside.

The TV was still there (Of course, who would steal something so old and heavy), the washing machine was also there (that's even heavier), my dad's desktop computer and my second-hand laptop were also there.

More importantly, the cash, bankbooks, and credit cards that were hidden in the pockets of clothes in the closet were all still there.

But there was a lingering feeling that someone definitely came in, but what went missing?

Don't tell me the adult goods worth over ¥200,000 was stolen? But you need a large truck to move those goods. Besides, if you were a thief, how would you even get rid of the goods, and what would you say to your wife and kids?

I briskly walked into the large room where we kept the goods and I realized the boxes have been moved.

When I was looking for the pair of silk underwear today morning, I remembered the boxes were arranged in a Á shape, but now the top box is missing. It's as big of a difference as the beginning of a level of Angry Birds vs the end of the level.

I stood in the midst of the scattered boxes and tried to think if any valuable merchandise was stolen. But because we didn't have a lot of capital, we always targeted the low to mid end of the market. We don't sell those ¥88,000 24K gold bars they sell on JD.com. (I don't understand who would buy those)

Even if the thief stole a pack of Trojan Fire & Ice or Okamoto 001, he would only be able to distribute to his accomplices and tell them to be safe.

One of the boxes wasn't stacked properly and came crashing down into the large screen (I kept the large screen in the room ever since Shu Zhe did the rope model photoshoots here). The screen shook and almost collapsed because of its low quality, then I suddenly had a shocking thought:

"Is the thief a super pervert who's actually hiding behind the screen right now? Is he just waiting for an opportunity to jump out and burst my chrysanthemum?"

After a momentary false alarm, I began to analyze the situation

A certain elementary school student said: "There is always only one truth." (TN: It's Conan). If a thief broke into my house, but didn't steal anything, then why did he come in?

My sight landed on a couple of old boxes that have been always kept at the bottom of the pile until today.

It was filled by a bunch of knockoffs of branded Japanese goods made by a certain Taiwanese company. I think a few years back there was a distributor who owed us product and used these to pay back his debt.

If we sold them as the actual products, we could sell it for over ¥10,000, but my dad was an honest businessman and he wrote these were counterfeit in the description and priced them at 14 of the authentic goods.

That's why these didn't sell well and became slow-moving product kept at the bottom of the pile.

Why did these goods get brought to the top of the pile? Did the pervert thief see these products on our store page and couldn't wait, so he came here to try it personally?

I suddenly remembered that a few days ago, there was a man who asked about these products. His username was a series of numbers and I suspected he was a virgin. He repeatedly asked me:

"Do you still have any of these goods? How much is left? When can you ship it if I order a bit more?"

When I first began managing the store, he asked me 'which condoms would easily make his girlfriend climax', so I marketed a lot of products to him, but he didn't buy jack shit.

That's why I replied half-heartedly to his question:

"These products& I might have some. If you place an order, I can go check our inventory. I'll immediately give you a refund if we don't have any."

I never thought there would be a follow-up, but who could have imagined the freakish case that occurred today.

I began to think a lot and my stomach began to grumble since I haven't eaten.

I have to find the connections between the suspected virgin and my house being broken into.

I swear on my grandfather's name&

First of all, it wasn't a random thief, he broke in with a purpose. Perhaps he's the same person as the suspected virgin, the one who kept asking about our products but never bought anything. Why did he come to my house to look through our goods? But if he never ordered anything from us, how did he even find our address?

Did he hire a private detective to do an investigation?

A private& detective.

I remembered that the first time the suspected virgin contacted me was shockingly similar to the time when the private detective was following me by the lakeside.

They might even be the same person! I come into contact with way too many customers a day, so I didn't really pay attention.

Maybe Ai ShuQiao hired a private detective to pretend to be the suspected virgin to find out information about me.

Damn, what did you even learn? Did you find the photos of Xiao Qin and the class leader hidden under my bed, or the nude photos of Shu Zhe saved on my laptop? Even if you reported it to Ai ShuQiao, she would only think her son is bisexual and it doesn't really affect me.

Which means the crucial point still revolves around the Taiwanese counterfeit goods.

My second aunt, who used to run a sporting equipment business, once told me she was reported by a store across from her who was in the industry. They said she was selling fake Wish tennis rackets and the Commerce and Industry Bureau (CIB) came and confiscated all her fake tennis rackets, then she paid ¥5000 in fines to get the rackets back.

It's hilarious how you can use money to buy it back. If they really wanted to fight back against counterfeit goods, they should just destroy it without letting them buy it back.

But it seems like they increased the punishment for counterfeit goods, so much so that they fine you 10-15 times the cost. As long as they receive a tip-off, they will visit for an inspection with no questions asked.

Shit, that means they want us to get fined! The three boxes of products are worth ¥15,000. If we get fined ¥150,000, then we will go bankrupt!

Not good, I have to move quickly. The private detective might have already made a report to the CIB, so I have to get rid of these three boxes before they arrive.

At 8 pm, as expected, a vice section chief from the CIB arrived with two subordinates. One of the subordinates was tall and the other one was short. The three of them knocked at my front door.

After displaying their ID, they said they received a tip-off and they need to search my home for counterfeit goods.

I tried to make my most amicable expression and gladly welcomed them inside. I poured the vice section chief a hot cup of tea and sat next to him. I chatted with him while smiling and watching the other two search our inventory.

I purposely didn't open the AC even though it was an extremely hot day. They were the ones who came to my house looking for trouble, so they were too embarrassed to ask me to open the AC. The vice section chief spent a long time holding the hot cup of tea without taking a sip. The two subordinates spent over 40 minutes searching and their entire shirts were drenched in sweat.

"There's nothing here." The tall one said, "Also, these goods are& how can they just leave it around and let a student watch the house?"

The short one didn't give up: "Section chief, let's try looking in another room. He definitely got tipped off and hid it."

I panicked. It would be pretty embarrassing if they found the sealed box full of pictures of Xiao Qin.

The vice section chief waved his hand, "No need. Look at how calm and composed this fella is. There's a high chance we got played. There are still two more places to visit and we should be able to fine them."

I'm not sure if he meant he got played by the private detective or by me. It's a good thing he was astute, otherwise, I would have turned on the AC to start blowing hot air.

The three of them admitted it was bad luck. I continuously bowed as they left and said:

"You're welcome to come again!"

The vice section chief got angry and almost sprained his ankle while walking down the stairs.

As for those three boxes of counterfeit goods, I gave a call to the courier who always comes to my house. I promised him to give him an extra ¥100 if he came immediately and delivered the boxes to Director Cao's home.

There's no point keeping these goods, so might as well give all of it to Director Cao. I hope he can put it to good use when filming AV in the future.

I might not be talented, but at least I made a meager contribution to the Chinese AV industry.

Oh, Ai ShuQiao, the detective you hired is a huge letdown. Why don't you send more people to take care of me?

By the way, there's a saying that you're not a man if you don't get revenge. Since I was able to take a picture of the private detective's license plate, and I also have a video of him 'bumping' into gramps. I might as well post the video online and ask people to dox him. I could even pretend gramps got a serious injury. I could say he was the one who injured gramps' waist& It'll be an online witch hunt.

After calming down a bit, I took into account that gramps might have a reputation in the martial arts world, so I didn't post the video. I went on a popular forum and uploaded the license plate number. I said that the owner of the car escaped after hitting a pregnant woman, but the driver had high-up connections and the police wouldn't catch him.

The netizens were very enthusiastic and people were eager to show results. But before anyone could dox him, another even more shocking post was made. Its title was "Driver repeatedly runs over two elementary school students which caused their deaths, while he also broke their father's legs". As a result, everyone's enthusiasm was attracted over there all at once. There were a lot of chivalrous discussions, things like how they would take revenge for the victims& Basically, there's no one left paying attention to my post.

When I went to check my post the next day, it had already dropped to the sixth page.

I felt frustrated but could only let it go.

I wasn't able to successfully retaliate against the private detective online, but I decided to finish the important things first. I'm going to change our front door's lock.

I went to a security store near our neighborhood and spent two hundred big ones on a secure lock and asked them to help me change it.

They were pretty happy they were able to make a sale right when the store opened at 8am on Saturday morning. They felt it was a good start to the weekend, so the asking price was fairly reasonable.

I didn't head to the lakeside to practice with gramps because I was busy changing the locks.

Since I knew the lock at my home could be picked easily, I can't leave before the locks get changed.

I don't have any concubines to help me because I haven't set up a harem yet, so I could only do it myself.

Even though I can easily give Xiao Qin a call and she would happily help me watch the house, but she wasn't able to recover well because she forced herself to go to school while she had dysmenorrhea. So it's better if she stays home and rests, and I can also get a quiet weekend alone.

The lock was changed successfully before 10am. I looked at the brand new key with a sense of accomplishment.

Hmph, I don't if it's the private detective or Peng TouSi, let's see you try to pick the lock now!

I decided to head to film city for a walk since I had nothing to do.

I wonder what Auntie Ren is like when she's not on site? I heard she was instructing them with video chat. Does this mean she has to actually do a flip in her hotel room as a demonstration? I can't hold back my curiosity without being able to see it in person.

I have to note: Although one of the reasons I came here was because I could see Ai Mi, it was not because of her underwear.

I had a dream last night where I forcibly took off Ai Mi's underwear. Then, I held the underwear above my head and drooled while yelling: "Twenty thousand bucks!". And I ran away leaving behind the terrified Ai Mi.

If I actually did that, then I wouldn't even be able to tell Ai Mi that I'm her brother!

Director Cao gave me a call right when I was doing some self-reflection.

"Xiao Ye Zi, why did you send three boxes of vibrators. I didn't order anything nor did I pay!"

"You don't need to pay." I laughed, "It's a gift to support your AV business."

Director Cao smacked his lips and said: "Don't tell me you had a guilty conscience because you decided to try to trick me and give me a random pair of underwear and pass it off as Miss Ai Mi'er's underwear? So, you gave me these to ease your conscience&"

Damn, can we have one conversation that doesn't revolve around underwear? Can you please stop giving me more unnecessary pressure? I've already had a dream where I did something vulgar to my little sister.

Thus I briefly summarized the CIB incident to him. Of course, I hid the things about Ai ShuQiao and the private detective since those are family matters. I have no reason to tell Director Cao if my dad hadn't even told him yet.

Director Cao came to a realization: "So that's what happened& but wouldn't they come to investigate me? I'm not afraid of fines, but what if I'm in the middle of a group film session&."

More like filming AVs& Don't worry, they only fine people who have the intent to sell counterfeit goods.

Director Cao breathed a sigh of relief when he heard all he had to do was say it was for personal use and not for reselling.

But then he said: "Damn, how would I even use this many myself?"

"Director Cao, these are toys for women. I don't think you can use them yourself."

"Um& that's true. I should host a raffle before I broadcast the second episode of Battle of Jin Ling and gave these as rewards."

Oh, the episode where the female protagonist gets raped by the Jin Ling Young Thug? Aren't the only ones who watch that show otakus who use it to jerk off? What do you want to achieve by sending them female love toys?

Before Director Cao hung up, he told me to hurry up and find a way to get my hands on Ai Mi's underwear. The bank card he specifically prepared holding twenty thousand is just eagerly waiting to be used.

I think you're the one who's too eager! If you can't control yourself, just pick up one of those female toys and use it on your own ass! I'm becoming more and more reluctant in giving my sister's underwear away.

It was already lunch time by the time I reached film city via the subway.

I didn't have to courage to head to Ai Mi's RV for free food before I could sort out my feelings, so I went to the cafeteria for the actors.

I sat by myself to eat the spicy beef curry, but unfortunately, Kyle and the old translator sat down right across from me.

Kyle greeted me through his

I kept my head down and continued to eat.

"Um, does Ai Mi have anything in particular she wants to eat? I keep inviting her for meals but she doesn't like my British chef. She said she would rather starve to death than come to my banquets&"

Well, if it's about what Ai Mi likes to eat, chips and cola are enough, but would you even believe me even if I told you?

Kyle kept bugging me when I didn't reply, so I listed off a couple of traditional Chinese foods at random:

"Steamed buns, dumplings, Zha Jiang Mian, Sichuan Boiled Fish, Zongzi&."

Kyle had a horrified expression when he heard Zongzi.

"Forget about Zongzi, that's not food for humans. I really don't understand Chinese people's eating habits."

Really? Are you really looking down on Chinese food when you have a British chef? Even though I don't think Zongzi tastes that good, but it's still better than English food! If you say Zongzi isn't food for humans, you should take a look at Bear Grylls' survival show where he eats cockroaches, scorpions, rotten seals, etc& now that's not food for humans!

Kyle continued to speak with lingering fears:

"It was the Dragon Boat Festival a couple of days ago and Ai Mi gave me some presents for the first time; it was a Zongzi without any fillings. At first, I was excited about trying a new traditional food, but once I tasted it, it was the worst thing I've ever ate and I never want to eat it again."

That's strange. A Zongzi without filling is normal, some people don't even like to eat Zongzi with fillings.

"No, that's not it&" Kyle waved his hands, "It's the type Zongzi without any rice. It only had disgusting vegetables and I could barely even bite it."

I was shocked and forgot to eat my beef.

Did Ai Mi give him a bundle of bamboo leaves wrapped in the shape of a Zongzi? How the hell can you eat that? How is that a present, it's a prank!

I shifted my gaze towards the old translator who was interpreting Kyle's words.

Weren't you next to him at the time? You're Chinese, so even if Kyle doesn't know about Zongzi, you should! Or do you only care about translating and nothing else? Kyle, you hired a British chef and a translator who doesn't stop you as you're about to eat bamboo leaves. How did you even survive this long with these terrible colleagues?

I received a call from my dad right when I finished eating. He said he was finally released after a week of quarantine. He wanted to come home to give me a surprise, but when he got back he realized the lock was changed and he couldn't open the door&

Well, if my dad's locked outside, I should hurry home and open the door for him.

I headed home in a hurry and saw my dad downstairs playing chess with some other elderly men. He waved excitedly at me when he saw me arrive.

"Xiao Lin, did you miss me?"

Why are you trying to act cute? I thought you would be thin and lethargic after being in quarantine for a week, but you seem even brighter than before. Did something good happen?

I brought my dad home and gave him the new set of keys. As for why I changed the lock, I told him a neighbor who had the same lock had some stuff stolen. My dad praised me for preparing in advance and said I inherited his brains. He wanted to go to our neighbor and express his sympathies, but I stopped him in a hurry.

Since my dad's already out, then that means Auntie Ren has also regained her freedom.

My dad invited me to eat a meal at a nearby restaurant to eat a reunion meal. I thought he was making a big deal over it, but I accompanied him since it made him happy.

"Oh, I have to return to the hotel tonight and make up for my missed work& but it feels a bit lonely since Auntie Ren won't be with me tonight&"

She only stayed with you because she had no choice.

Although I would be supportive if you got remarried, the partner definitely can't be Auntie Ren. Please stop giving me more trouble.

There was a lot of dust being blown around on Sunday morning. Even though it was annoying, I still ran to Dong Shan lake and planned to train with gramps. He might get angry if I miss two days in a row.

But I didn't see gramps when I arrived. Instead, I saw a piece of paper under a rock and it said, "You bailed on me on Saturday, so I'm bailing on you today."

Please stop trying to act cute. If you didn't come, then when did this piece of paper get here! Don't tell me you wrote it on Saturday and no one moved it after being left here for an entire day?

Clearly you came today but went home after seeing all the dust and sand being blown around. Then, you left the note behind to purposely piss me off. Can you not act like a kid?

But today's weather wasn't really suited for outdoor activities.

Actually, I already had a gist of today's weather based on last night's weather report. Even Ai Mi canceled all her plans with the film crew for the day and stayed at home to protect her skin.

Strictly speaking, it's not her home, but the VIP building at Qing Zi Academy.

Peng TouSi gave me a call this morning and told me Ai Mi wanted me to go over to her place. She also called Xiong YaoYue and told her to come with me if it was convenient.

I don't even know where Xiong YaoYue lives, how would I know if it's convenient to go together! Also, if Ai Mi personally called Xiong YaoYue, why did she make Peng TouSi contact me? Why couldn't she tell her own brother to come over and play!

I headed home and took a shower to rinse off the dust and sand on my body. Then, I received a call from an unknown number.

I came out of the shower stark naked and made preparations to curse at them if they were trying to sell insurance.

In the end, it was from Xiong YaoYue. I guess Ai Mi told her my phone number.

"Ah, I'm really sorry." The first thing Xiong YaoYue did was apologize.

Huh, what happened? Did she see me taking a shower? But this isn't even a video chat! Otherwise, I would have been the one to apologize for showing you my mushroom.

"I originally agreed I would head over to Miss Ai Mi's place, but I just got a call from the captain of the 'Wasteland Wolves'. Something came up and I have to head to an internet cafe to assist my team in a team battle!"

"Wait, slow down. What's 'Wasteland Wolves', and assisting what?

"It's a team in a game." Xiong YaoYue seemed to be in a rush, "Because the second best in our team was dragged home by their parents, the captain called me in to fill the vacancy. It's a 5v5 ranked team battle. If I don't go, then their going to lose to a group of elementary school students!"

LOL, so League of Legends? So Xiong YaoYue is the type of person Xiao Ding would never get along with. I never thought you would also be pretty good at games other than fighting games. Also, you said you guys were facing elementary school students, why does it feel like the main force of your team who was dragged home probably never even graduated from elementary school too&

"Anyway, I'm sorry, but I can't let my teammates down. I'll have to skip our meeting with Miss Ai Mi today. Please don't hate me, I'll make sure to visit and apologize at a later date."

"It's alright, it's not like we had anything important." I said, "Your team battle is more important, hope you guys win."

"Don't worry." Xiong YaoYue said confidently, "I'll definitely win. Watch me teach those elementary school students a lesson&"

Thus I put on my Qing Zi Academy uniform and slipped through the school gates. Then, I arrived at the VIP building.

Peng TouSi helped me open the door to room 101. I was shocked at the scene I witnessed as I entered the room.

There wasn't a lot of sunlight today because of all the sand being blown around, but the curtains were drawn shut as if to prevent even a single ray of light from entering the room. (Although I could understand Ai Mi's sensitivity to UV light)

But why did she not open the light? There's no way Ai Mi was trying to save electricity like the class leader. What are you burning so intently while holding a lighter and standing barefooted in front of your dressing table?

When I took a closer look, it was fucking cash! Ai Mi had nothing to do and was burning money! Do you think you're amazing because you have too much money?! It's illegal to destroy currency, so please do not imitate her. If you have money you don't want, then please mail it to me.

Every time she burned a bill, she would whistle with a joyous expression. She watched as the last corner of a one hundred dollar bill slowly fall onto her expensive carpet. Her stool was already surrounded with ashes.

"Do you have nothing better to do?" Ai Mi didn't reply, she took out another bill from her drawer and began to burn it. The atmosphere was a bit strange.

"Xiao Xiong& Winnie, can't make it today." I said.

"I know." Ai Mi's voice in the pitch-black room seemed a bit cold, the only light source was when she used the lighter in her hand to burn money.

"Winnie already called to apologize. It's fine even if she doesn't come, it's not like I was looking forward to you guys coming."

Ai Mi said even though it differed from her real feelings. Then she almost got burned by the lighter and she began sucking on her pinky.

Ai Mi was clearly shrouded in an aura of disappointment. I don't think Xiong YaoYue bailing on us would have such a huge impact on her.

She continued to burn money and she had already burned two thousand bucks since I arrived.

The atmosphere felt really awkward, then I coughed a couple of times due to inhaling too much dust on the way here.

"Did you take medicine?" Ai Mi didn't turn around and her tone didn't seem like she really cared.

"Why do I have to take medicine if I'm not sick. Even if I was sick, I wouldn't take medicine. Usually, I would drink some hot water and go to sleep. Then, I would be better the next day. That's how all warriors do it."

Ai Mi laughed, but no joy could be seen on her face.

"You'll die if you don't take medicine when you're sick&"

I disagreed, "Humans aren't that weak."

"It's true. My grandfather refused to take medicine when he was sick and ended up going to heaven&"

Is your grandfather, the father of John, the one Ai ShuQiao eloped with? According to Peng TouSi, he was poisoned because he was against his son getting married to Ai ShuQiao. It was camouflaged as a heart attack because she used some sort of undetectable extract from tomatoes, so she was able to escape punishment. Why did Ai Mi say he died because he wouldn't take medicine? Didn't he breathe his last breath after he drank a bowl of tomato soup?

Ai Mi began to recollect past memories while continuously burning money.

Because the AC unit was filtering the air, the room didn't smell like smoke. Nor did the smoke alarms in the room get triggered.

"I was four years old at the time& no, maybe a bit younger than four. According to my mom, my grandfather hated how she would always remind her to take his medicine, so he didn't let her near him. My mom said he had heart problems and would die if he didn't take medicine. I didn't want my grandfather to die, so I asked my mom if she had any ways to prevent him from dying&"

"My mom told me the next time I go to my grandfather's house, I could secretly slip some medicine into his food. She even gave me a convenient pendant to hold the medicine. But it seems I was too young, perhaps I forgot, so my grandfather still died&"

"Then the pendant my mom gave me also disappeared. I would sometimes doubt if my memory was wrong. Maybe I never even received a pendant, and my mom would always deny my claims. She said I was too young to differentiate between a dream and reality&"

It felt like I was struck on the chest.

I now understand why Peng TouSi siad John doesn't want to reveal the details of the case even when he already has enough evidence. That's why he said Ai Mi would suffer shock if the case was revealed.

Since Ai ShuQiao was hated by John's father and he never let her get close to him, it was impossible for her to poison him.

Then the truth was: Ai Mi loved her grandfather, so Ai ShuQiao used her four-year-old daughter to poison him!

It's& way too cruel. Ai ShuQiao, I don't really care that you abandoned me since I don't really want your love, but Ai Mi was the new life you chose. You watched her grow old from infancy!

Even if a four-year-old won't be determined to be guilty by a jury, how could you let your own daughter murder her beloved grandfather? You've already all lost all qualifications as a human being.

And you even used this as a trump card against John? You probably knew John already kept evidence from those years and it would be troublesome if he started an investigation, so you decided to drag your own daughter down with you? If John decides to get justice for his father, then the courts would summon Ai Mi as a witness. Then she would have the face the truth of poisoning her own grandfather in court!

Ai Mi was raised in a sheltered environment. She's allergic to almonds and sunlight, she has acrophobia and gets lost easily& How could a girl who seems tough on the outside but has a tender heart be able to withstand this shock? Do you want her to live the rest of her life while carrying the burden of knowing the fact she poisoned her own grandfather and was tricked by her own mother?

I've never felt this rash before. I even wanted to take the custody of my sister away from Ai ShuQiao.

That's enough. How long are you planning to treat your own daughter as a chess piece? Ai Mi's hands are already stained with her grandfather's blood, what else do you still want her to do? Please leave Ai Mi's life.

The darkness in front of Ai Mi couldn't be removed regardless of how many bills she burned. It's just like Ai ShuQiao's evil cage that's currently trapping her.

I have to rescue Ai Mi from her invisible cage. Regardless of how many years it takes, how much I have to sacrifice, or the dangers I have to face. Only then, would I be able to prove my worth as her older brother.

I made a vow.

My dear sister. Even if the only relationship between you and me is Ai ShuQiao's wicked blood, but I decided I won't abandon you.

Please give me a bit of time. No, it might take a lot of time, but I won't give up halfway.

Because the job of an older brother is to protect a younger sister's smile.

According to Ai Mi, she was in low spirits because her mom told her she had to immediately return to America once she finishes filming. It's mainly because she still has numerous commercials and one concert still waiting for her.

"I thought I would get some time to rest, I haven't even been able to experience winter or summer breaks."

Ai Mi complained.

"She said I would be forgotten by the fans if I don't make an appearance back home& who cares about those disgusting fans who rush onto the stage to touch my feet, I wish I was forgotten by them."

I still haven't calmed down, so my words inevitably carried some sarcasm which blamed Ai ShuQiao:

"Don't tell me your mom said it's because she loves you?"

Ai Mi was angered to the point she laughed. She ordered me to turn on the lights, then she threw her lighter on top of her dresser and stopped burning money for fun.

"Love? Don't make me laugh." Ai Mi said with a maturity that transcended her age, "There's no such thing as love between two people, there's only necessity. You're either needed or not needed."

"My mom made me like this because she needs me. I listen to my mom because I need her help to solve my problems."

"I don't even need to mention those so-called fans. They say they love me, but they probably already raped me a numerous amount of times in their minds."

"&. Even Obama, he only follows me because he needs me to feed him."

I couldn't stand that she felt there was no love between people. It's probably because she was influenced by Ai ShuQiao after staying with her for too long.

"What about Peng TouSi?" I asked, "Didn't he take a bullet for you?"

Ai Mi hesitated a bit, "He& he doesn't love me either. He only wants to repay my mother for saving his life and they are in a mutual relationship where they take advantage of each other."

If that's what you think, then you're greatly mistaken. Peng TouSi watched you grow up and might be closer to you than your real mother (The only reason I didn't mention father is because Peng TouSi is a catcher).

I thought it was dangerous having this outlook in life and I had to demolish her misconceptions.

Thus I took a step forward with stirred up emotions. Ai Mi sat on her stool and looked at me strangely because she didn't know what I wanted to do to her.

"Then& what about me? Do you think I got close to you to use you?"

Ai Mi thought for a bit, "Pretty much."

"Pretty much&"

"You&" Ai Mi said as she began to sway her two bare feet, "Although you might not desire money, but your motives for getting close to me aren't pure."

I was a bit upset, "What's my motive?"

Ai Mi began giggling liked I was an idiot.

"Do you even need to ask? If you don't have an interest in money, then you're aiming for my body!"

Ai Mi placed her left hand on her soft and pink neck, then she traced her finger down her body, past her breasts, her abdomen, her waist, her navel, and displayed the perfect curves of her body.

"Manservant, you're actually just a lolicon."

"You probably fantasize about raping me like my other fans."

"But I'm used to it since you're not the only one who has improper thoughts about me&"

"I'm generous and allowed you to fantasize about me. Try to win my favor in the future when staying near me."

"So, we achieved a perfected relationship of needed and being needed&"

It wasn't my imagination that Ai Mi seemed a bit hurt when she said the last sentence.

"You're wrong." I said seriously, "I didn't get near you because I need you. You also shouldn't think everyone has improper thoughts about you because you look good&"

"I'm not wrong." Ai Mi stubbornly retorted, "Do you think those damn lolicons would like me if I was ugly? Do you think they would push my songs to 11th place on the Billboard Hot 100? Did you know I want to puke every time I hear myself sing those childish songs?"

"I'm not the same as them&" I couldn't come up with a good argument on the spot.

"Excuses&" our argument provoked the negative feelings she was trying to suppress. She suddenly leaped off the stool and picked up the lighter from her dresser.

Since the light was now open. I noticed the lighter in Ai Mi's hand was coated with a luxurious metallic gold cover, it might even be pure gold.

Ai Mi raised the gold lighter near her own face.

It was as if there were shooting stars passing through her blue eyes as the flames flickered.

She stood barefooted on the ashes of the burnt money and said with an expectant tone:

"No one will like me if I use this lighter to burn my face."

"What& are you doing."

I wanted to pounce forwards and snatch the lighter, but Ai Mi lit a flame and brought it closer to her chin threateningly.

"Worried?" She had a smile of ridicule. She looked excited as if she corrected a teacher's mistake during class.

Her following words contained hints of sorrow.

"As expected, you're the same as them& if I'm not a beautiful doll anymore, then you would immediately abandon me& I only have worth because I'm beautiful. If I wasn't beautiful, then no one would need me&"

"That's not true." I yelled, "Hurry and put the lighter down."

Ai Mi brought the lighter even closer. The strands of hair near her ears began to warp due to the heat.

"Are you worked up because you can't bear to part with my face?"

Ai Mi began smiling happily as she saw me anxious expression.

"Ai Mi, put the lighter down." I forced myself to calm down, "I don't care what you think about others, but our relationship is not as simple as using each other and you will understand later."

"Ha." It was like Ai Mi heard the world's best joke, "A mere manservant wants to establish& a relationship with me closer than my mom and Peng TouSi? If our relationship isn't using each other, then what is it?"

Ai Mi furrowed her brows.

"Or are you trying to say you love me?"

"That's right, I love you." I blurted out.

Even though it's only brotherly love, I don't think it would lose to real love.

Ai Mi took a step back and the shooting stars in her eyes became even more chaotic.

I stepped over the ashes of the burnt money without letting her escape.

"I love you. It has nothing to do with your appearance."

"Liar." Ai Mi retreated to a corner of the room, "All those stalkers in American said they loved me, but they only want to take advantage of me."

I spread out my hands to show I had no malicious intentions.

"Ai Mi, you may be half-right& we are in a relationship of necessity, but it's not because I need you, but it's if you need me, I'll come running even if I have to tread through fire. My love doesn't need any returns."

"Nonsense, it's becoming more and more unbelievable." Ai Mi waved the lighter in her hands to prevent me from getting any closer, "If you love me, why did you accept the violent girl as your girlfriend."

I didn't hesitate and answered decisively:

"Xiao Qin is an outsider. She can't interfere between us. Even if I was forced to get married to Xiao Qin, I would still love you."

"&. if you& say it like that&."

Ai Mi didn't know what to do. She dropped the lighter and tried to escape out the door.

She wasn't fast enough, I reached out and hugged her from behind. I was gentle but resolute, otherwise, I would never be able to unburden her.

"Ai Mi, I swear that I'll always protect you. It doesn't matter how you change or how I change, and it doesn't matter how the world changes& you've already been hurt enough and I won't allow anyone else to hurt you anymore."

Ai Mi struggled for a bit before giving up, but she could see tears running down my cheeks.

Men don't cry easily, but I couldn't control my tears. It continuously dripped down on to my sister's flawless face.

Ai Mi stood there vacantly at a loss.

After a while, she lowered her head so I wouldn't be able to see her expression. Then she reached out one of her small hands and clutched my large hand.

We stood for a while silently and at one point I almost felt that time had stopped.

Finally, Ai Mi's ponytail's began to quiver and I think I heard quiet sobs.

She pushed my arm away and went to the washroom.

I'm not sure why, but Ai Mi turned on all the taps in the bathroom and the sound of running water concealed everything else.

She only came out after half an hour after having washed her face and hair. Her ponytail was split apart and her new hairstyle made her seem a year older.

She didn't speak to me and headed to the fridge on the side.

I began to review my prior words to see if I could have said any words that were easily mistaken. Then, I felt something cold on my neck and almost shrieked.

"What& is it?"

It turns out Ai Mi took out two cans of sugar-free iced coffee from the fridge. She sneaked up behind me and surprised me by pressing it against my neck.

Ai Mi's mood got better after surprising me.

"I really looked down on you. I never expected you could make lies so pleasant."

So she still didn't believe me.

"You even said you loved me and would protect me forever. It was so corny I almost laughed when I heard it."

After she ordered me to open her can of ice coffee, she walked to her dressing table and began to write something with a marker.

"Hmph, since you decided you're my number one fan, I'll give you a souvenir."

TN: Just saw there was someone translating the manhua, so if anyone's interested&

I was curious on what Ai Mi was scribbling, was it her signature?

It wasn't her signature! I thought she would be signing her own own name on a sheet of paper and putting a kiss on it as a souvenir, but it wasn't. Ai Mi signed her name on a pair of light pink underwear!

It might be due to the fact her Chinese writing wasn't up to par, so she signed her name in English. It was written in beautiful cursive, but unfortunately, I have trouble recognizing all the letters. I could only make a guess it's the English word for 'Ai Mi'er' based on the spelling. Since it was for a fan, she could only sign her artist's name.

Actually, if it's a gift for me, I prefer if you would sign your real name. A while back, I used a VPN to watch one of your opening acts on youtube (my English was god awful), I couldn't understand anything and couldn't even differentiate if it was good or bad. Also, I couldn't even keep watching when you were dressed so skimpily with all the cheering fans. It's better if you stop being a celebrity, or at least stop doing those concerts.

No, what am I thinking about? It's not the right time to be thinking about her signature. A younger sister giving her older brother her underwear isn't normal!

I asked while trembling: "Ai Mi& what are you doing?"

"It's a signature."

"No&. I mean what are you writing on?"

"Underwear."

Can you not reply as if nothing is wrong? Even if you've lived an open life in America for 12 years, can you at least have some shame?

"Who's underwear?"

"Mines." Ai Mi finished signing her name and looked at me strangely, "Who else could it belong to? Peng TouSi?"

Damn, please don't mention that possibility. Now I can't help imagining Peng TouSi wearing girly underwear and it killed off millions of my brain cells.

"Why& are you signing your name on underwear?"

"Didn't I say I wanted to give you a souvenir?"

"I& I'm not a pervert, why would I want that as a souvenir?"

Ai Mi looked at me mischievously and we both stood there in silence.

"If my underwear could be removed by your gaze alone, it would have already been removed at least twenty times in the past couple of days. Don't think I didn't realize you were staring at them."

Is it a women's sixth sense? I feel ashamed&

"Just tell me if you want it. If you can say you love me easily, why do you have to act so shy over a pair of underwear?"

Shy? I think that's a normal reaction. On Valentine's day, there are a lot of boys who confess to girls, but I don't think there's a single one who asks for a girl's underwear.

"Ai Mi, you can't just give away your underwear randomly&"

"I didn't. Obama was the one who gave them away randomly. As for me, it's the first time I've ever personally handed a fan my signed underwear, just be grateful and accept it."

"But, your worn underwear&" I refused while I subconsciously reached out to receive it.

Then, Ai Mi suddenly moved the underwear further away and I grabbed air. Ai Mi mischievously hid it behind her back and laughed.

"Even though you say you don't want it, it seems your body is pretty honest."

She gleefully brought the underwear in front of her. Then, she stood on the stool and raised the underwear as high as she could like she was baiting me like a fish.

"Come on, I'll give it to you if you bite it with your mouth."

It was like she was getting revenge for the time when we first met at the supermarket where I raised the chips and only gave it to her when she said good things.

Who would use their mouth to bite their sister's underwear? Don't seduce me onto a dangerous path.

"Ai Mi, stop fooling around, it's dangerous." I said, "How could you take your worn underwear&."

Ai Mi sat on the stool with disappointment when I wouldn't play the fishing game with her. she then rolled the underwear into a ball.

"Manservant, this pair of underwear is indeed from my closet, but I never said I've worn it before."

"Huh?"

"I have hundreds of pairs of underwear I choose daily based on my mood. I can't remember which ones I've worn or not&."

"Do you have a requirement that it must have been worn?"

Ai Mi's current expression made her seem like she was a Alien Queen conquering Earth.

"Hehe. If you kneel and beg me, I'll wear this underwear, then take it off and hand it to you."

"No, no need" I waved my hands in a hurry, "It doesn't have to be worn, it's fine as long as it's your underwear&"

Since I'm going to sell it to Director Cao, I would feel less guilty if it's never been worn.

Ai Mi, on the other hand, thought I confessed. She pointed at me and laughed:

"Hahaha, as expected, you're a lolicon with fetishism! Do you get excited as long as it's my underwear, even if it's never been worn?"

"No, you're misunderstanding&"

"Why are you being shy? Didn't you just brazenly profess your love for me? Hey, are you going to take this underwear home and use it to jack off?"

Who would use their sister's underwear to masturbate? I only want to sell it for money&

"I'm warning you." Ai Mi suddenly became serious, "You can use it to jack off, but you are not allowed to wear it. I hate perverts who wear female clothing. Stay away from me in the future if you do wear it."

Ah, aren't you talking about Shu Zhe? He's fond of your money and might even try to get into a relationship with you.

"I don't care about what you do with it as long as you guarantee you won't wear it." Ai Mi told me her condition as she handed it towards me. I hesitated whether or not I should accept it.

It's twenty thousand bucks! It's the money I've decided to use to cut off all relations with Ai ShuQiao. I could only battle her without restraint after I returned the money I used. And since this pair of underwear was willingly given to me by Ai Mi, you can take it as a declaration of war from the two of us.

I accepted my sister's underwear with uninhibited excitement.

I put it in my pockets for now. I don't have to worry about it losing its smell since it has never been worn.

Ah, what am I thinking about? It's already bad enough I'm selling my sister's underwear, I have to make sure no one gets their hands on my sister's worn underwear!

"You can come ask me for another pair when that one tears."

Ai Mi said magnanimously.

What do I have to do in order to tear it?

"Of course, it's when your by yourself on a quiet night furiously jerking off while using your imagination. You'll definitely rip it since you're strong."

Ai Mi said happily.

"I'm actually a bit curious on how you would fantasize about me when using my underwear to jerk off. Would you jump on me and tear off all my clothes or attack me when I'm sleeping?"

Stop, I have never and will never use your underwear to masturbate. The scene you're imagining will never happen between the two of us. It's a crime just thinking about it.

Ai Mi was in a good mood after teasing me. She instructed her French chef to prepare me an extravagant lunch. While we ate, we both laughed at Kyle's stupidity, complained about our mother's harshness, and Auntie Ren's pickiness.

Peng TouSi reminded Ai Mi after we've eaten quite a bit: "Miss, you've already surpassed your daily recommended caloric intake." Ai Mi left the table in a bad mood.

There was a ton of fruits and desserts in the afternoon. I pretty much ate all of it since Ai Mi had calorie limits.

In order to not gain fat, I took off my shirt and began doing push-ups in Ai Mi's room in my vest.

"1, 2, 3, 4, 5, 6&&"

"7&&7%å@#å,.,,,&.."

Something heavy was suddenly put on my back and my nose almost hit the floor.

It was Ai Mi who had sat on my back.

There are a lot of chairs and sofas in the room, go sit in another spot. Although you're not heavy, your butt being pressed against my back is distracting!

"Is it too much for you?" Ai Mi taunted me, "Peng TouSi could do 1000 push-ups with me sitting on him."

Of course I believe it since he's a man with God as his target. The most important thing is that he's gay, and it doesn't matter if you guys have physical contact. But it's not fine for me since even if I'm your brother, my body will still have natural physiological responses!

But I guess it's unavoidable for siblings to have physical contact. I might as well get used to it now.

I quietly accepted the fact Ai Mi was sitting on my back.

"25, 26, 27&.."

"You're not as stable as Peng TouSi." Ai Mi said fussily.

No shit. He's two meters tall and wide as hell. If you think I'm skinny, then get off!

Ai Mi turned on the TV while treating me as a chair. She started laughing while watching a foreign TV show called The Powerpuff Girls.

And you still say you're not a child while watching such childish cartoons.

Due to various reasons, I dropped down from exhaustion after doing 40 push-ups with Ai Mi sitting on me.

Ai Mi still didn't get off and finished watching three continuous episodes of The Powerpuff Girls.

Then she called Peng TouSi and told him to teach me killing techniques. Peng TouSi shook his head and said 'It's not good to kill'. He refused to teach me even when Ai Mi went and pinched his face.

Gradually, it was already 8pm. It was time for me to say my farewells since the wind wasn't blowing outside anymore.

Ai Mi was reluctant to part and she told me to come see her more often which I agreed to do.

It was hard to calm my emotions on the way home.

It was like Ai Mi's underwear that was in my pockets was calling out to me to take it out and appreciate it under the streetlights.

I resisted the bad urges and walked into an alley that seldomly has people passing through it. Then, I heard the hurried footsteps of someone running. He was carrying a large bag and his face mask had fallen off and it was hanging on one of his ears. It was like he was being chased and he was running for his life.

Wait, isn't that the small-time gang leader, young master Xu, a.k.a the outdoor jacket-wearing panty thief?

He was even holding onto a recently stolen pair of underwear. He was sniffing it while running with a satisfied expression.

It seems like it's true you can't escape if you're guilty. Watch me punish this perverted underwear thief in the name of the citizens!

I saw young master Xu sniffing a pair of underwear and I subconsciously reached into my pockets to verify if my sister's underwear was still there. (TN: Sorry, his last name is Xu, I think I used Shao accidentally before. Honestly, I may still be getting his name wrong as idk if his name is part of a title or something, but will change it if I find out it's wrong.)

Young Master Xu immediately recognized me when he spotted me walking towards him. His entire body began to tremble and the face mask hanging from his ear fell on to the ground.

As an underwear thief, you should feel insecure if someone sees your face. Young master Xu didn't pick up his face mask, instead after some quick thinking, he wore the underwear that he was sniffing over his head.

Damn, you're already straying further and further into the path of a true pervert. Bank robbers use stockings as a mask, so are you going to use underwear? Besides, I already saw your face. It wouldn't have helped much even if you used the underwear as a mask before I saw you. Anyone will know you're the panty thief if they see you walking through the city while wearing a pair of underwear over your head!

Wait& a second. What's going on? Why is his body surging with fighting spirit after putting on the underwear even though he once lost to me within one move? His fighting spirit was as still as a mountain and as sturdy as bamboo. It would terrify others if it ht them in the face. It seems as if the two brick walls were also shaking in this narrow alley.

Are you hacking? Why do you turn into ultraman when you put a pair of underwear on your head? His fighting spirit was even stronger than the class leader's Justice Devil and my Metal Blooded Lone Wolf.

Is this the true power of a pervert?

No, I have to make the first move, you can't lose in terms of spirit in a fight. If you have panties, then I have my berserk mode. Let me turn on my fearless berserker mode and we can fight till the end.

Eh, it seems I don't have enough anger. I was a bit happy because I was able to get my sister's underwear. Also, young master Xu was a laughable pervert, I couldn't really bring myself to hate him&

Damn, this won't work. Let's punch him first even if we can't turn on berserker mode.

I took my hands out of my pocket and intended to give him a punch on his cheek&

But the pair of underwear came out too and it fell towards the ground! Forget the punch, I have to save the precious underwear first!

I was able to breathe out in relief after catching it in midair, then I carefully put it back into my pocket.

Young master Xu exhaled a devilish breath and said:

"Return the underwear to me&."

"What?"

"I said return the underwear to me. All the girls' underwear in Dong Shan West District belongs to me."

It seems like you have no sense of shame. Also, how did you know it was a pair of underwear from a quick glance? Are you saying you have enough experience to become a world-renowned expert in underwear?

"Give it to me." Young master Xu rudely extended out his hand.

Keep dreaming. It's a brother's duty to protect their younger sister, it's also his duty to protect her underwear!

I spat on the ground towards him, "Hmph, for someone who lost to me&"

Before I was able to finish my sentence, a sudden gust blew towards me and I quickly evaded. Young master Xu's hiking boots struck the red brick walls with a bang and sent fragments flying.

Why are you wearing hiking boots in this hot weather? Is it because it makes it easier for you to scale buildings? The problem is once you remove your shoes, it will stink up the entire taekwondo dojo.

But, damn, your kicks are strong, you chipped the brick wall! You might have broken my ribs if I didn't dodge it!

He stood on one leg and left his other leg on display in mid-air.

Stop acting cool, I'm the protagonist! Why are you showing off simply because you have long legs?

I kicked off the ground in an instant to get close to him. He wouldn't be able to use kicks if we fought at close range.

But he didn't fall for it. He changed his right leg movements in an instant and kicked at my left flank.

Shit& it's not easy to dodge in this tight space. I'll have to use Yin Yang Sanshou to counter your attack.

I inclined my body back a bit while pressing both my hands against his tibia. I wanted to use Hua Jin to direct the force towards the wall.

Ah, young master Xu actually stopped his attack when he felt I was about to 'absorb' it. But he didn't change his posture, and he sent three consecutive kicks at me after only waiting half a second.

That's way too fast. I haven't practiced enough with Yin Yang Sanshou, there's no way I can receive all those attacks.

After I avoided two kicks aimed at my chest, I knew I couldn't avoid the third one. I could only tense my arms and receive the hit with my shoulder muscles.

Fuck, it hurts. Did you train your leg strength by climbing buildings all day? You were able to learn a miraculous skill without even properly training for martial arts.

Even though he saw me in pain, he didn't give me the final strike, instead, he got closer and tried to reach into my pocket for the underwear.

Bastard, don't even think about laying a finger on my sister's underwear!

I threw a punch at him, but he had no intention of dodging. He wasn't able to take away the underwear because he was struck by my fist.

How persistent. If this keeps up, he might actually be able to take it away from me.

He licked his red and swollen backs of his hand with a crazed expression. The underwear on his head accentuated his pervertedness to a higher degree.

I heard there was movie released in Japan recently called HK: Forbidden Super Hero which is about a young man who's able to gain super strong by wearing panties as a mask. Is young master Xu perhaps from the same faction?

Or is it because a cute girl's underwear has an insane amount of magical power and can instantly elevate you into a master.

Young master Xu sent another flurry of strikes at me without giving me any chance to think. He forced me to keep dodging left and right and almost drove me into a corner.

His attacks were fast and fierce. Yin Yang Sanshou might be very effective against opponents who only rely on strength (like Li ErLeng), but I didn't have enough control to use it effectively against trained martial artists who rely on technique. It looks like I have to give up on using Yin Yang Sanshou today.

Another hole appeared on the brick wall with a bang. It was twice as large as the last one. Are you trying to demolish a house?

He sent another side kick at me and the wind that accompanied it actually cut my face.

Ah, I'm sorry for underestimating Taekwondo before. I never knew it would be this powerful.

No, wait a second. Isn't this the power of the underwear rather than Taekwondo? In the past, you weren't even able to land a single move on me without the underwear on your head. So rather than calling yourself a Taekwondoin, you should be a member of the underwear martial artist group.

Your moves aren't even delayed at all even when you're carrying such a large bag. It's obvious it's filled with women's underwear and it's giving you a boost. This is written all over your face: I'm proud of the underwear and anyone who dares to offend my underwear must be punished. My underwear is an inseparable and sacred part of me&.

Ah, he tried to take Ai Mi's underwear again. But this time he learned to back off before I punched him but I was at a disadvantage.

It seems I've almost accumulated enough rage to invoke berserker mode, but the problem is I would lose all reasoning. Even if I did beat him in the fight, it would be my loss if he got the underwear.

"I'll let you live if you put down the underwear." Young master Xu roared as he sent another flurry of consecutive kicks at me.

I stooped down to avoid his ferocious attacks. Then, I brought out my sister's underwear.

In this situation, there's only one place I would be aware of even if I activated berserker mode.

I looked at the pair of underwear on young master Xu's head with a bit of sorrow.

It can't be helped. Even though I don't want to do it, but it's for my sister, for victory&. for justice.

I could only wear Ai Mi's underwear on my head too.

Ah, what is this feeling? It's snug with a surprising amount of elasticity. The light shining through it enlightened me as if it was here to deliver all creatures from their sufferings. I could feel the tightness around my temples and it seemed to have instantly recovered my stamina.

I could feel power surging out of my limbs. Is this me? Am I still human? Why does it feel like I'm in an empty void where I'm the master of the universe? Even if there was a tsunami or a volcano erupted, it would seem like nothing to me.

I was actually able to use a clear-headed berserker mode. I could keep all the advantages of the berserker mode while keeping my sense of reasoning.

Is this the power of underwear? I just want to yell out loud: "Give me strength, long live panties!"

You, who's wearing panties of an unknown origin. I'll show you the strength of wearing my sister's panties!

After I started using the clear-headed berserker mode, I placed my wrists together and sent a Kamehameha wave at young master Xu.

He shrieked as he was swept up by the wave and became a distant star in the night sky.

Nope, that was only my imagination. In reality, I didn't evade his kicks and I punched him on his knee causing him to stagger backward.

It was the so-called using force against force, but my fist didn't hurt at all. I don't feel any pain in berserker mode even if my bones break.

I have to punish this shameless underwear thief in my sister's name!

How could you steal something as private as underwear, then wear it over your head?

It's not the same for me, because I'm doing it for justice and love!

Young master Xu sneered as he saw me also wear underwear on my head:

"I never thought you would still have some good tricks up your sleeves."

"Hmph." I returned his compliment, "Same goes for you."

The hair on both our heads were parted in two by the underwear and was swaying with the wind.

"Who does that pair of underwear belong to?"

He suddenly asked.

"Hmph, you don't need to worry about who it's from. All you need to know is that I can gain more power from this pair than yours. As for someone like you who takes underwear without consent, if the underwear could think, it would probably despise you."

Young master Xu muttered quietly.

"Are you saying the underwear on your head was given to you voluntarily?"

"Of course." I answered proudly, "It's a pair of underwear filled with love and confidence. It can't even be compared to your nameless underwear."

He seemed disappointed and frustrated but wasn't willing to admit defeat:

"Even if you're wearing your girlfriend's underwear&"

I laughed out loud: "It's not my girlfriend's underwear and she will never become my girlfriend, but I will always love her and she will always love me."

Young master Xu was left speechless for a period of time.

"You& you're a master who enjoys romance."

"It's not romance, our relationship was decided since birth."

"Now you're talking about fate& you must have brainwashed that girl."

"Hey, you're an underwear thief, when did you start caring about women's rights? You should just admit defeat if you think you can't defeat me."

Young master Xu gritted his teeth, then he unzipped his backpack and took out another pair of underwear.

As expected, the backpack was packed to the brim with stolen underwear. There were probably around two hundred pieces of bras and underwear.

He took a deep breath and put the new pair of underwear over his head right on top of the old pair.

Two-sword style, no, two-panty style? Are you trying to use quantity to beat quality?

It wasn't a misconception, he got stronger again.

A sudden gust hit my face. His attacks were as relentless as a storm, but I was able to see his moves clearly with berserker mode. I let him attack freely as I evaded and counterattacked.

The two of us was left panting and sweating heavily after seven or eight exchanges.

Ah, damn, the underwear on my head is probably already soaked with my sweat. I don't even know if it's been worn by Ai Mi, yet I'm going to impart it with my smell.

Young master Xu advanced again after a bit of rest. I didn't give up either and we exchanged blows twenty more times.

Fist vs fist, leg vs leg. He used snake's strike while I fought back with a tiger's bite.

Ah, who was the one who said Chinese martial arts is on the decline! Needless to say, young master Xu's are no longer even taekwondo moves. He used a lot of self-created techniques with his fists and legs.

To be honest, even though we both looked laughable with underwear over our heads, it was still a high-level fight.

If it was recorded, it could become good teaching materials for the younger generation.

Of course, I would first have to ask a professional to edit the underwear on our heads out of the video.

Otherwise, it might leave a bad impression on youth that you would get superpowers by wearing underwear over your heads.

After numerous exchanges, even if he was trying to act tenacious, he was showing signs of fatigue.

I didn't let this chance pass and was able to make him fall back onto the ground with a quick swipe of my legs, and his backpack also fell off his shoulders.

He wasn't very injured. He supported himself up with his arms and stared at me, who was panting as heavily as him, with sluggish eyes.

"You're& nothing."

It looks like he's all talk.

I rushed forwards in a fit of anger. I wanted to kick him back on the ground.

But a pervert definitely has strange thought patterns. He thought I was aiming for his bag of stolen goods, so instead of protecting himself, he used his body to protect the bag.

I kicked at his back, he groaned but still didn't let go of the bag.

"Let go, you pervert." I didn't know how to react and kept kicking him from behind.

I wasn't sure when my berserker mode had ended and I felt muscle aches all over my body. But, right now, young master Xu doesn't even have any strength to resist.

Who knew he still didn't give up. He took out another pair of underwear from his bag and wore it over his head.

Now it's three sword style? Although underwear might energize you, but don't think it actually works as a stimulant!

As expected, even though he entered three-sword style, he couldn't stand up anymore.

He began to sob and took out two more pairs of underwear but there was no place for him to wear it.

I was also getting tired of kicking him. Seeing as he looked beaten, I relaxed my vigilance and asked:

"What, are you trying to do five sword style now? As long as you admit defeat, confess your sins, and guarantee you won't do it again&"

Young master Xu's eyes suddenly flashed, then he tried to put a pink laced underwear onto my head.

I wasn't able to dodge in time.

Fuck, you're too aggressive when putting it on, it almost ripped! More importantly, it's covering one of my eyes because it's slanted!

Did he do it on purpose to block my view?

Ah, the world I see through my left eye is drastically different. It's so fuzzy yet warm at the same time. But the main question is who does the underwear belong to? Since you said you're only active in the West district, it's likely it belongs to a classmate, or at least someone from the same school!

Xu made a happy expression after he succeeded. I'm not sure if it was because he didn't have the strength to punch anymore, but he brought the remaining underwear in his hand towards my head.

Are you trying to cover my right eye too? I can't let him have his way, so I snatched the underwear from his hands (he didn't have much strength left). I was hesitating on whether or not I should put it back into his bag when I saw him take out a pair of cartoon underwear from his bag and tried to put it on me again.

You're still playing around? I got angry and put the pair of underwear in my hand straight onto his head.

I put in a lot of strength. Even though it didn't cover his eyes, it still covered his nose and didn't let him breathe properly.

"Ahahahaha."

He was wearing four pairs of underwear over his head and I kept laughing because it looked too comical. He leaped up unexpectedly and put the cartoon underwear over my head.

4:3, are you trying to play a game you created?

Since he had tons of underwear, I took the largest pair I could find from his bag and put it over his head.

5:3. Ye Lin contestant leads by two points, please give him a standing ovation!

In the night alley, there were two youngsters who exhausted all their strength to continuously put underwear on each other's heads.

When it was 11:9 with me in the lead, I grabbed onto a pair of bras. Right when I was fretting about how to put it onto his head, I heard a furious women's voice coming from the entrance of the alley, behind young master Xu.

"I finally caught you."

The woman who was obscured by the shadows slowly crept closer.

Young master Xu trembled after being hearing the women's voice. He used his remaining strength and flung his bag towards me. Then he took the chance to bolt away into a different nearby alleyway.

There were all sorts of female underwear hung from my head, shoulder, hands, and legs. I had 9 pairs of underwear on my head (the innermost one belonged to Ai Mi). I was also holding onto a pair of sexy purple bras and I had no idea what to do.

The woman realized Xu had fled, but she didn't chase him and instead headed towards me.

As she got closer, I realized it was fucking Auntie Ren! Why is she trying to do police work by catching the underwear thief the first day she was released from quarantine?

Auntie Ren didn't recognize me at first (I had 9 pairs of underwear on my head). Her face flushed red with anger when she saw the bra in my hand.

"You scum lack discipline. Do you think you guys would be able to escape safe and sound after stealing underwear form my balcony?"

The closer Auntie Ren came, the more I frowned. Plus, I looked like an over-decorated Christmas tree with all the underwear hanging off my body.

I shook of all the undergarments from my body in a hurry. Then, I took off the 9 pairs of underwear off my head and put the innermost one (the one that belongs to Ai Mi) back into my pockets. As for the one in my hand, the bra that likely belongs to Auntie Ren, I stuffed it back into the bag while trembling with fear.

By the way, her bra was at least a C cup. Xiao Qin, why couldn't you inherit some of your mother's breast genes? If you were a bit more developed, I would have realized earlier you were a girl.

It was a bit dark outside and I was wearing a Qing Zi Academy uniform, so Auntie Ren wasn't able to recognize me right away. She mistook me as a common pervert who steals underwear.

"Ah, a student from Qing Zi Academy. Who would have thought there would a talent who could scale buildings with their bare hands in a school filled with useless people&."

Auntie Ren spoke sarcastically with a stern face.

"You better not run, otherwise, I'll tell your principal to expel you."

I had nothing to fear since I was innocent. I stood still proudly and waited for Auntie Ren.

After taking a quick look over my uniform, I realized I made too many large movements and caused a lot of the buttons and even the school crest to fall off. Qing Zi Academy's uniform isn't suited for fights, and the class leader isn't here this time to help me mend it.

Auntie Ren gradually came closer and realized the underwear thief she caught was her daughter's boyfriend.

"Why is it you?" Auntie Ren was both angry and shocked, "Do you and your dad have nothing else to do other than cause trouble?"

I made a o(o¡p)o expression, "Auntie Ren, how did I cause trouble, and what does this have to do with my dad? Please don't wrongly accuse me, the person I was fighting with earlier is the thief."

Auntie Ren's eyebrows jumped when she heard me mention my dad. It was like she heard a pest like cockroaches or mosquitoes.

Do you need to hate my dad to such an extent? Didn't you have a turn of heart and offered him to sleep for a night in his own room? It was a standard hotel room with two single beds, so he wouldn't even dare make a move on you. Was it because he was snoring in his sleep and disturbed your sleep?

"I never saw you guys fight." Auntie Ren stood in front of me like an interrogator, "Weren't you guys splitting the loot and seeing who can put more underwear on their heads&"

We weren't comparing who could wear more, but who could put more on each other's heads. Did you actually think we put these underwear on our own heads? What kind of loot splitting party were you imagining?

"Confess." Auntie Ren said, "What's your relationship with the outdoor jacket guy? He crawled up to the fourth floor balcony to steal our underwear and scared Xiao Qin half to death."

Huh, so are you saying Xiao Qin's underwear is also in this bag? Which pair is it, the cartoon one he put on me first looks like her type. Don't tell me I wore my sister's underwear and my girlfriend's at the same time? Why does it make me seem even more perverted even though it was for justice?

Besides, why would Xiao Qin be scared? Wasn't she the one who dominated me for years? She could use her Hokuto Shinken and hit him down four floors and turn him into a meat paste.

Then I slowly came to a realization: Young master Xu is the same age as us and it triggered her androphobia. When will she be able to get over her fears?

Based on Auntie Ren's description, she didn't see the thief's true identity. She only saw Xiao Qin sitting paralyzed on the balcony after hearing her shriek. She questioned her and found out all their washed underwear was stolen. So, she left Xiao Qin at home and chased after the thief for a long time.

"Auntie Ren, believe me, I'm not his accomplice."

Auntie Ren crossed her arms in front of her chest and snorted: "There are no good men."

Ah, why did it escalate to an issue of gender? Why does Auntie Ren seem like a resentful woman?

Then she picked up the bag filled with stolen underwear and hooked it around her own shoulder.

"These can't be used anymore since it's been dirtied by the two of you. I'm going to bring it back and burn them."

"Don't burn it!" I stopped her, "It's important evidence, especially the bag. I need it to find the true perpetrator."

Auntie Ren hesitated a bit because I seemed sincere, then she asked:

"Then tell me, who's the true perpetrator?"

I pointed towards the direction young master Xu escape to. "Although I don't know his full name, I'm sure he's the son of Xu JinSheng, the owner of the Golden Victory Taekwondo dojang. People refer to him as young master Xu and he's the one committing the crimes in this past month."

"Xu JinSheng." Auntie Ren frowned, "He has six or seven chain dojangs in this city and over a thousand members. Don't slander him."

"I'm not. I fought with young master Xu once under the bridge by Da Ning River. He became an underwear thief after losing to me."

"Why would he become the underwear thief after losing?" Auntie Ren was full of doubt.

"No, I didn't force him to become the underwear thief. I'm assuming he already had an interest in women's underwear and his miserable loss to me only caused his built up stress to implode."

"Fine." Auntie Ren grabbed onto my shoulder, "In order to prove your innocence, you have to come with me."

"Wh- where?"

"Of course, it's to Golden Victory Taekwondo."

"But didn't you say they had six or seven chain stores? And it's not like he definitely escaped to one of their dojangs&."

Auntie Ren clenched her fist. "He can run, but he can't hide. We can go to their main dojang in and demand them to give him up. If Xu JinSheng wants to defend his son and refuses, then I'll& knock down their signboard."

Eh, is this the so-called martial arts challenge? Why do I feel like Chen Zhen right now? I'm full of excitement and expectation.

Of course, since I'm all out of stamina after our fight, I will hide behind Auntie Ren&

Auntie Ren brought me out of the alley and hailed a cab. She told the old driver to take us to Golden Victory Taekwondo in the DongChen district.

"Ah, so the main dojang." the old driver said as he began to drive leisurely.

Since there was a pile of goods stacked on the front passenger seat, Auntie Ren could only sit with me in the back seats. She put the bag of underwear between us to prevent us from being too close.

Auntie Ren didn't say anything for the first half of the trip, but then she seemed to have remembered something as she felt her own pockets. Then, she said with a slight hint of embarrassment:

"You have to pay when we get there. I didn't bring my wallet because I was in a hurry to chase after him."

"No problem." I agreed. For someone as solitary as me, I'm never without my cellphone, keys, and wallet.

"You'll also have to be responsible for any money we need for the day."

Auntie Ren gradually became more blunt.

"Of course, of course. It's natural for me to pay for you~"

Actually, I was thinking I still owed Xiao Qin ¥4,000 for helping me copy the Bible. Although this money was already bundled up with the ¥20,000 I said I would use to break ties with Ai ShuQiao, I still feel like I owe Xiao Qin a lot. If I don't pay her back, I feel like I would have to work like a horse to pay her off in my next life.

Auntie Ren, on the other hand, thought I was trying to take advantage of the situation when I said it was natural to pay for her.

"What did you day? Xiao Qin might not even marry you in the future, but you're trying to call me your mother-in-law?"

"No, no." I lowered my head timidly.

Then, the driver who has been silent for the entire time, spoke:

"Excuse me for asking, young man, are you 18 years old?"

I replied honestly: "I'm 14."

"Ah!" The old driver's hand slipped and the taxi almost crashed into the guardrail on the right, "You don't look 14."

After a while, he sighed: "It might be because young people nowadays have better nutrition& but I thought I was early when I got married at 17. I never thought you would be discussing marriage with your mother-in-law at 14."

Auntie Ren angrily hit the driver's seat, "Who are you calling his mother-in-law? Watch your mouth, or I might not pay you when we get there."

The old driver chuckled, "I know you didn't bring your wallet and the young man has to pay, isn't that right?" He said as he winked at me through the rearview mirror.

Soon after, the taxi stopped across the street from Golden Victory. The reason we didn't stop closer is because a vehicle was parked in front to pick up the students.

Auntie Ren got off the car first and went towards the nearest trash can. She flipped through the underwear bag and pulled out a few pieces and threw them into the fly-infested trash.

It should be the ones that belong to Auntie Ren and Xiao Qin. It would no longer fall into the hands of a pervert, now that it's in the filthy trash. Amen.

I paid the driver, but he didn't even count the money, instead he smiled and said:

"Young man, make sure to treat your wife well."

I didn't know how to respond and left the car with a bitter smile.

As we got closer to the dojang, we could see more and more young children wearing white uniforms. They all cheerfully got on to the parked bus with their parents.

Their business is insanely popular and it's easy making money off of kids. Why aren't the products from our Happy Valley Love Shop suitable for kids?

After walking through a hallway that would fit four people side by side, Auntie Ren and I arrived at the waiting room. Standing behind the shining front desk was an equalling shining female receptionist.

Along the way here, my face caused the passing kids to stiffen with fear and some even began to cry.

They're useless. The most important is courage, then strength, then martial arts. Even if you learn some flowery moves, it would be useless without courage.

But I guess it's already good enough they didn't implode under the pressure of my Metal Blooded Lone Wolf aura. They can come looking for me after training for another one or two hundred years.

I had a twisted smile on my face as I followed behind Auntie Ren.

The female receptionist trembled and she first determined the location of the emergency exit. Then, she forced herself to put on a professional smile and spoke to Auntie Ren:

"Hello madam, is it your first time here? Are you here to register your son?"

"He's not my son!" Auntie Ren slammed both her hands on the counter and almost caused the receptionist to bite her tongue.

"Then, may I ask why you're here? It's already late and most of the students and instructors have already left. How about tomorrow&"

"Tomorrow doesn't work." Auntie Ren raised her voice, "Tell the master to come out, I have questions for him."

"Madam, who are you looking for?" the receptionist blinked with confusion.

At this time, three to five students who looked like middle school students came out from the training grounds. Auntie Ren found it hard to communicate with the receptionist, so she yelled at those students:

"Tell master Xu JinSheng to come out! I'm here to challenge him!"

Damn, don't be so emotional! Didn't you say you would only challenge him if he tried to defend his son?

When those students heard someone was here for a challenge, it was probably a first experience for a lot of them. They decided to not go home, instead, they ran back to the training grounds with excited and yelled:

"Brothers, someone's here for a challenge!"

"Hurry up and call instructor Wu and instructor Huang before they get too far!"

"It's gonna be a good show. It was worth paying the thousands of dollars of tuition."

"What school are they from? I don't see a banner&"

"They're probably travellers, they don't seem like they are easy to deal with&"

Auntie Ren somehow calmed down a bit more after the clamor. She flung the underwear bag onto the counter and asked the receptionist:

"Do you recognize this bag, does it belong to young master Xu?"

"Um& he might have a bag like this, but I'm not sure&"

The receptionist felt awkward.

"Fine." Auntie Ren tossed the bag towards me and told the receptionist: "If you don't know, then call Xu JinSheng so he could personally verify it. Tell him Ren HongLi is looking for him. If he doesn't come quickly, I'll tear down his dojang!"

The receptionist picked up the phone while trembling with fear.

Auntie Ren sent a glance at me and said:

"Let's play with them before Xu JinSheng gets here. I'm not sure why, but I feel like hitting someone."

Auntie Ren cracked her knuckles as she stepped into the bright training grounds.

I was carrying a bag of underwear while walking closely behind like an attendant.

We suddenly came to a wide clearing. The training grounds of the main dojang was as large as twelve volleyball courts. Shock absorbing floor mats, sandbags, resting benches, drink machines, automatic sanitized towel dispensers& it was filled with various facilities.

There were also changing rooms, rest rooms, washrooms, showers, and an empty office.

The office was at the end of the training grounds. It was facing a stage that was elevated by one meter. The stage was surrounded by railings that seemed to be used in MMA or boxing fights. I guess it's mainly for putting on exhibition matches in a taekwondo dojang.

We were surrounded by thirty or more students as we entered. They weren't ganging up on us, but more like they wanted to get the first glimpses at the challengers.

"Huh, how come it's a woman?"

"Don't look down on women. Just look at the difference between the men's and women's national soccer team."

"The guy behind her has a really fierce look."

Even though I was wearing the uniform from Qing Zi Academy, the emblem already fell off. It was also really dirty from the fight and didn't feel like a prestigious private school's uniform. Also, Qing Zi Academy is in the southern district, while this is the eastern district, so it makes sense no one would question my identity.

By the way, my dad's hotel is also in the eastern district. I'm not sure how close it is from here.

I was observing the students as they observed me.

They were all young and curious faces. At the moment, only four of them were older than 17.

A middle-aged man with a black belt on his white uniform walked towards the unsatisfied Auntie Ren.

"My last name is Huang, I'm the only instructor here at the moment." he spoke prudently, "I heard madam's last name is Ren. May I ask if you have any connections to the mayor's personal fitness advisor?"

"I don't have any relations with that old man." Auntie Ren snorted, "So, you're Xu JinSheng?"

"My, my last name is Huang&" the middle aged man repeatedly awkwardly.

t

"Stop blabbering." Auntie Ren waved her hands and posed as if she was the owner of the dojang.

"I came here looking for someone, but since Xu JinSheng is going to hide, I changed it to a challenge. Do any of you guys have the guts to challenge me? Anyways, if he doesn't show up by midnight, I'll tear down your sign and turn it into firewood."

Instructor Huang's face turned blue right after she finished her sentence. Also, quite a few students' faces were filled with anger.

"What is she saying? It's like she's implying master Xu is afraid of her!"

"Hurry up and call Instructor Wu. Instructor Huang's skills are shoddy."

"Shhhh~~~ don't let him hear you."

"So, is her son here to spectate or will he also fight?"

Auntie Ren couldn't hold it in anymore after hearing them repeatedly refer to me as her son, she stamped on the ground and yelled:

"He's not my son, he's& my son-in-law. Laugh while you can since he'll take care of you guys later."

Wow, did she already accept the marriage that quickly? I only followed behind to watch the show, I don't even have any strength left.

All the students who were initially ignoring me all put their sights on me.

"Isn't he at most 17? He's already a son-in-law at such a young age?"

"His mother-in-law is beautiful, so her daughter must be pretty good-looking too."

"Hey, where can you find such a young mother-in-law, unless& her daughter is a minor. I can't believe he has a beautiful minor as a wife, I'm pissed!"

"Truc, I'll cripple him if he has the guts to compete against us. My heart's in pain just thinking about a beautiful minor being pressed under him every night."

"What do you mean by beautiful minor? Don't you just mean loli? I already know the two of you are lolicons& Ow!"

The small boy was hit on the head by the other two students, "You shouldn't badmouth fellow students."

At this time, instructor Wu also came over. He had a skinny build, but he was ruthless. He didn't say anything when he saw the challenger was a woman, instead, he jumped onto one of the elevated stages and beckoned Auntie Ren:

"Come up, don't say I don't treat women well after I knock out all your front teeth."

Auntie Ren grinned while baring her teeth. Both her smile and gaze made you shiver, "You're the one who should wear a mouth guard, or better yet wear a full body of protective gear."

She took off the running shoes she wore to chase the thief. Then after instructing me to also take off my shoes, she got onto the stage with a gentle leap.

I was already drenched in sweat from my earth-shattering battle with young master Xu. When I removed my shoes, all the students around me covered their noses and backed away.

Now do you understand my savagery? Stay away from me if you don't want to implode!

"Don't just stand there." Auntie Ren shouted at me, "Get onto to the stage next to mines. I'll take care of the ones older than 18 and you take care of the ones under 18. Teach them a lesson for making fun of my daughter."

It was difficult for me, but I was too embarrassed to say I had no strength left to fight, so I said:

"I could take care of them, but I don't know how to hold back, what if&"

Auntie Ren interrupted me: "I'll take responsibility for everything as long as you don't kill them."

Every single one of the students sent me doubtful and hostile gazes.

"Then, what about the bag&"

"Leave it to Huang." Auntie Ren said impatiently, "Don't ask me everything."

I handed the underwear bag carefully to instructor Huang. I told him to not look inside as it's filled with stuff that should not be seen.

Instructor Huang's face was filled with worry, he waved at instructor Wu and yelled:

"Xiao Wu, hold back a bit, she might be well-connected."

Instructor Wu laughed mischievously, "Sorry, but my kicks are as fast as lighting, once I&"

Before he finished speaking, Auntie Ren dived in and struck his chin with a high kick. He rolled back as he fainted while frothing at the mouth.

A large crash reverberated through the room.

"What's wrong with her? The instructor wasn't even ready!"

"That's right! Instructor Huang, go show her our strength."

Instructor Huang may have been called shoddy by his students, but he was still a 3rd degree black belt. He was able to ascertain her true skills and only stood there shaking his head without a word.

I naturally became the focal point once instructor Wu was taken away for treatment.

My entire body was sore from the previous confrontation. Even if I did recover a bit on the taxi, I still felt like I was completely spent.

The stage was actually pretty high. I wanted to imitate Auntie Ren and lightly leap onto the stage, but I didn't use enough strength plus my legs were short. I stepped into air and fell on the ground with a miserable cry and bruised my nose.

Laughter immediately erupted from my surroundings.

My face was flushed red, I could only use my hands and feet to clumsily crawl onto the stage.

"Why is he coming to do a challenge when he can't even get onto a stage?"

"I thought he would be strong when I saw his eyes, but his skills are way worse than young master Xu."

"I'll fight him."

"Why? I'll go."

"Um& sorry, can you let me try first?"

The one who spoke last was a female student with double braided pigtails and freckles on her face. I didn't notice her because she was standing at the back.

Everyone's looking down at me! Even the slightly reserved female student thinks I'm an easy target to test her skills!

None of you are my target if I was at full strength, unless you can beat young master Xu.

Ah, I can't even stand still anymore if I get too excited.

The female student had already jumped onto the stage. She smiled bashfully and bowed at me. Then, she took a defensive position while staring into my eyes.

What's the point of even guarding? I can't even move. It's going to be so embarrassing once I get kicked off the stage and I wouldn't even be able to face Auntie Ren anymore. I might as well shave my head and become a monk. I'm going to leave behind my mortal desires and stop playing harem games.

The female student took a defensive pose and stood there for a while. She began to lose her patience when I didn't attack.

"If you're not going to attack, then& please excuse my rudeness."

Once she finished her sentence, she leaped up and sent a revolving kick towards my chest.

Damn, what a ruthless attack. She may be reserved, but her attacks are not reserved at all!

I didn't even have the strength to dodge as I watched her bare foot coming towards me. I was exhausted and leaned against the vinyl ropes to prepare to take her hit.

But although her strike was proficient, I could tell she was lacking in a certain area after my battle with young master Xu.

And that is Zanshin.

Zanshin originates from kendo and refers to one's ability to return back into proper posture after an attack.

A certain kendo master used a full cup of tea as an example. If he turns the teacup upside down, the tea would naturally pour out, but there would still be droplets remaining in the cup, and that is Zanshin.

Not only was young master Xu's attacks stronger, he also had an endless variety of follow-up attacks. That's why I couldn't really use Yin Yang Sanshou and had to fight to the death with berserk mode.

I leaned against the railing and only had enough strength to move my arms. I couldn't dodge at all, but it feels bad to take the hit without doing anything. I recalled the feeling of when I practice with gramps. I raised my left hand languidly and set it in the predicted path of movement of her ankles.

I didn't necessarily have to use force against force, mainly because I didn't even have the strength left to exert any force. Right when our skin came into contact, I immediately used my body as a guide to shift her strength towards the vinyl ropes I was leaning against. The ropes immediately 'counterattacked'.

I did the same as previously and guided the strength from the ropes back onto the young girl's ankles. She screamed out with shock and turned pale from the fact I sent her flying with one hand.

When the surrounding students saw her beautiful attack and my dejected appearance, they all thought she would easily win a round and recover from the fact their instructor Wu was KO'ed. No one expected me to easily send back the young girl's flying kick with a flick of my arm.

They people all stopped cheering and began whispering among themselves:

"What's that strange martial art? I even saw both his feet trembling, but how could he exert that much force&"

"Could it be a superpower&."

"Shut up, you read too many comics."

"Ah, a tiny amount of strength for a lot of power& it's Taichi! It's the first time I've seen Taichi in an actual fight."

I really wanted to yell out "Screw Taichi, is Taichi the only thing you know. Pretty much all other martial arts knows how to use Hua Jin and Fa Jin!" in stead of gramps.

But gramps already told me numerous times he doesn't recognize me as a disciple and I can't recognize him as my master. I'm not even allowed to mention the name Yin Yang Sanshou to others.

The female student looked at me with doubt after she regained her balance with some difficulty. I still looked like I was half dead.

She clenched her teeth and inched closer to me. This time she sent me a straight kick instead of a revolving kick. She abruptly sent a kick towards my waist with her heels as she leaned her upper body slightly backward.

This attack is even crueller than the last! This girl might look reserved, but she's actually extremely competitive. Did she fly into a rage after failing one attack?

But for a Yin Yang Sanshou practitioner, the more rage your attacks contain, the easier it is for me to bring you into my movements.

I once again clutched the ropes with my right hand and set my left hand open on her predicted path of travel. When we came into contact, it was as if my hand and her foot were repulsed by each other. The two traveled closer towards my abdomen until the back of my hand was already stuck against my stomach. She had a joyful expression because it seemed her attack had connected.

I tightened my abdomen and transferred her force behind me.

It seems the ropes played a huge role again this time as all her power was returned back to her and sent her flying. Before her foot left my hands, I played a prank and tickled the bottom of her foot.

What's even worse is that from an outsider's point of view, it looks like I used my abs to reflect her attack.

The female student lost her balance in mid-air and fell down sprawled out on all fours. She made an annoying yet lovable cry from the ground. I think her real personality is partially leaking out.

"Let's switch." A tall and muscular man who had a full beard spoke to the female student.

Damn, how old are you? If you're over 18 go to Auntie Ren to meet your death!

Currently, Auntie Ren was leaning against the ropes on the neighboring stage and watching my moves with a face full of suspicion.

"I'm not switching." the female student said stubbornly, "I've never lost this badly before. I have to beat him no matter what."

She said as she ran towards me.

Hey& your too close! Even though Taekwondo does have some fist techniques, are you actually going to use your fists? Young master Xu did his best to keep his distance from me.

The female student already grabbed onto my shirt before I could respond. She raised her knee and sent it flying at my lower abdomen.

A knee strike? It is a valid move in Taekwondo, but isn't the place your aiming at a bit&.?

It was an emergency and I didn't have any experience using Yin Yang Sanshou in a grapple. In a panic, I made a quick-witted decision and used my height and weight as an advantage to hug around her neck. Then, I let my weary body naturally fall forwards.

She originally thought I was trying to break free so she pulled harder on my shirt. She wasn't able to respond quickly enough and she was flattened under me on top of the stage.

Her knee strike was also powerless because she had no support. She fell with her legs apart as if she was allowing me in.

"You& pervert." her face was flushed red and she struggled to break free.

"Get off of me. Don't get so close, you reek of sweat."

I swear it's not on purpose, I'm just way to tired. I really want to sleep& the cushion under me right now is really soft, but why does it keep shaking.

After watching me fall on top of the female student and refusing to get up, the students below cursed at me angrily:

"Are you trying to do a challenge or act like a pervert? If you don't stop, I'm going to call the police."

"Why call the police, let's all beat him until his mother won't even recognize him anymore."

I thought in a daze that Ai ShuQiao actually might not recognize me. You guys don't have to move a muscle since I never had a mother that would recognize me in the first place.

I suddenly heard Auntie Ren yell from the neighboring stage: "If you guys have to guts to gang up on Ye Lin, then he and I will fight all of you."

It seems Auntie Ren could tell I was too exhausted and I wasn't laying on top of the female student on purpose. Otherwise, she would be the first to teach me a lesson as my mother-in-law.

I tired to support myself up with my arms so I could let her out, but I lost strength halfway and fell back down again.

I hit her pretty hard this time and she let out an "Ahhh~~hhhh" scream.

Don't make sounds that would cause misunderstandings. We're already in an awkward position, if you stretch out a scream like that, it would make it seems as if we're filming an AV.

The female student was in an extremely uncomfortable position. She didn't care about my sweat anymore and began to bite, claw, and scratch me. She did everything she could to try and get out from under me. It actually had some effect as her loose uniform opened up a bit right around her chest area.

Fuck, I became energetic the instant I saw them, two white rabbits even whiter than her uniform! She's not even wearing a bra under her uniform!

It doesn't seem like something a reserved person would do. Even someone as extroverted as Xiong YaoYue would usually wear a sports bra. Are you purposely not wearing a bra among all these boys so you can become the center of attention?

According to Eunuch Cao: she would be consider a wild girl on the inside.

Auntie Ren couldn't keep watching anymore. She jumped onto the stage and rolled me away like I was a dead fish and saved the female student.

The female student tidied up her uniform, then hesitated a bit. It seems she felt she exposed too much of her true personality and it might not be favorable for her among the boys, so she began to sob.

"I, I was bullied~"

The boys in the front row were all itching to jump in and peel off my skin to comfort the female student.

Even though all the male students were glaring at me, no one had the guts to come onto the stage with Auntie Ren standing next to me. All they could do was curse at me in their minds.

The female student cried on the stage for a while but walked off stage in disappointment after no one came to help her. She swatted the hands of a few fellow students who reached out to help her and walked to the shower room by herself.

Auntie Ren asked me while I was still seated on the ground and panting heavily: "Who's been teaching you martial arts these past couple of months?"

I quickly denied it: "No-, no one. I learned it from watching Taichi on TV. I only seemed strong because that female student was too weak."

The male students became angrier as they heard me call her weak.

Auntie Ren clicked her tongue, "If you can learn it that easily by simply watching TV, why don't you do and learn the Eighteen Subduing Dragon Palms?"

I stammered, "That's& a bit& difficult&"

Suddenly, the male student with the full beard yelled at Auntie Ren:

"Didn't you say anyone under 18 can fight against Ye Lin& are you going to keep your word?"

Auntie Ren asked in return, "How old are you?"

Full-Beard: "I'm 17."

"Ah?" Auntie Ren had a face of disbelief.

Full-Beard awkwardly scratched his chin: "It's true, I can show you my ID if you don't believe me."

Auntie Ren turned around and said to instructor Huang: "Go bring us some water, a folding chair, a bucket, and a wet towel."

Instructor Huang didn't know why he couldn't refuse her words. He handed the underwear bag to a boy with glasses (the one who was called a lolicon), then he went to gather the items as if he was one of Auntie Ren's servants.

All the items were gathered fairly quickly. Then, Auntie Ren helped me onto the folding chair and fed me water and wiped my sweat like she was my boxing coach.

I took off Qing Zi Academy's jacket under Auntie Ren's orders. The black vest I was wearing over my muscular body was exposed.

The crowd exclaimed in surprise and someone whispered: "I never thought he would be so built. Was he playing with us by pretending to be sick?"

Full-Beard seemed to be shrinking back a bit in fear.

"What's wrong? It's a great opportunity to get revenge for our junior (TN: the female student)."

"That's right. He might look built, but I think he's actually sick. As someone once said: The right time to strike is when they are already down. So that means now is the best time."

Auntie Ren wiped the wounds on my face (caused by young master Xu) while looking down the stage with a threatening gaze. No one had the guts to pick a fight while she was still on the stage.

"Can you still fight if you rest for ten minutes?" Auntie Ren asked me.

I smiled bitterly: "I don't think I can even if I rest thirty minutes."

"So you weren't lying, you actually fought with the underwear thief."

"That's right& young master Xu is strong&"

I didn't mention he was only strong after wearing panties on his head, nor did I mention I only beat him because I also wore panties over my head.

Auntie Ren suddenly intentionally raised her voice: "Which part of young master Xu do you think is the hardest part to deal with?"

Initially, I didn't understand what she meant and I responded: "I guess it would be his dedication towards underwear&."

"No, no, no." I quickly changed my mind when I saw Auntie Ren's change in expression, "It's his unpredictable kicks and it's hard to guard against."

Auntie Ren raised her voice even higher: "Then, how did you defeat young master Xu?"

The area below the stage immediately turned silent. Each of them pricked up their ears and couldn't believe their hero could have been defeated.

I was finally able to understand Auntie Ren's intentions. She wanted me to describe young master Xu's past so we could stall for time and also intimidate them.

Thus I purposely spoke slowly:

"Well, we would have to start from the time when I first met young master Xu. It was a warm spring day&"

Thus I retold the story of meeting young master Xu and the other hoodlums. I talked about how they were picking on a couple and I beat all of them 1v5. Especially about how I used my lawnmower attack to deal with peaked cap guy and Tang Jiang, and how I kicked away young master Xu's knife. I described it vividly and colorfully without leaving out a single detail.

Some of the students said I was bullshitting: "Young master Xu isn't that kind of person, stop making things up!"

But a few of the students began to mutter when I mentioned Tang Jiang and the injuries on his face.

Full-Beard clapped his hands together as he came to a realization: "You& you're the strong homosexual Tang Jiang mentioned!"

"You're the one who's a fucking homosexual." I cursed, "That was a rumor Tang Jiang started because he couldn't beat me."

"That's true&" one of them said, "If he was a homosexual, he wouldn't have done perverted things to our (female) junior&."

Then I began to talk about our next confrontation. Of course, I had to omit some facts and I didn't mention anything about the underwear.

It's not like I'm trying to cover up for him, but if I mention the panties on his head, then I would have to mention I wore it too.

That's why I removed all the unnecessary details and changed the fight into a scene from a wuxia movie. I added a lot of embellishments to my memory and made it seems like it was an evenly matched, hair-raising match.

Even though a lot of what I said may have been unreliable, I still made an impartial assessment of young master Xu's martial arts skill. I was also able to perfectly summarize his style of fighting so the crowd had to believe I definitely crossed paths with young master Xu.

I drank some water to re-hydrate while Auntie Ren stared at a wall clock in the distance. Then, she whispered:

"Keep talking. It's almost 10, Xu JinSheng should be here soon."

As if to validate Auntie Ren's room, instructor Huang ran back towards the stage after checking out the waiting area and said:

"The master is already here, he'll come in after parking. Madam Ren, please talk to the master about your concerns&"

Footsteps echoed from the entrance earlier than expected and everyone's eyes gathered at one spot.

A 1.8m tall man walked into the training grounds.

His white uniform reflected the dazzling white lights. What's strange was his feet showed no signs of training and was as white as his uniform.

His hands actually gave off a refined feeling and he had an oval callus on the middle section of his right middle finger. Not really sure what he practices to get those calluses.

Finally, I looked at his face. He had glasses with a black frame and looked like a scholar&

By the way, he seems really familiar.

Even Auntie Ren was stunned.

Isn't& he my dad? He got the callus on his right hand from writing for prolonged periods of time.

Wh-wh-wh-what is this situation? Why is he the master? Is Xu JinSheng your other identity? I always thought you were a miserable man, but I never thought you would establish a large business behind your son's back. How come I don't know that you know martial arts? Also, you must have another family and wife. Is young master Xu my half-brother? Then that explains perfectly why we both power up unnaturally when we wear underwear over our heads.

I was still working really hard to manage the Love Shop! If you have such a large business, at least hire a housekeeper who knows how to properly season dishes to cook dinner for me! I'm starting to break down when I think about those long nights where you don't return home, but you're actually just spending time with a warm and harmonious family. There's no god, both my parents are scum. I want to retaliate against society. I'm going to force myself on the class leader, Gong CaiCai, Xiong YaoYue, Xiao Qin (actually I don't really need to use force for her), then I'm going to head into the forest and live in the wild.

Instructor Huang and the thirty plus students were as surprised as me.

"May I ask who you are?"

My dad stood there awkwardly and blushed. Then, he pulled a fat man who was also wearing glasses and a uniform to the front.

"I told you we went the wrong way. There's no washroom here."

My dad blamed him before I realized the fatty was his old classmate, the vice-principal of some university who invited him to write teaching materials.

Damn, why didn't you guys mention sooner you went the wrong way, you almost scared me to death. Although this place isn't far from the University area, why did the two of you come here? Didn't you only get released from quarantine yesterday?

Auntie Ren was one step ahead of me and asked:

"Why& are you following me?"

This was when my dad realized his son and old neighbor were on the stage.

"I, I never followed you." my dad said, "My classmate invited me here to the dojang to loosen up after being released from quarantine. To tell you the truth, the area they have for professionals to vent their anger is amazing. They have specially designed wooden boards and bricks that would break in one hit. There are a lot of people relaxing there while still wearing their suits!"

Auntie Ren turned away and ignored him. I chatted with my dad for a bit and he was extremely interested when he heard Auntie Ren and I came as challengers.

Then, the real master, Xu JinSheng, who was close to 1.9m tall, walked in wearing a suit.

Xu JinSheng wasn't alone. Young master Xu, his son, was following behind him quietly.

Young master Xu had already changed into a different set of clothes but he still had a wound on his face that I caused. The surrounding students were all curious, but were afraid to ask any questions due to the heavy atmosphere.

As for the real Xu JinSheng, he had a good looking face, but his eyes were really small.

Although they were small, they still shined brightly and showed his self-cultivation.

Actually, I can't tell anything about his skills, but they say it in wuxia novels all the time, so I just went with the flow.

"Aren't you the second daughter of the Ren family?" Xu JinSheng made a slightly apologetic smile and pointed at the office towards the ends of the training grounds.

"Let's talk over there. I kind of already have a gist on how my son offended you."

Auntie Ren leaped off the stage while holding the ropes and walked with Xu JinSheng towards the office.

After walking a few steps, she called out to me:

"Ye Lin, bring the bag to me so they can't say we don't have any evidence."

I recovered a bit of strength after sitting down for a while. My dad helped me off the stage and I went to ask instructor Huang for the bag.

Instructor Huang pointed to a boy sitting on a nearby bench, "I handed it to him."

I staggered towards the boy who was wearing glasses and I saw him staring sluggishly at the bag on his legs as if he suffered a great shock.

Damn, he probably looked inside the bag. I specifically told instructor Huang that people shouldn't look inside the bag! This boy looks like he's in elementary school. If you let him see this many stolen underwear (some of which may even be worn), it will definitely affect his views and change his future!

I took the bag from his hands and said to him:

"Little boy, which you just saw was an illusion, don't steal underwear when you get older!"

The little boy repeated: "Underwear, underwear&"

Why does he seem like a zombie from Plants VS Zombies were they keep muttering "Brains, brains&."! Why did young master Xu turn into an underwear thief after losing to me? Does this mean this little boy might also walk a dangerous path because he came into contact with me? Why do I have a strange ability to incite others to steal underwear? I don't want this useless power!

I caught up to Auntie Ren and passed her the underwear bag. Then, the two of them entered the office and shut the door.

I thought she would use me as a witness, but I guess it's better if I wait outside, otherwise I might get into a fight with young master Xu again.

I sat on a nearby bench while drinking the free bottled water. My dad and his vice-principal friend sat next to me and began to affectionately chat with me.

After I took a closer look, I remember I've seen his friend before and everyone used to call him by his nickname Gou Sheng&

Thus, I respectfully lowered my head and gave my greetings, "Uncle Gou Sheng&"

My dad quickly punched me on the head, "What are you saying? Call him Uncle He."

Then, my dad smiled and apologized: "Kids don't know any better. Gou Sheng, don't take it personally."

Uncle He had an awkward expression and his face wrinkled up.

"Lao Er, you're also being disrespectful, you can call me Lao Liu."

Uncle He mentioned their rankings when they lived in the same dorms in University. (TN: Yeah, in this case they literally refer to each other as second and sixth, I'm going to leave it in Chinese.)

"Sigh, Xiao Ye Zi has grown a lot in these couple of years&" Uncle He looked at me and lamented at the passing of time, "Xiao Ye Zi& looks much more manly&"

Ah, why is your face filled with regret? You should be happy for me if I'm more manly. Oh, that's right, you're not complementing my muscles, but sighing at the fact my face got fucked up! No wonder he's the vice-principal, he can still have tact when calling someone ugly!

"If I recall, when Xiao Ye Zi was eight or nine, he was short and pretty. My wife was really fond of you at the time and always told me we should arrange a marriage between you and our daughter."

"But you're already so tall, and my daughter's only 1.6m, so she won't be a good match for you."

Damn, are you going to break the marriage immediately after you saw my fucked up face? I don't even care about your daughter , since I'm going to create an unprecedented enormous harem!

The female student who was defeated by me earlier walked over. She had changed into a new white uniform and beads of water hung from her hair. She tied her green belt tightly around her waist and made herself more noticeable with her protruding breasts and buttocks.

She walked straight towards me after looking at me with doubt.

Did she still not get enough? I was borrowing the strength of the ropes earlier, but I'm not her match with my remaining strength without assistance.

I never thought the one she was looking for was Uncle He. She walked in front of him and pouted:

"Dad, why are you here? Isn't mom the one who usually picks me up?"

"Ah, Ling Ling, your mom sent her car in for a yearly checkup." Uncle He laughed and scratched his sparse hair.

Before I could react, she politely bowed towards my father, "Hello Uncle Ye, you also came."

"Yeah." my dad said cheerfully, "Your dad brought me to the place to vent anger for professionals."

Sh& shit, she was Uncle He's child! I hope she doesn't tell her dad the stuff I did to her on stage.

As expected, after greeting our dads, she pointed at me with an unpleasant expression:

"Who is he and why is he sitting here?"

I lowered my head with shame.

Uncle He quickly introduced the two of us: "He's Ye Lin, the son of Uncle Ye. He's currently attending second year of middle school in the west district. Ye Lin, this is my daughter and her name is He Ling. Her mother and I both call her Ling Ling. She's in the third year of middle school at a girl's school that's in between the east and west district."

A girl's school. So is that why she comes to a dojang to be doted on by men, because she can't see any boys at school? She appears polite in front of her elders, so Uncle He might even think she's a virtuous girl.

When He Ling heard her dad's words, blood rushed to her head and she almost stopped breathing.

But Uncle He didn't notice her daughter's abnormal expression and teased us:

"Look, your names actually rhyme, Lin and Ling& Lao Er, do you remember that poem?"

"Oh yeah, that's right." my dad began to recite the poem&

Stop reciting, can't you see He Ling wants to strangle me?

"He's only in middle school." After a long pause, He Ling said, "I thought he was in high school."

"Sorry, my son is a bit abnormal." My dad patted my shoulder and urged, "Uncle He's daughter is older than you by a year, so you should call her sister."

I stammered: "Sister Ling Ling&."

He Ling's face flashed red and white after being called 'Sister Ling Ling'. I'm guessing she wants to kick me to death in her mind but she can't do anything in front of her father.

"So, you're Ye Lin? Your skills are pretty impressive."

I was embarrassed: "It's nothing much&"

He Ling became angrier. I guess if my skills were nothing and I defeated her, that means she's worse than nothing.

"Then Ye Lin, I'll be in your care."

She said with hidden meanings, then she told her dad to immediately drive her home.

"Can you wait for a bit?" Uncle He asked, "I want to bring Uncle Ye back to his hotel too."

My dad shook his hand in a hurry, "Don't worry, I'll walk with Ye Lin. Lao Liu, you head back first so your child can rest."

Uncle He couldn't withstand her daughter's urging, so he left first with an apologetic expression.

While our fathers weren't paying attention, He Ling turned around and made a warning at me with her fist.

Does she still want to get payback? It wasn't even on purpose, it was her own fault she didn't wear a bra!

The male students began to scatter and head home after He Ling left and it didn't seem like Auntie Ren and the master was going to get into a fight. The only ones left were a few curious students and instructor Huang who was waiting outside the office.

The main lights were also closed since there was nobody still using the training grounds. There were only a row of small lights left to illuminate a path for walking.

The doors to the office were thick and soundproof, but you could hear still indistinctly hear Auntie Ren's high pitched shouts of blame.

After about 40 minutes of discussions, the remaining students couldn't stand the boredom and went home. Only instructor Huang stayed along with me and my father.

10 minutes later, Auntie Ren finally walked out full of vigor like the victor, but Xu JinSheng didn't have much of a defeated expression. It seems they were able to make a compromise.

According to Auntie Ren, even though Xu JinSheng had an eighth degree black belt, he was still extremely courteous towards her. He kept saying it was his failure as a parent and eventually Auntie Ren wasn't angry anymore and accepted his apology.

It turns out Xu JinSheng already noted his son's abnormal behavior in recent days. He thought it was good his son no longer led people around causing trouble in the streets, but then he found hundreds of pairs of underwear hidden at home. His son is afraid of him, so after some interrogation, he admitted he was the rumored underwear thief.

But even if he admitted, he still couldn't hold back his urges. Whenever his father wasn't keeping an eye on him, he would run out and continue his businesses. Xu

JinSheng had already scolded him numerous times, but he couldn't change his son's mind.

I never would expected that after our fight, he went home and told his father he was finally able to see how shameful it was to steal underwear. Especially when he saw a certain person wearing 8 or 9 pairs of underwear over their head with bras hanging off his body. He became aware of how perverted he was and he wanted to change himself before it was too late like a certain somebody.

Fuck, are you talking about me? I can't believe an underwear thief thinks I'm perverted. If you wanted to change yourself before it was too late shouldn't you have done it as you looked at yourself in the mirror while sniffing underwear?

Xu JinSheng first told his son to apologize to Auntie Ren, then he offered to pay 10 times the compensation for her losses. She said it was unnecessary and told him to donate to UNICEF when he makes more money.

In conclusion, Auntie Ren was able to get rid of the unpleasant feeling in her chest, and Xu JinSheng was happy his son was able to repent. He was also grateful Auntie Ren didn't damage his reputation by injuring younger students or announcing his son was an underwear thief.

Xu JinSheng also showed kindness to me, the one who was able to make his son turn over a new leaf.

"I heard Miss Ren called you her son-in-law, haha, it looks like your luck is pretty good. Come, shake hands with my son. The martial arts world isn't that large so you two should get to know each other more."

Then he beckoned his son over.

"Tian Ming, don't keep silent the whole time. Come shake a hand and apologize."

Since Xu JinSheng called him Tian Ming, I assumed young master Xu's full name was Xu TianMing. He walked closer but was unwilling to shake my hand.

"He's too&. I don't want to touch him&"

"What did you say?" Xu JinSheng used his thick and rough hands to grip his son's shoulder and caused him to grimace in pain.

"It's true, Ye Lin is even more perverted than me! If I didn't meet him under the bridge last time, I wouldn't have gone to& steal&"

"I'm already determined to quit now, but if I touch him again, I might develop some other bad hobbies."

Xu JinSheng didn't listen to his excuses and forced him to shake hands with me.

Both our hands were covered with small injuries caused by the other party. We were only forced to reconcile so we both had fake smiles while feeling awkward on the inside.

"Please excuse my previous actions." Xu TianMing said, "You're the strongest opponent I've faced from my age group."

"Same to you." I said the same words of courtesy, "I have to rest at least three days at home."

Xu JinSheng was a straightforward person. While we were both shaking hands, he patted our backs intimately and said:

"Since you guys are pretty similar, why not become brothers."

"No&. need."

Xu TianMing and I both blurted out simultaneously.

I'm the one who thinks he's a pervert! If we were to be sworn brothers, what would be our name, the panty alliance? If we ever face the same enemy, are we expected to wear underwear over our heads to power up? That's way too embarrassing.

Xu JinSheng could tell he couldn't force the two of us, so he gave me a coupon for trying out the junior classes at his dojang. He also gave me a large number of coupons for the professional stress relief are so I could share it with my friends.

After I finished speaking with Xu JinSheng and his son, I went to look for my dad and Auntie Ren, but they were both missing.

Instructor Huang saw my confusion and told me: "They both went to the washroom, they should be out soon."

Huh, why would a man and a woman go to the washroom at the same time? Wasn't Auntie Ren annoyed when she saw my dad? This is in someone else's dojang, so you guys better not be doing anything strange in the washroom.

Xu JinSheng asked if we needed instructor Huang to send us home, but I didn't have the nerve to accept when I saw instructor Huang's bitter expression. I told them I'll leave with my dad after using the washroom.

Then I ran into the dark and quiet washroom with worry.

The washroom was larger than some of the ones found in airports and train stations. There were a total of six sinks at the entrance that seemed to be shared between the men's and women's washroom. I stood there and concentrated my senses to listen in.

Fortunately, there weren't any "Ah~ah~ah~oh~" sounds.

But there was a man and woman speaking to each other and they were obviously my dad and Auntie Ren.

"Lend me some money. I forgot my wallet so I can't get home."

Auntie Ren spoke angrily.

Huh, were you embarrassed to speak in front of others so you guys came to the washroom?

"Okay." I could even imagine my dad lowering his head, "We're old neighbors, so you don't need to return it."

"What do you mean?"

"I& didn't say anything&"

"How much money did you bring with you?"

"Around& five or six hundred&"

"Why do you carry so less?"

"I could withdraw some more with my bank card if it's too less&"

"How much will you give me?"

"As much as you want?"

"What do you mean as much as I want? Do you think I'm trying to sell myself?"

"But, I was just following along to what you said&"

"Forget it, just give me fifty bucks later. But keep in mind, I'm only borrowing it, I won't take even a cent from you."

"I know, I know&"

"And&"

"Yeah."

"About the night before&"

Oh, she lowered her voice. What happened the night before? Dad, didn't you say nothing happened between the two of you that night?

Auntie Ren then raised her voice again.

"Anyway, you can't tell anybody about what happened. If you tell anyone, I'll kill you."

"I won't tell anyone. My lips are sealed." My dad quickly guaranteed.

"You can't tell your son either."

"Okay, I won't tell Xiao Lin."

"I'm not joking, if Ye Lin finds out& I'll kill you."

"I already said I won't tell him&"

"I can't believe a man's words. Listen closely. If you blabber, you'll end up floating down DaNing river as a headless corpse."

"But what will happen to Xiao Lin if I die."

"I'll take care of him. You can rest in peace."

I quickly backed away as I heard them walk out.

I don't even remember how we parted ways with Xu JinSheng. My dad decided to head home tonight with me instead of returning to the hotel.

Once we got home, my dad went to the fridge to get some beer. I blocked his way and put on an interrogative pose and asked:

"Dad, are you hiding something from me?"

"Eh, Xiao Lin, where did you hear that from?" My dad shifted his glasses with unnatural movements.

"Auntie Ren, she&"

"Xiao Lin, don't misunderstand, nothing happened between us."

My dad denied it as he timidly touched his neck.

What, are you afraid of being turned into a headless corpse?

"What did I misunderstand? I didn't say anything yet, but you clearly have a guilty conscience&"

My dad turned serious and asked: "Xiao Lin, what do you think about Auntie Ren?"

"She's okay." I replied, "She might be easily irritable and fussy, but she has a soft heart&"

My dad immediately made a vulgar smile: "She is pretty soft-hearted&"

What the hell happened, did you peek at her in the shower or something?

My dad coughed as he was being pressured by me and by the fact he wanted to share, "Actually, something happened the night before&"

"What happened?" I asked in a panic, "Didn't you say nothing happened between he two of you?"

"That's right, nothing happened at first."

"Then what."

"Then&. started making love&"

"What?"

"No, the people above us& started making love&"

I was seething with anger and grabbed my dad's collar, "Don't scare me like that. Hurry up and get to the main point."

"Ah, I'm thirsty. Can I have a can of beer first?"

"No, here's a bottle of water. Drink it and spit it all out."

My dad gulped down half the bottle and wiped his mouth with regret, then said:

"The hotel wasn't soundproofed well, and the people above us were really loud when making love. Both Auntie Ren and I couldn't sleep, so we got up&"

"And then&?"

"Then& Auntie Ren yelled at the people above us, but they were still really loud, so she put on headphones and started using the computer&"

Based on my dad's narrative, here's what happened the other night.

It seems like the guests above them really had some issues. Not only were they really loud, they also took a long time. After Auntie Ren and my dad were finally able to wait until they were done so they could sleep, they started their second round.

Auntie Ren looked ashen after hearing the female's screams. She wanted to head upstairs and pound on their door, but my dad persuaded her to not go since a lot of people came to hotels for those reasons anyway.

But my dad felt a bit uncomfortable after saying that, since they were also in a hotel room together, would they also do it?

As expected, Auntie Ren nitpicked as his reasoning and said: "Since you won't let me go, then you're responsible for making them shut up."

My dad had a bitter expression: "What can I do? They won't pick up even if I call their room&"

Auntie Ren clicked her tongue, "Haven't you heard those jokes online? They say if your neighbors make too much noise when making love, then all you have to do is scream louder than them to make them shut up."

My dad was pleased by the turn of events: "Are we& going to make those sounds too?"

Auntie Ren was sitting on her bed in pajamas while using my dad's laptop. A faint white light from the LCD screen illuminated her body, and my dad said she looked like a goddess.

But the goddess only glared at him, "Keep dreaming, I'm telling you to scream."

"Huh?"

"What are you dazing out for, hurry up and scream. I just read online that as long as a man yells 'Oh my god, you're an incredible husband' or 'Husband, do me harder', then they will immediately quiet down."

My dad said awkwardly: "That's too embarrassing&"

"What's embarrassing? If you're not going to scream, are you going to make me scream?"

He didn't have a choice, so he cupped his hands around his mouth and shouted bashfully:

"You're an incredible husband~~?"

Auntie Ren spoke while glaring at him: "Harder."

My dad continued to yell: "Husband, do me harder."

"No, I meant use more force and yell louder."

"But& I'm already using a lot of effort&" My dad drooped his head and said, "I can speak louder when I'm teaching a class, but this, I'm too embarrassed&"

Auntie Ren said with disdain: "Hmph, you can't even make some screams, how dumb. You're so useless."

Auntie Ren hit a nerve and my dad lowered his head: "That's right& I'm useless&.."

The people upstairs finally finished their second round, but now my dad and Auntie Ren couldn't really fall asleep.

So Auntie Ren continued to use the computer while my dad began to read an issue of Scientific American.

Half an hour passed with neither of them saying a word.

Auntie Ren regretted her harsh words a bit when she saw my dad's mournful expression from the corners of her eye, but she couldn't stoop herself low enough to apologize. She got bored using the computer, so she got a 6 pack of beer from the fridge.

My dad bought this and kept it in the fridge before the quarantine happened. He didn't have a chance to drink it as he was chased out of his room the same night. Auntie Ren also likes drinking beer, but she couldn't really buy any during quarantine, so she held back on drinking.

My dad completely forgot about it, but got cravings once he saw it, so he asked pitifully:

"Can I also have a can?"

Originally, the beer was bought by my dad anyway. Auntie Ren would have shared it with him if he asked confidently. But my dad didn't even voice his objections, so she replied:

"No. What happens if someone like you gets drunk."

Then Auntie Ren gulped down all six cans right in front of my dad.

Not only did she drink a lot, she also drank it quickly as if she was afraid my dad would laugh if she drank it slower.

It's easier to get drunk if you drink too fast. Auntie Ren got the hiccups and went to sleep after shoving the computer to one side.

My dad was a gentleman and didn't try to do anything to Auntie Ren while she was drunk. According to him, all he wanted was to sneak over and check if there was any beer left in those cans. But he didn't do it because he was afraid Auntie Ren would misunderstand.

After a while, when it seemed Auntie Ren was already in a deep sleep, my dad turned off his bedside lamp and prepared to go to sleep.

Who knew the people upstairs would start their third round after an hour of rest. If they are not going to die of bird flu, they are going to die from an excessive amount of sex!

It was in the middle of the night where men were usually stiff. My dad's body reacted naturally to the screams coming from above. Right when he was feeling awkward, he saw Auntie Ren sway shakily off her bed. The silver rays of moonlight passed through the curtains and illuminated Auntie Ren's thin pajamas. It outlined her sexy body and made my dad even more excited.

"You bastards think you're so amazing?" Auntie Ren cursed while pointing towards the ceiling ina drunken stupor. Then, she accidentally tripped and fell onto my dad's bed.

My dad hid his awkward part while supporting Auntie Ren.

Auntie Ren pressed down on my dad's chest and pushed him down.

"Don't touch me." Auntie Ren was drunk and in a half awake state.

She sat on top of my dad without any explanation and pointed at him:

"There's not a single& good man."

She scolded him as she ripped off my dad's shorts.

My dad couldn't resist, so he tried to call out her name, but he got slapped in the face in return.

"My name isn't something you can call! You scum, why did you go to brothels?"

"I, I didn't&"

My dad tried to explain but was pressed down by Auntie Ren as she ripped off his vest and underwear and tore them into shreds.

At this time, the people upstairs were still going at it, but they only seemed to be background noise.

Auntie Ren had a conqueror's look in her eyes as she looked at my naked dad who was held under her. She laughed for a bit before she threw off all her clothes and accurately rode on top of my dad.

It was like my dad was watching the perfect AV as he was describing the scene.

On the other hand, I felt as if I just received the death penalty.

Other than the fact Auntie Ren rode my dad like a horse, she also swung her bra in the air like a lasso. At the same time, she was making embarrassing sounds towards the people upstairs.

"Do you hear that? Do you think you're the only ones who can do it?"

"Come down and I'll gladly fight you, if you have the guts!"

Of course, she wasn't forming full sentences, but my dad cut out some words he shouldn't tell me.

Fuck, you shouldn't even have told me this story since it's not suitable for me. You were pushed down and raped! Why are you laughing instead of being upset!

I'm not sure if Auntie Ren was especially competitive or something, but she did it with my dad four times, exactly once more than the people upstairs. Then, she was finally able to go back to sleep.

And of course, the people upstairs realized their inferiority compared to Auntie Ren and never did it again.

The next day, after Auntie Ren sobered up, she discovered her clothes scattered around the room. She held her aching head as she remembered the dumb thing she did last night.

Coincidentally, it was also the day they were notified by the health bureau that the quarantine was over. A racket could be heard outside in the hallway as people began to leave. My dad's new friend, the fatty, knocked loudly on the door to try and notify them the quarantine was over. Auntie Ren was afraid of being seen, so she wrapped a blanket around myself, then she glared at my dad and ran into the washroom.

My dad didn't know how to face Auntie Ren either, so he left to eat breakfast with his fatty friend. Then, he went back home to check up on me so he could also give Auntie Ren some space.

Auntie Ren was already gone by the time he returned to the hotel on Saturday night. But he found an incredible menacing note placed with his documents. My dad said it was too terrifying to read, so he burned it in the sink.

After telling me what happened, he rested his chin on the table as if reminiscing that wonderful night. At the same time, he asked pitifully on what he should do.

Why are you asking me? I'm the one who wants to ask how I should face Xiao Qin at school tomorrow! Obviously, Auntie Ren wouldn't tell Xiao Qin, but it would feel more awkward for me because she didn't tell her! She always respectfully calls you Uncle Ye, but she has no idea Uncle Ye screwed her mom!

Wait, no, it seems like it's Auntie Ren's fault this time, since she pushed down my dad. China's justice system is imperfect, so we can't report you, but you're the ones who should be ashamed.

Well, since we're all mature here, we don't need to investigate who's at fault& let's just never discuss it again.

Because no matter what, I don't want Auntie Ren as my step-mom. I mean anyone's better than Ai ShuQiao, but then I wouldn't be able to escape from Xiao Qin. Who wants a step-sister who only thinks about marrying you?

I might even have to live with Xiao Qin if Auntie Ren and my dad gets married.

On Monday morning, my dad was still sleeping soundly. Based on the red glow on his face, he must have secretly drank some beer while I wasn't watching him.

I woke up at five in the morning. I was deeply worried about future developments, so I ran dejectedly to the lakeside to practice with gramps.

Gramps who bailed on me on Sunday had his hands behind his back while gazing at the bluish-green lake.

I'm not saying the lake is bluish-green because of the scenery, but rather, there's a vegetable market nearby. The vendors would sometimes dump their rotten veggies into the lake. So, the main reason the lake is bluish-green is due to the spinach leaves.

My complexion probably looked just as bad as the spinach leaves. When gramps saw me, he frowned and said:

"Why do you look so worried at so young? Did you get AIDS?"

"No, no&."

"Then what are you worrying about?"

I couldn't tell him my dad did it with my classmate's mom and I don't really want to face her.

Besides, this is personal. Gramps isn't related to me and we don't even know each other's names. Even if my dad and Auntie Ren did it four times in a row, it has nothing to do with gramps.

"Since you don't have an incurable illness, we can continue practicing."

Perhaps gramps was still pissed I bailed on Saturday, but his hits seemed much harder. I shot onto the trunk of the tree multiple times and it left bruises on my body.

Plus, my entire body was sore from the battle with young master Xu TianMing the other day. That's why the results against gramps was even worse than usual.

Gramps played with me for a bit in high spirits. Then he watched me as I sat down in front of the tree to catch my breath and said with curiosity:

"I never expected your Hua Jin skills to improve even more when you didn't come to practice for two days."

"Eh." I was astonished, "I was clearly beaten terribly."

"Hmph, that's because I usually only use twenty percent of my strength, but today I used forty percent. I can only say you're learning at lightning speeds if you are already able to withstand forty percent of my strength."

So you were planning on pushing me into the lake and covering my entire body with spinach? How much do you hold a grudge?

Does my quick developments have anything to do with the battle yesterday with Xu TianMing?

Wait, that doesn't make sense, since I couldn't use Yin Yang Sanshou due to his fast kicks.

Maybe it was because of the battle with He Ling on the stage at the dojang? At the time, I could only depend on Yin Yang Sanshou because I had used all my strength. Did I accidentally level up in that instance?

Wahahaha, I'm a genius! Based on how fast I'm learning, there's no one else who can learn martial arts like me! Gramps, you should hurry up and come to a realization so you can pass on Fa Jin to me too. I might be willing to accept if you beg me to learn it while hugging my legs.

Gramps clicked his tongue as if he read my mind and said:

"You don't have to come here to learn from me anymore."

"Huh?"

"Even if you come, I might not even be here."

"Huh?"

"Take your time to understand the thing I've taught you."

"Huh?"

"The most important thing is don't tell anyone that I'm your master."

I suffered a huge shock. Is gramps trying to break off our relationship? I haven't even learned enough yet!

"Master, master, I was wrong. Please don't chase me away."

I hugged onto gramps's legs and yelled while sobbing..

Gramps' face turned purple as kicked me aside and shouted furiously:

"I already said don't call me master! There's a reason why I won't train you every day anymore."

"Huh?"

"If we're only talking about Hua Jin, your skills in Yin Yang Sanshou is almost on par with my daughter&"

"Even though I said my granddaughter is a genius and there's a huge difference between you and her, she completely refuses to learn. She keeps saying learning Yin Yang Sanshou with me will make her legs shorter. But I've already tricked her into learning a lot when she was a kid."

"Martial arts is like rowing a boat upstream. If you stop moving forwards, you'll be pushed back. At that time, you may actually surpass both of them."

I felt a bit depressed after hearing his words. Does this mean gramps doesn't want an outsider's skills to surpass his family?

"More importantly, the smell of vegetables in the summer is awful&"

Wow, you really changed the topic really quickly.

"I recommend that you shouldn't run every day. According to the mayor, they're planning to build a slew of resting pavilions around the lake to attract tourists. That means you would be breathing in a lot of dust and dirt when running around the lake, and that could lead to lung cancer."

"Are you perhaps&" I was touched, "Do you want to change a location to teach me because you're worried about my health?"

"You really have no sense of shame. I'm obviously worried about my own health."

After fuming at me a bit, gramps said:

"A master can teach you the basics, but the rest of the work depends on yourself. Besides, I'm not even your real master. Just slowly try to experience the profound nature of Yin Yang Sanshou while construction is underway. The most important thing you should remember is don't rashly use it against other people. Your skill in Hua Jin may have reached new heights, but Hua Jin and Fa Jin are both integral components. If you suddenly discover Fa Jin and use it without the proper experience required to handle it&.."

"What's going to happen?" I was in a panic, "Am I going to go mad with power? Are my veins going to burst?"

"The hell, I already told you not to read that many wuxia novels." Gramps hit me on the head, "It's even worse than going mad."

Gramps said with a worried expression:

"Fa Jin is a common occurrence in martial arts. Even the best boxers in Europe use Fa Jin, but obviously they call it something else."

"When my ancestors created Yin Yan Sanshou, it was still during the Warring States Period. That's why they prioritized destructive power for the Fa Jin in Yin Yang Sanshou& if you use it on a regular person near their vitals, they can easily die."

I didn't really believe him, but had to agree to be careful because of his solemn expression.

Besides, you never even taught me Fa Jin! How would I even discover it myself?

"Then, when the construction ends, do I still come here to look for you? What if you don't come?"

"That's an easy problem to solve, just give me your phone number. I'll give you a call when the time is right."

After I told him my number, he said he can't remember it and he didn't bring any paper.

"I'll tell you my number, but don't call me randomly. You can only call me when you get stumped during training."

I was elated and shocked: "Gramps, you have a cellphone?"

"Why won't I have a cellphone? Do you think I'm an old fossil? Not only do I have a cellphone, it's also a 5th gen iPhone my son bought me. I also hold the highest Fruit Ninja record in my martial arts association."

After separating from gramps, I felt a bit disappointed I won't be able to see him for a while, but I was also secretly happy to know my skills improved.

I was late to school since I got held up in the morning. I couldn't attend the morning flag-raising ceremony and had to sneak into class. I found Xiao Qin sitting in class with tears running down her face while holding a thick math problems textbook.

Damn, there's no need to be that sad even if you can't even do a single problem.

Wait, there's no way Xiao Qin would care about her own grades. It would make sense for Gong CaiCai, but Xiao Qin wouldn't feel guilty even if she scores a zero. So, there's no way she would cry over math problems she can't solve.

Is it because of something else? Did you coincidentally remember something when you opened the textbook? What made you this sad?

Shoot, don't tell me you found out about Auntie Ren and my dad? You were still telling me a few days ago how I shouldn't get any dirty thoughts about my own sister and incest is gross, but are you getting sad now that we're about to be step-siblings?

It's fine if my dad didn't keep it a secret, but why did Auntie Ren tell her daughter? Is it something to be proud of? Is four times a night something amazing?

I walked over awkwardly, but found Xiao Qin reading a novel that had the cover of a math textbook. There wasn't a single formula, it was only filled with words.

"Sob sob, Ye Lin classmate&"

I thought she would say, "How could our parents do that?", but she said:

"This book is really moving."

"I'm reading books to gather inspiration for manga, and this novel is really touching."

"The female protagonist is so brave. She's willing to kill all her rivals in love to stay with the male protagonist. Why did the Nobel prize in literature go to Mo Yan, this novel is clearly better."

"Isn't that right? Hey, why are you shaking? Is it because you like Mo Yan and I made you mad?"

Shit, if you don't know about our parents, don't cry randomly! Also, stop trying to send me warnings while reading these violent novels.

I had a guilty conscience because my dad did 'that' to Auntie Ren, so I let Xiao Qin play with my phone. She happily started to play Angry Granny from her last save.

To be fair, my dad really didn't do anything. Auntie Ren was the one who attacked, so why should I feel guilty?

"Huh, why is there a crack on the top right corner?"

Xiao Qin asked.

I took a closer look and there was indeed a slight crack on the top right corner of the screen. It doesn't really affect usage other than a bit of light leakage.

It was probably broken during the fight with Xu TianMing. Even though Xu JinSheng would compensate me, it would make me seem annoying when I make a fuss over minor matters. Besides, he already gave me a lot of coupons and vouchers.

After thinking about it for a bit, I decided to forgo asking for compensation. I didn't really care a lot about aesthetics anyway.

Soon, the flag-raising ceremony ended, and the class leader and PE committee member led everyone back to class. The class leader looked furious when she saw me sitting next to Xiao Qin and teaching her how to get more points.

"Ye Lin." She walked straight towards me, "Why didn't you come to the flag-raising ceremony?"

Our class probably lost points again, but I didn't skip on purpose&

The class leader would never believe me if I said I was late because I was practicing with a master in martial arts.

Thus I lied: "I went to the recreation center near Daning River& to practice basketball. It's easier getting a spot in the mornings."

Niu ShiLi was chatting with You Chen in the row in front of me, but he instantly retorted my remark.

"You Chen, Xu LiJun, and I all went to the recreation center this morning, but how come we didn't see you?"

"That's& that's because I was moving to fast, so you couldn't see me with your naked eyes. Haven't you guys watched Dragon Ball before?"

My nonsensical explanation made the class leader look at me even more coldly.

"Ye Lin, the first class is Physics, so come with me to help the teacher move his tools."

"Huh, isn't Niu ShiLi the Physics class representative, why doesn't he go?"

"He sprained his ankle this morning while playing basketball, but he still went to the ceremony this morning. Don't you feel ashamed as the PE committee member?"

Then, the class leader saw Xiao Qin who was engrossed in the mobile game.

"Xiao Qin, class is about to start. Put away your phone, wait& that's not your phone?"

"That's right." Xiao Qin admitted happily, "It's Ye Lin classmate's cellphone. He lent it to me because we have a good relationship."

The class leader glanced around and noticed a crack on the top right corner.

"Why don't you get it repaired when the screen is cracked this badly?"

Please, how is it even cracked? It's a crack smaller than a fingernail, please stop bringing your OCD everywhere.

Anyway, Xiao Qin obediently returned my phone, and I also obediently followed the class leader to pickup equipment and tools from the Physics room.

Shit, why is this toy electric motor so damn heavy? Why is it even called a toy when it's so heavy, is it a toy for Hulk's son?

Usually, it would be fine if I carry some heavy things. But in the past couple of days, I've been hit by Xu TianMing, hit by He Ling, and hit by gramps. It hurts with every step I take.

As we got closer to the classroom, we bumped into Xiong YaoYue who came to help out. The class leader lowered her head suddenly in embarrassment as if she was afraid Xiong YaoYue would rebuke her. But then she furled her brows in confusion when she saw Xiong YaoYue intimately help me carry the things.

Xiong YaoYue was awesome, maybe it has to do with the fact she felt guilty for ditching Ai Mi and me on Sunday, but she helped me carry the heavy motor back after class ended.

The class leader was always beside us and seemed upset Xiong YaoYue was joking around with me.

After another class passed, I saw Xiong YaoYue sighing and leaning against the window sill during the break.

You rarely see Xiong YaoYue with such a sad expression. Did she get scolded by the class leader because she helped me?

I got closer to her and asked:

"What's wrong? Is it because of the class leader?"

"Oh, it's you." Xiong YaoYue seemed unenergetic, "The class leader didn't say anything, but she did ask me some strange questions. She said something about how you already had someone you liked, so I shouldn't act so intimately. ~~~ But the class leader doesn't know you're gay and have no interest in me& I can't believe she would get mad over that&"

Who's gay? Who said I had no interest in you?

Xiong YaoYue held her cheeks and sighed again.

"Compared to the class leader, what happened yesterday was worse&"

I wanted to ask, but she said:

"I got my ass raped yesterday&"

What, don't tell me that stuff even if you consider me as a good friend! Didn't you say you had no experience, but the first thing you do is ass play? Are you discussing this with me because you want to share experiences?

I don't really want to be someone who's considered an expert in this field! Also, if he forced you in any way, you should hurry up and report him to the police.

After seeing my strange expression, Xiong YaoYue changed her previous statement:

"Oh, it's more accurate to say that 'we' got our ass raped&"

You guys? Who else was there? Other girls from our class? Who's the piece of shit who brought middle school girls to hotels so he could burst their chrysanthemums!

"Who is that bastard?" I asked with clenched teeth.

"Oh, so you know they're bastards too!" Xiong YaoYue said strangely, "I called them bastards at the time, but I still couldn't hold them back&"

Them? So, it wasn't a single person? Where was the police? Where was the minor protection law? Why did they go into hiding when the minors actually needed to be protected?

"Hey, Ye Lin, it has nothing to do with age, I think they were minors too&"

"Huh, minors vs minors?"

"Yeah, they might even be in elementary school."

What, you guys were raped by elementary schoolers? That's so embarrassing, please don't tell anyone you guys are in the same class as me! Xiong YaoYue, you have as much speed and strength as an athlete, why didn't you resist? It would have been fine if you were the only one to escape so you could have called the police!

"No, I can't be the only one to leave even if we get raped, it has to be together. That's one of the pains of the maturing process."

I don't think you have to be self-sacrifice in that situation. Did the other side have a lot of elementary school students? How outrageous did they have to be to gang rape a group of middle school students? Are these the ones who will become the backbone of our nation in the future?

"What? They also had five people, how could there be more than five? A 5v5 only allows that many people."

What, 5v5, are you talking about LOL? So, you were playing a game with elementary school students, not being gang-raped.

"Ah, what were you thinking of?" Xiong YaoYue laughed out loud while pointing at me, "Another team caught up to us and we got raped, and we dropped to third place in the rankings."

She said as she knocked angrily on the window, "Third place! It's unprecedented! We've been disgraced and humiliated. We have to practice more, then rape the second place team to take back our ranking!"

Is it worth it getting so worked up over your rank in LOL? I remember you were placed third from last in last semester's exams and you still folded your exam papers into a paper airplane and threw it around. I might not be the study committee member, but I really want to say loudly next to your ear:

"A student's duty is to learn. Take your mind off games and focus on your studies!"

During lunch, I sent a text to Shu Zhe and told him to come to the cafeteria to exchanged the goods and pick up his money.

He jostled over eagerly and handed over the silk panties. Then, based on our agreement, I handed over ¥500 from the client to Shu Zhe.

This was Shu Zhe's first official business transaction as 'Ms. Red Berries', so he was delighted. He even began to brag: he had nothing to do the past couple of days, so he was able to successfully pit 'Popeye' and 'Cilantro Buns' in a price war. In the end, 'Cilantro Buns' won the opportunity for Shu Zhe to wear a pink bikini thong for ¥600.

"Men are so stupid. All I have to do is sound a bit coy and they'll agree to anything, hahaha~~~"

Shu Zhe then seemed to have noticed he was also considered a man, so he awkwardly changed the topic.

There were a few new customers who wanted to order worn pantyhose. But he thought he would definitely be exposed if he wore pantyhose in the summer so he didn't agree.

So, the main problem is that you would get caught? That means you would agree if it was winter? It looks like you really would do anything for money!

Even though the class leader also ate in the cafeteria, she didn't come over when she saw me together with her brother.

It seems Shu Zhe told his sister he was asking me for advice on how to improve his PE grades. That's probably why the class leader didn't intervene when she saw us speaking with each other.

Xiao Qin also planned to eat together with me, but she saw Shu Zhe standing nearby. She glared at him for five minutes before finally shivering and going to eat with Loud Mouth and Little Smart.

Is Xiao Qin actually that keen? Since Shu Zhe wasn't currently wearing female underwear (he might not even be wearing any underwear), does that mean he can invoke your androphobia?

How fussy. I can't really tell the difference from the outside when Shu Zhe switches between men's and women's underwear.

After thinking about underwear-related topics, I abruptly remembered I would help Shu Zhe explain to Xiong YaoYue that he wasn't the underwear thief.

But the underwear thief had already turned over a new leaf (probably). As long as there aren't any more incidents of missing underwear, Xiong YaoYue won't be always keeping an eye on him.

I returned to class after lunch right when the class leader was handing out peaches.

It turns out the class leader's aunt went to visit them yesterday and she left behind a huge box of peaches for them. The class leader thought the peaches would spoil quickly so she brought it to school to share with her classmates.

Actually, Loud Mouth had already realized the class leader brought an extra bag today and it seemed to have food inside. But no matter what, the class leader refused to let her look inside until after lunch.

Can you only eat fruits after a meal? I think you're OCD is already out of control. Since you weren't being stingy, you should have given some to Loud Mouth earlier. I mean she wasn't even able to focus properly in class!

We have a two hour break for lunch, so not all students would immediately return to class after eating. Thus, there were still a couple of peaches left out of the twenty she brought.

It was excruciatingly hot today and I was also thirsty, so I went to ask the class leader:

"Can I also have a peach?"

"There's no more." The class leader said as she passed the remaining bag of two peaches to Loud Mouth.

I returned to my desk empty-handed and saw that Xiao Qin had a peach placed on her desk. She was holding a pencil and a sketching pad and using the peach as a model.

"So Ye Lin classmate wants to eat the class leader's peaches&"

Xiao Qin said bitterly.

You're the only one who's not allowed to say that line! I remember when you used to compare the class leader's breasts to peaches, are you trying to say I want to kiss the class leader's breasts?

"The class leader also gave me this peach, but there's only one, so it might not satisfy you&"

One is enough. Why do normal words sound extremely wrong when you say it.

Since you already got a peach, why didn't you eat it? The class leader already washed it, so you could eat it right after peeling off the skin. Why are you trying to use it as a model? I mean you clearly have a potato drawn on your pad, but it really doesn't matter if it's a peach, because you would draw a potato even if a banana was placed on the desk.

Xiao Qin pouted.

"Ye Lin classmate, did you forget I don't like peaches?"

"If you want to know why, it's because it has hair on it."

All peaches have fuzz! Besides, it's already been washed cleanly by the class leader! Why would you not eat a perfectly good peach? If you don't want it, then give it to me. I want to eat the class leader's peach&

Xiao Qin handed over the peach when she saw my gluttonous expression, but she reminded me:

"Be careful of poison."

"Although the class leader gave everyone else normal peaches, my peach could possibly contain Antiaris Toxicaria."

"If Ye Lin classmate ate it and was poisoned to death, then I&."

Then what? Are you going to get revenge? Are you going to kill the class leader? Please don't because she's a Justice Devil and would never use poison.

I remember there was a homicide last semester in Dong Shan city where a student was the victim. The perpetrator was extremely cruel and shocked the rest of society. At the time, I asked the class leader by chance what she would do if someone from class 2-3 was killed.

"Of course, I would do everything I can to make sure the murderer gets punished by the law." she answered without any doubts.

"But what if he doesn't get punished?" I argued.

"Then&" She had a gleam in her eye that sent cold chills, "I'll personally punish him."

I didn't even know the class leader had a gun when I asked this question. If I think about it now, does it mean she would use illegal weapons to punish the perpetrator?

By the way, I'm also a part of class 2-3. If I was killed, would the class leader get revenge for me?

Why do my insides feel a bit warm? Just the thought of the class leader searching for the murderer on a cold winter's night while holding a gun seems really cool.

No, no, why am I jinxing myself.

Besides, if I was killed, Xiao Qin would get revenge for me. Now death doesn't seem that bad when there are two girls who would get revenge for me.

I returned to reality and continued on with the topic of the poisoned peach.

Xiao Qin said seriously without blinking:

"If Ye Lin classmate was poisoned, I would eat the rest of that peach. Then, I would die with you while hugging you tightly so we would be together forever."

Huh, so you're not going to get revenge? Then, the class leader would lose a helper. Why would you die together with me?

"Hey wouldn't it be better to stay alive to get revenge?" I reminded her.

Xiao Qin sighed and lowered her head:

"What's the point of living if you're already dead. I don't want to stay another second in a world without you."

I ate the succulent peach while trying to understand Xiao Qin's words.

Why would she place her entire life on me? It's completely irrational and extremely dangerous! If I betrayed her, wouldn't there be a high chance she would take me down along with her?

How bothersome. Xiao Qin's too prejudiced, and I have no idea what's going to happen between my dad and Auntie Ren. I'm going to have to get past it, but I should finish this peach first.

What a waste, I can't believe Xiao Qin doesn't want to eat this delicious peach.

I suddenly had a realization.

Something's not right, Xiao Qin should love peaches. I remember how she even stole my peach when I was seven years old. To my younger self, it was a gigantic peach given to us as a gift when a relative came to visit. I was standing on the side of the road thinking about where to start eating when you suddenly came up from behind and snatched it away! You ate in in big bites while you stepped on me! You even threw the pit at my nose before you left!

Not only did the Little Tyrant love peaches, she also excelled at climbing trees. I had short legs and acrophobia, so I couldn't even climb the smallest tree.

That's why sometimes when the Little Tyrant climbed up a tree to get shade, or catch bugs, or pick fruits, I would run under the tree and sing at the Little Tyrant:

"Monkeymonkeymonkey? Oooh ooh aah aah~~"

Then I would try to escape when the Little Tyrant got infuriated and came down the tree to beat me up.

Of course, the Little Tyrant gradually decreased the amount of time it took to get down the tree. Sometimes, she would jump straight down and give me a beating.

Every time I get beat senseless, I would feel like she's a violent gorilla instead of a monkey.

Xiao Qin loves eating peaches yet she pretends she doesn't. Is is so she could leave it for me to eat? I& I'm touched, even more so than when you said you would die together with me. At least eating a peach is easier than dying.

"Xiao Qin& you used to love eating peaches, did you leave this just for me?"

"Ye Lin classmate, did you forget? I don't like eating peaches after that incident."

"Huh, what incident?"

Xiao Qin seemed to get slightly embarrassed, "It was the incident when we cooperated to steal peaches."

Ah, I remember now, but we weren't cooperating, it was you who forced me. You threatened me by saying you would take away my Optimus Prime if I didn't keep watch under the tree (but you still took it away in the end).

There were a lot of bungalows across the compound where we used to live. A lot of them had backyards, and there was a really mean old granny who planted a peach tree. It would produce a lot of bright red and tasty looking fruits.

The Little Tyrant could have simply asked Auntie Ren to buy her some peaches, but instead, she got some crooked ideas and thought hand-picked peaches would taste better,

Thus, on a moonless and windy night, she forced me to climb the wall (I'm sorry, but because I had short legs and was shorter than her, I had to be dragged along).

The Little Tyrant climbed up the peach tree with ease and left me keeping watch on the old granny's window.

She picked a lot of ripe peaches before she realized she forgot to bring a bag to carry them in.

It was early autumn and still hot outside. The Little Tyrants was wearing a vest and shorts, the same as me. We didn't have any large pieces of clothing, so we couldn't take off our clothes and use them as wrapping cloth even if we wanted to.

But it wasn't a problem for the Little Tyrant. With some quick thinking, she tied a dead knot at the bottom of her vest around her waist, then she began tossing the peaches inside.

Freshly picked peaches have prickly fur. The Little Tyrant might not have felt it with her hands (since it was numb from climbing the tree), but once it hit her soft white chest, it began to itch and she immediately shrieked.

She screamed loudly into the silent night. It was still a time when most people weren't used to nightlife.

The peaches scattered out from her vest and dropped around the bottom of the tree. One peach even hit me on the head.

I secretly picked it up and stuffed it into my pocket. I was thinking in my mind how she deserved it because she didn't get to eat any peaches and also got pricked. I was already thinking about how I would take the peach home and have a delicious treat&

That's why I was a bit slower at running away. The peach tree owner was startled awake and came running out with a broom. The Little Tyrant endured the itch and jumped onto the wall and escaped. I was left behind staring up at the top of the wall with my short legs. The old granny gave me a beating and even confiscated the peach in my pocket.

I went with her to steal peaches but didn't get to eat any, but my butt did end up as red as a peach.

"&right." Xiao Qin said, "Peaches gave us a painful memory, and I want to engrave Ye Lin classmate's pain in my mind, that's why I chose to never eat peaches again&"

Nonsense, it has nothing to do with my pain. It was because you got baptized by fresh peach fuzz and it gave you a psychological trauma. But no matter how much time has passed, I still want to say: "You deserved it. It's karma for always bullying me."

Wait a second. At the time, I thought the Little Tyrant was a boy, so I didn't even pay attention to the fact the peach had rolled over his chest then dropped on my head. Which means I was planning on eating a peach that had rolled over a girl's chest. Why does it sound so perverted when I think about it now?

Xiao Qin flipped a page in her sketch pad and said with a smile:

"Ye Lin classmate, since you ate my peach, you can substitute it as my model."

Isn't it the class leader's peach, that's what you've been saying too. I mean, you only have flat pancakes.

"Draw me?" I laughed, "Whatever you draw only turns into potatoes."

"No way, because I love you, so my drawings will also be filled with love. Even if it does turn into a potato, it will be a potato sprouted from our love fluids."

What the hell are love fluids? Don't use words people would easily misunderstand!

"Oh right, Ye Lin classmate, um&" Xiao Qin gripped her pencil tighter, "You don't have to keep still as my model, but I have a small request&"

"What is it? I'm assuming it's something completely unreasonable."

"It's& can you take off your clothes and be my nude model?"

"What..?"

"It's because the peach wasn't wearing clothes. I was drawing a nude peach, so that's why&"

"The peach's clothes is its skin! I was just removing its clothes when I peeled its skin as I ate it! Before peaches are washed, they even have furry clothes, I mean, haven't you experienced it first hand?"

Xiao Qin shivered as I mentioned that event and she didn't request me to be her nude model anymore.

After a while, she went to the class leader and asked respectfully:

"Class leader, can I draw you?"

"Eh, so you were learning how to draw? Let me see your skills."

The class leader took her sketch pad and flipped through a couple of pages. She had a befuddled expression on her face.

"So you were practicing on drawing vegetables the entire time? I never knew you cared a lot for the basics."

It's not the basics, she was trying to draw other things, but in the end, everything she draws turns into potatoes or carrots.

"Don't worry." Xiao Qin said seriously, "I'll draw you seriously and even make you a hundred times prettier. After I give you my drawing, you'll never want to look in a mirror again."

Her sentence was worded weirdly as if she was trying to imply the class leader was ugly.

Although the class leader felt a bit awkward, she still said warmly:

"There's still a bit of time left before lunch break ends. If you want to draw now, I can cooperate with you, but we have to stop when the bell rings."

Xiao Qin made a crafty smile after the class leader accepted.

"But, I have a small request&"

"What is it? Do I have to stay still?'

"No, since I'm a beginner, I still can't draw the wrinkles on clothes&"

As the class leader heard her clothes had wrinkles, her OCD caused her to quickly look at her clothes and straighten out her sleeves.

"Um, it's not just wrinkles, I just can't draw clothes.."

Xiao Qin admitted her lack of ability in an unprecedented manner.

The class leader replied: "It's fine if you can't draw it well, I don't mind."

"No, I mind." Xiao Qin raised her voice, "As the future Celery Sensei who will move millions of people, how can I leave behind an imperfect drawing? If I can't draw clothes, then I should just avoid it!"

The class leader blinked blankly as she couldn't understand her words nor did she know who Celery Sensei was.

"Umm& can you not wear clothes when being my model?"

Ah, the class leader's face darkened and she finally realized Xiao Qin was teasing her. She stood up and kept tickling Xiao Qin furiously to the point she wished she was dead.

I completed an extremely important task on Monday night before my dad returned to the hotel.

And that was to hand wash Ai Mi's signed underwear three times.

That way when I hand it to Director Cao, there wouldn't be any of my sister's scent left on it.

I'm not feeling reluctant because I have a strange hobby for collecting my sister's underwear, but voluntarily handing over my sister's underwear is breaking my brotherly heart.

Shit, why didn't I make more money from Shu Zhe's worn underwear instead of trying to cash in my sister's underwear to repay my twenty thousand dollar debt!

Wait, I think my reasoning is a bit off. If I never wanted to return the money, then I would have never thought about taking my sister's underwear, not would I have actually gotten my hands on it.

It seems it would be better if I kept the underwear instead of giving it to a fanatical fan like Director Cao.

But I swear on the name of my ancestors: As Ai Mi's brother, my love towards her is COMPLETELY PURE. I would never hide her underwear under my bed and it take it out at certain inappropriate times.

Of course, I should hurry up and pass this underwear off to Director Cao before an alien controls me and makes me do those horrid things.

Although I can't guarantee Director Cao wouldn't immediately wear it over his head and do lolicon stuff with it, Ai Mi might not even have worn this pair before. Afterward, I even put it on my head and now I washed it three times, so it's already not much different from a new pair of underwear.

I didn't have the guts to dry the underwear on the balcony. One reason is because it's almost night and it would run out of sunlight soon. Another reason is in case Xu TianMing only pretended he repented but instead became more intensified. I would cry if he came and stole my hard-earned underwear.

Thus, I carefully dried the underwear with a hair dryer.

The underwear felt warm in my hands after being blow-dried. Even if it wasn't fresh off her body, it can still reach the same warmth.

Hey, what are you thinking about, clear your mind. You should only have loving and protective thoughts towards your sister and any other thoughts are prohibited.

Oh right, I should check to make sure the smell is gone. I have to make sure Director Cao is basically getting a new pair of underwear other than Ai Mi's signature.

I brought the underwear towards my nose and sniffed it for a second before I realized.

What the hell are you doing? Sniffing your sister's underwear? Even though it only smells like soap, it's still crossing the line!

Chinese netizens gave the male protagonists in Japanese siscon anime, manga, and games a nickname of 'sister fucking demons'. I really don't want to walk down that path. Since I had some extra time, I washed the underwear again and dried it with the hairdryer.

The next morning, I didn't follow my usual routine of running around the lake, and instead called Director Cao while doing one-armed push-ups.

Even though he was woken up in the morning, he instantly became energetic when he realized it was me.

"Xiao Ye Zi, if you called me this early, is it perhaps about Miss Ai Mi'er's underwear&"

I replied in a bad mood: "That's right, I was able to get a pair. So bring your bank card and drive over, you can also drop me off at school on the way back."

Director Cao readily consented and soon arrived downstairs.

He was driving a light yellow van. According to him, he bought it because it's convenient to transport film equipment, and it's also spacious enough to shoot car AV scenes.

After painfully handing Ai Mi's signed white panties with a decorative border to Director Cao, he actually knelt down and shed tears of gratitude.

"I recognize this signature, it's actually Miss Ai Mi'er's writing. You didn't lie to me, if you got her signature& then she gave it to you as a gift?"

I said: "Anyway, it was a gift Ai Mi gave to her number one fan. You seem pretty fanatical if you're willing to pay twenty thousand dollars, so it's not like I can't give it to you&"

Director Cao was deeply grateful and bowed towards me a couple of times before getting up and passing me his bank card.

Then he took out a gold gilded box and carefully placed the underwear on the black felt inside.

Director Cao clenched his fists and pledged:

"It's such a valuable gift, so I'll live up to my name as a lolicon and pass it down to my successors as a family heirloom."

Shit, aren't those Xiao Qin's lines? Damn fatty, don't steal the female protagonist's lines!

I looked at Director Cao as he closed his golden box and carried it around like Scrooge carrying a bundle of money. He glanced around as if he was afraid of someone coming to steal it from him. But just thinking about the contents made me feel unpleasant.

"Director Cai, your box looks pretty expensive." I tried to change the topic to shift my attention.

"Of course." Director Cao said proudly, "It cost me over ten thousand dollars! It would be rude to use anything less than ten thousand to store Miss Ai Mi's underwear."

Hmph, it's not like you're spending your own money. You're just using that investor's money, so I guess you don't feel that bad spending it.

After Director Cao dropped me off at school, I sat through two classes while feeling at unease. I suddenly remembered I also forgot to bring Shu Zhe's bikini to school, so I could only delay the shipment.

I climbed over the school walls during lunch after radio calisthenics and went to the bank on the corner (the reason why I went after radio calisthenics is because I don't have the guts to skip, otherwise the class leader's gaze would freeze me to death)

I stood in front of the ATM and gave Commissioner Wang from American Express a call.

"Mr. Ye, do you require our services?" Commissioner Wang said politely as usual.

I spoke with pride and some self blame:

"I already prepared the twenty thousand dollars I would give Ai ShuQiao."

"Twenty thousand in one month." Commissioner Wang was a bit perturbed since he knew I was only in middle school.

"That's right, it's all hard-earned money from stacking bricks and distributing posters. My house is already stacked full of coins."

I joked with Commissioner Wang and tried to forget it was obtained in exchange for my sister's underwear.

Commissioner Wang laughed professionally, "Mr. Ye is very humourous. Did you call to ask about how to transfer the money."

"Yes, if I don't transfer it away, then I might spend it all treating other people to meals."

Actually, I would never use the money to treat others to a meal because that would be equivalent to eating my sister's underwear.

Under Commissioner Wang's guidance, I transferred the twenty thousand dollars to a special no-fee intermediate account temporarily held by American Express.

I felt my entire body relax. Now I cut off all connections with Ai ShuQiao and we can now battle face to face without any feelings of being mother and child.

"Mr. Ye, I have received your payment. It will be handled along with Madam Ai ShuQiao's rebate at the end of the month, and it will be concisely written on the receipt& oh that's right, you can still add a six-word message, do you need me to help you add one?"

I thought about it and sneered: "Just write 'cutting off ties'."

"Alright, then to confirm, this amount will be transferred at the end of the month along with the message 'cutting of ties', is that correct?"

"That's right Commissioner Wang. I feel great right now."

I then hung up with a laugh.

After returning to school, I notified Shu Zhe I didn't bring his bikini, so he has to delay the delivery to Cilantro Buns. He said unhappily:

"I already made a promise~"

The he realized he spoke like a girl, so he told me angrily and awkwardly to not forget to bring it tomorrow. Then he tossed a piece of gum in his mouth and walked away.

When I saw him chewing gum, I remembered I was preparing to start a new balloon blowing venture. Maybe he should come to my house to grab the underwear while helping me blow up a few balloons.

But I don't know which day is convenient so I put that plan aside for now.

I ate lunch with Xiao Qin on the food stalls street. We bumped into Xiong YaoYue who mooched a piece of fish from us, but treated us to yogurt.

Xiong YaoYue said to Xiao Qin after lunch when we returned to school: "Do you want to go to the washroom together? It seems because Xiong YaoYue scolded the class leader to not separate Ye Lin and his lover, so Xiao Qin had a good impression of her and the two of them left together."

As for me, right when I returned to class 2-3, something bad happened.

Loud Mouth was watching a video online on her cellphone and burst out laughter, then she even called the class leader over to watch with her.

"Hey, class leader, check this out. These two people are fighting while wearing underwear over their heads! It looks like the underwear thief and his accomplice were splitting the loot and began to fight!"

"It turned out a nearby resident filmed the whole thing on their phone. They put it online and called it 'Underwear on their head with matchless martial arts'. The views skyrocketed and quickly climbed to first place!"

"Although you can't see their faces, one of them is wearing a uniform from Qing Zi Academy!"

The class leader's face froze after she watched the video on Loud Mouth's phone.

There's no time to lose! If I can't watch the video with them, then I have to take out my own phone and search for the video on the top rankings of that site.

It was in second place! What an awful title, and the contents of the video were just as awful.

The netizens successively left comments under the video:

"Damn, doesn't the guy with the outdoor jackets have kicks as skillful as Donnie Yen?"

"The other guy is also crazy! He's using his fists to counter knees!"

"Are they martial arts students? It's fine to compete, but why are they wearing underwear over their heads?"

"Haha, it's actually something that occurred in Dong Shan city. These two are the infamous underwear thieves who ravaged our city, and they got into a fight because they couldn't distribute their loot evenly."

"Where is Dong Shan city, I've never heard of it before. It's probably a tiny third-rate city."

"Yeah, cause obviously you're city is the best s. Everyone from Beijing Shanghai, or Guangzhou are all so snobbish."

"I'm not from any of those cities, I'm from Hangzhou. Beijing, Shanghai, or Guangzhou are too polluted, they can't even compare to my city."

"Southerners are all weaklings. You should come to the north and we'll easily beat you up."

"Please don't attack people based on where they live, I hate those kinds of people."

"I heard Xinjiang had another terrorist attack, good thing I don't live there."

"How did you guys stray so far off topic, talk about the video!"

"I heard from a relative who lives in Dong Shan city that the one who's wearing a private school uniform and uses his fist might be a trust fund baby."

"And he still won in the end. There's no god, why couldn't he have gotten kicked to death."

Damn, I'm begging you guys to stop making the video even more popular.

In addition, the class leader turned around at this time and stared at me with an ice-cold glare.

Even though the video was low quality and taken from a distance, it still had a frontal view of me.

The face was unclear enough that Loud Mouth couldn't recognize me, but the main reason was probably because the Qing Zi Academy uniform threw her off.

But the class leader is different because she's seen me wearing that uniform before. More importantly, I've worn that uniform in front of the class leader while fighting Zhao GuangTou and the Xia B Li in berserk mode! (TN: It was the fight near the pet hospital I believe, where they cornered the class leader in an alley)

I also used berserk mode in the video! The class leader could probably recognize me based on my movements alone! The class leader now believes I'm the underwear thief's accomplice who had a life or death battle with underwear over our heads because we couldn't split our loot evenly.

Also, Shu Zhe also blamed the underwear thief when he took his sister's underwear. Now, she might even think I was the one who stole it!

I'm innocent! Even though your underwear did end up in my hands, I gave it to Xiao Qin! Didn't you see her wearing it at her house? (Although you thought she coincidentally bought the same pair)

Not good. The class leader's black pupils darted around as she glanced at my face, then she immediately bit down on her lips. Did she realize something? Perhaps that it wasn't a coincidence Xiao Qin was wearing the same underwear and it was actually one of my schemes?

If I think about it, it seems Xiao Qin told the class leader that the underwear was a gift. Then, that means I would be her first suspect.

The class leader would piece the puzzle together and might come to this unfortunate conclusion:

That the underwear thief was two people, me, and the guy wearing the outdoor jacket in the video.

And that I was the one who stole her underwear and gave it to Xiao Qin, so that I would steal it back after it's filled with Xiao Qin's scent.

Then I would be able to obtain a pair of underwear worn by two girls. And if I used that pair of underwear to rub one out, it would mean I was humiliating two girls at the same time.

Ah, she's walking towards me. She was able to guess I was also watching the video, so she returned the phone to Loud Mouth and walked towards me empty-handed.

Is she planning to use her hands to strangle me?

I paused the video in a hurry, then I raised my collar and contracted my neck like a turtle.

"Class leader& what are you doing? Don't come any closer."

She acted like she was a teacher as she placed one hand on my desk and one hand on her hips as she looked down on me as I was sitting down.

At first, she used a disappointed tone of voice:

"Ye Lin, I even defended you when everyone else thought you were the underwear thief. I said you were sleeping in the classroom when the underwear thief was spotted&"

"So it turns out there were two of you! You guys split up to give each other alibis. No wonder you weren't caught for over two months!"

"Tell me why you became the underwear thief. Also, where did my underwear go? Don't tell me you gave it to another girl?"

It was good she at least spoke quietly, otherwise, the entire class would have heard.

"Class leader, it's a misunderstanding. Your brother was the one who stole your underwear&."

As matters stand, I can't cover for Shu Zhe anymore.

"Are you still shamelessly pushing the blame onto my brother?"

The class leader's eyes were a bit red.

"Do you like girl's underwear that much to the extent you wore it over your head? Did you&. already use my underwear to jack off?"

"You're never allowed to step in our home ever again."

I was at a loss and wanted to explain, but Xiong YaoYue appeared at Xiao Qin's spot. She was sucking on a popsicle while listening in to our conversation.

"Why did you come back alone, where's Xiao Qin?" I blurted.

"Xiao Qin was unlucky and bumped into the math teacher. She was called to the office so they could discuss her poor grades and if she's interested in math or whatever& I was afraid I would get scolded together, so I ran back first."

You have pretty good foresight since your grades aren't much better than Xiao Qin's.

"Oh right, what were you guys arguing about?"

"Ask him." The class leader folded her arms in a fit of anger.

Xiong YaoYue looked down and saw my paused video.

"Ah, it's that! I already watched it yesterday." Xiong YaoYue laughed, "For some reason, one of them looks a bit like Ye Lin, but why would Ye Lin have a Qing Zi Academy uniform? Hahaha~~~"

The class leader snorted, "That person is Ye Lin. He has a Qing Zi Academy uniform at home, I've personally seen him wearing it."

Xiong YaoYue opened her mouth wide in shock.

"Are you perhaps suspecting he's the underwear thief?"

"Who else could it be?" The class leader said bitterly.

"No way! It's clearly your brother&"

Xiong YaoYue quickly shut her mouth when she saw the class leader's murderous gaze.

"I guess it's reasonable to say these two are the underwear thieves&"

Xiong YaoYue frowned and thought for a while before coming to a conclusion and said:

"But Ye Lin might not be an accomplice, he might be trying to stop him."

I'm moved that Xiong YaoYue believes in me.

The class leader remained unmoved, "If he was acting for a just cause, why did he put underwear over his head."

Xiong YaoYue scratched her face, "It might have been an accident?"

"There's tons of underwear blown down buildings every year, but do any passersby on the ground end up looking like Ye Lin? He's clearly a pervert who uses the underwear to jack off."

"Class leader, that's where you're wrong." Xiong YaoYue's face turned more serious.

"I can't guarantee that Ye Lin was acting for a just cause, but I can guarantee he doesn't jack off with the underwear."

Xiong YaoYue patted her chest and said seriously. The class leader could only quiet down after seeing her earnest expression.

After a while, the class leader asked quietly: "What evidence do you have?"

"I have evidence, but I can't really tell you. But I guarantee he didn't steal underwear to jack off or may I never get married!"

I'm grateful you believe, but you need to stop jinxing yourself.

The class leader was still skeptical. By this time, Loud Mouth had shown the video to many other people. Some of them seemed to realize the one in the Qing Zi Academy uniform looked like me but were too afraid to say anything.

But it looks like we couldn't keep the secret because Xiong YaoYue was too loud. Right when the class was about to suspect me as the underwear thief, Eunuch Cao suddenly stood up.

"My master didn't steal underwear, nor is he the underwear thief."

"The person he's fighting isn't the underwear thief either."

"My master is filming a movie with my dad, it's a sacrifice for the sake of art!"

Not only did Eunuch Cao confuse the class leader and the entire class, he also left me at a loss.

"Why do you even have to ask?" Eunuch Cao said, "How can two talented martial art youths fight over stolen underwear?"

"It's completely illogical. The only explanation is that we purposely uploaded the video online, it's a form of art& no, we did it to bring attention to our film."

Eunuch Cao blabbered on and on. I wasn't sure if he was actually even able to fool anyone, but now everyone knew the one in the video was me.

"I thought he looked familiar!" Loud Mouth stared at her phone, "But what movie are you guys promoting?"

Everyone in the class gathered around Eunuch Cao. Loud Mouth, Little Smart, the class leader, Xiong YaoYue, and I were in the inner circle. Everyone else was in the outer circle waiting to hear what Eunuch Cao was about to say.

What's rare was that even Gong CaiCai came over curiously to see what was

Made in the USA
Las Vegas, NV
16 December 2024

14370407R00168